MW00463301

my sacred pause

my sacred pause

DAILY REFLECTIONS

On Looking Within,
Loving Who You Are,
And Living Out Loud.

Melinda Scime

First edition December 2019

Book cover design by Jacquelyn Tierney
Author photo on back cover by Sarah Bridgeman

ISBN 978-0-578-60427-5

www.melindascime.com

For my daughters, Megan and Melaina

acknowledgements

This book would not have been possible without the guidance and support of many people. Thank you to Stacy de la Rosa for your support and expert consultation on this book from the beginning. Thank you to Jenna McGuiggan for editing the book. Your feedback was invaluable and your kind words throughout the process offered me encouragement when I needed it most. Thank you to Jacquelyn Tierney for your loving design of the book cover. Your beautiful work made this book real in my mind long before I ever held it in my hands.

I want to acknowledge some of my many teachers in this life who have helped shape me into the woman I am today: Melinda Alexander, Dr. Catherine Cook-Cottone, Elizabeth DiAlto, and Hannah Marcotti. Your influences can be felt throughout the pages of this book. I am deeply grateful for your guidance and support on my own path of personal and spiritual development.

This book grew out of my weekly love letters that I started writing in 2012. Many people would reply to let me know how much my words meant to them or that they saved the emails in a special folder to revisit as needed. Some even encouraged me to write a book. I am indebted to my readers for their support over the years. Thank you.

I am lucky to be surrounded by amazing friends and family. Thank you to Sue Vester for being my confidant and number one cheerleader since we were young girls living next door to each other. Thank you to my YaYas— Kimberlee Beach, Ann Courts, Delinah Heim, and Maria Knoebel—for always being there and loving me through the many phases of life we've navigated together. I also want to acknowledge the women of *Connect, Inspire, Grow*—a local women's circle that has been a source of encouragement and inspiration for me over the past several years. I look forward to many more hours together sipping tea and sharing our truths.

Thank you to the village of women who helped me when I was a young single mother raising my daughter Megan—especially my mom, Elizabeth Smallwood, grandma Margaret Pittorf, aunt Edith Weaver, and sister, Maureen Remus. Neither of us would be the women we are today without your love and support. To my grandma Margaret Pittorf, thank you for being a steady source of comfort and a safe place to land in the hardest moments of my life. To my mom, Elizabeth Smallwood, thank you for always believing in me and loving me unconditionally. You taught me from a young age that I can do anything I set my mind to and that belief is the foundation I stand upon as I pursue my dreams.

Thank you to my daughters, Megan Scime and Melaina Lewis, for being the source of more love and joy than I ever thought possible. I love you more than words can say and I'm so grateful that I get to be your mom. Finally, thank you to my husband, Michael Lewis, for your unconditional love and support. Thank you for believing in all of my wild ideas and always encouraging me to pursue my goals. I am grateful to have a true partner in this life. You are my rock and the love of my life.

welcome

This book is an invitation to pause and take a few minutes for yourself each day. My intention is to offer you a moment of mindfulness amidst the chaos of daily life. My hope is that the simple ideas and practices within these pages will add up to create a powerful impact in your life. I encourage you to create a ritual around the reading of this book. Give yourself space to turn inward and reflect on the message of the day, perhaps over your morning cup of tea or snuggled up in bed in the evening. You don't need any special tools to engage with this book. However, there are many journal-writing prompts, and I encourage you to invest in a notebook where you can record your answers. Give yourself the gift of using a beautiful journal as part of your self-care.

A few notes: First, my use of the words *woman* and *women* throughout the book refer to anyone who identifies as a woman and is not meant to be exclusive. Second, although I am a licensed psychologist, this book is not a substitute for therapy. Please practice self-care and seek out professional help from a therapist if you are struggling with your mental health. Lastly, oftentimes personal and spiritual development focuses on the individual to the point of ignoring the impact of systems. I have done my best to not do that in this book.

The daily reflections within these pages are a culmination of my work as a therapist, yoga teacher, and Badass Self-Care® coach. The stories and strategies that I share have grown out of my experiences as a woman navigating self-care in this patriarchal world. I believe they will resonate deeply with all women but particularly with those who identify as sensitive and empathic. Throughout these pages you will learn how to give yourself the same beautiful care you so easily give others. You will reclaim self-love and self-trust and learn strategies for taking care of your needs, setting healthy boundaries, and honoring your truth. We do this work for ourselves and we do this work for our world. Because women taking care of themselves creates powerful shifts within and without. Let's begin.

January 1

You Are Not a Problem to Be Fixed

Modern life can feel so full of noise. The constant stimulation of electronic devices and social media regularly overwhelms my sensitive soul. At the New Year, the noise seems to increase. The messages about declaring resolutions and making changes seem ever-present. *"New Year, New You!"*

Here's the thing: you don't need a new you.
You are not a problem to be fixed.
There is nothing wrong with you.
In fact, everything you need is already within you.

I want to help you connect with your inner wisdom.
I want to help you remember your worth, your truth, your joy.
I want to help you create a sacred space within yourself where you can seek solace no matter what is going on around you.

That is the purpose of this book: the work of reclaiming self-love and self-trust so that you can live your life guided by the deep inner knowing that has always been within you. Let's begin by sitting with the idea that you are not a problem to be fixed.

What comes up for you when you read that sentence? If you accept that you do not need to be "fixed," what will that mean for your life? Take a few minutes to reflect on these questions in your journal. For now, simply observe your thoughts and feelings without any judgment or expectation.

January 2

Choose a Practice to Help You Connect with Your Inner Self

The process of reclaiming self-love and self-trust begins with turning inward and reconnecting with your own wisdom. *Everything you need is already within you.* Today, I invite you to do something different this year. Rather than declaring resolutions or setting goals, I invite you to dedicate this year to reconnecting with yourself and your inner wisdom.

What helps you connect with your inner self? Perhaps it is meditating or writing in your journal. Maybe you find that walking or practicing yoga work for you. Or that the outer noise falls away when you are painting or in nature. There is no right or wrong answer. Take some time to think about a practice for looking within. Consider committing to doing it (whatever it may be) daily, for this week or this month or this year. Please choose something doable for you in your life right now. This practice can be as little as five minutes per day. *You'll be amazed at what can shift in five minutes*, especially over time.

Once you choose your practice (let it be just one thing for the sake of this exercise), decide when and where you will do it. Research tells us that when creating a new habit, it is most effective to pair it with an existing habit. For example, I will meditate for five minutes every morning after I brush my teeth, or I will write in my journal for five minutes every night after I wash my face. Give yourself the gift of dedicated time to turn inward and look within.

January 3

Your Body is a Compass

Many of us live our lives from the neck up, cut off from the wisdom of our bodies.

Your body knows things in a way your mind can't comprehend. This knowing is beyond logical thought. Some call it instinct or intuition. We all have the ability to tune into the body and access this knowing that transcends rationality.

Try this: think of a time when you were in a situation that felt off, wrong, or misaligned. Take a few moments, close your eyes, and really imagine it as if you were back there right now. The job you hated, the relationship that felt off, the party you didn't want to go to last week—whatever it is, close your eyes and go back there. As you revisit this memory, notice what you feel in your body. Name the sensations: is there tension in your jaw, heaviness in your chest, a knot in your gut? Put words to it.

Now, do the same thing for a situation that felt right and aligned, like you were exactly where you were meant to be. The job you loved, an amazing vacation, a celebratory day—close your eyes and go back there. Notice what you feel in your body: is it tingling in your hands or a lightness in your heart or warmth in your cheeks? There is no right or wrong answer, just observe whatever is true for you.

This is your body compass, a concept I first learned about through the work of author Martha Beck. You now know what "yes" and "no" feel like in your body. Most things may not feel as strong as what may have come up for you in this exercise, but you can still use your body compass to help you make decisions big and small. If you're thinking of taking a new job, imagine yourself there and see how it feels in your body. When you're deciding where to go for dinner, observe how each option feels inside your body. Experiment with making decisions based on how they feel in your body. Practice connecting with the wisdom that lies within your cells and observe the impact on your life.

January 4

You Can Trust Yourself

Most women fight wars on two fronts, one for whatever the putative topic is and one simply for the right to speak, to have ideas, to be acknowledged to be in possession of facts and truths, to have value, to be a human being.
~ Rebecca Solnit

Women in our society are repeatedly told that they are crazy, too sensitive, and out of touch with reality. Gaslighting, when someone manipulates you into second guessing what you know to be true, is a widespread phenomenon. As women, we are conditioned to question our own perceptions.

Maybe you fell down when you were young and it hurt like hell and you cried and your parent said, "It's not that bad." Maybe your dad got drunk and swore and broke things and the next day everyone acted like it never happened. Maybe your coach gave you a pat on the butt that made you uncomfortable and your teacher said you were making a big deal out of nothing. *Maybe you experienced all three of those things and more.*

Little by little our faith in ourselves chips away, until we are left in a state of confusion and uncertainty. It's time to reclaim our power, our voice, our truth. We can trust ourselves. *You can trust yourself.*

Spend some time with your journal today. When did you first learn to discount your truth? Let's name the old stories so that we can release them and move forward into fully embodying our wisdom as women.

January 5

White Space

No need to hurry. No need to sparkle. No need to be anybody but oneself.
~ Virginia Woolf

When is the last time you did nothing? Today, give yourself 30 minutes of white space. If you absolutely can't do it today, take the time to schedule it into your week. White space is empty space, time to do nothing.

Why take time to do nothing?

Because it is too easy to get distracted by all the to-do lists.
Because our culture glorifies busyness and reveres productivity.
Because we are always connected to our screens.

Because possibility lives in the empty space.

Because we need quiet to truly hear ourselves.
Because empty space is essential to nurturing our dreams.
Because the answers we seek often appear just on the other side of some silence.

Be a rebel.
Schedule some time to do nothing.
Be brave and claim it for yourself.

Today (or this week), create 30 minutes of white space for yourself: alone, quiet, no electronics. *Schedule it in your planner.* These 30 minutes are yours to spend as you wish. You might write, read, draw, sit quietly, or go outside and watch the sunset. Notice what arises during this time. What is present when you can finally hear yourself think?

January 6

Dialogue with Your Body

Our bodies are truth-tellers, and they will be our guides throughout the journey of reclaiming self-love and self-trust. My therapist is always reminding me to check in with my body, to just feel what I am feeling and where and how it is showing up. One of her favorite questions is, *"And if that tightness in your chest (or ache in your gut, or pain in your head, or anger in your hands) could talk, what would it say?"* I am consistently impressed by the wisdom that arises from this question.

Our bodies are speaking to us all the time. Are we listening?

Today, try an experiment.

1. Think of a distressing situation or incident, maybe the thing that keeps coming up.

2. If it's comfortable for you, close your eyes. Let your mind go to the distressing situation and observe what comes up in your body. Name what you feel.

3. Dialogue with the feeling in your body. Give it a voice. Ask it what it wants you to know. Keep an open mind; be willing to receive knowledge from your body (not just your mind). You might sit in meditation and allow the conversation to unfold or write the dialogue out in your journal.

The Truth Is...

Some women get erased a little at a time, some all at once. Some reappear. Every woman who appears wrestles with the forces that would have her disappear. She struggles with the forces that would tell her story for her, or write her out of the story, the genealogy, the rights of man, the rule of law. The ability to tell your own story, in words or images, is already a victory, already a revolt.
~ Rebecca Solnit

You are here.
You matter.
You deserve to be heard.
You deserve to be seen.
You deserve to be known.
You deserve to be adored.
Don't let others define you.
Don't let others erase you.
Tell your own story.

Tell the truth about your life, in words, images, or both. Tell the truth to yourself in your journal, or to someone you trust in conversation, or to the whole world on social media—whatever feels supportive for you today.

I like to start with, *"The truth is..."*

January 8

Dear Self...

Let's make a promise to ourselves, a promise to tune into and trust our internal wisdom. Today, I invite you to write vows to yourself. You know what you most need to hear, the promises and words that will soothe your soul.

Here is an example to help you get started:

Dear Self,

I promise to love you unconditionally,
I will acknowledge and honor all the parts of you with kindness,
I vow to continue to work on self-forgiveness and self-compassion.

I promise to trust you,
I will believe your gut feelings even when there is no rational evidence,
I vow to honor your intuition, the place within that simply knows.

I promise to take exquisite care of you,
I will tune into your needs and nourish them accordingly,
I vow to respect and honor your boundaries and self-care practices.

All my love, now and forever,

Me

Read your vows regularly to help you stay connected with your promises to yourself.

The Goal Is Not to Live Fearlessly

Guide your heart to your throat, and open. Empty your ghosts. Let the words catch air and set fire to the horizon. Run toward the warmth of it. We must learn to be braver. ~ Victoria Erickson

I am not a fan of the idea of living fearlessly. Fear, in some forms, is an adaptive emotion. It helps us keep ourselves safe. I think of this type of fear as instinctual. This is the fear we feel that lets us know we are in danger. This is the fear that keeps us alive, that tells us not to run in front of that car or eat that weird-smelling thing. This is the fear that makes your heart race after you almost get into a car accident. This is the fear we experience as a feeling in our gut that might not make any logical sense but we know we have to listen. You are walking alone and you feel the pull to take a different route. Something tells you to not get on the plane or take the meeting or make the deal. This fear is our intuition speaking to us. It is present moment focused. We need this fear to keep us safe; it is useful data to have as we navigate life.

As humans, we also struggle with another type of fear that is not helpful—the fear of "what if?" This is the fear that keeps us up at night imagining all the worst-case scenarios. This is the fear that is not based in logic or instinct. This is the fear that is maladaptive and creates unnecessary pain. I think of this as anxious fear. Worrying that you are not good enough. Thinking you aren't capable. Obsessing that they are going to betray you without any evidence of a real threat. Imagining that every strange look someone gives you is them disapproving of or disliking you.

Creating negative stories about your future. This fear is future focused. Unchecked, it can create havoc in our lives.

When instinctual fear pops up, listen and honor the message. When anxious fear creeps in, simply greet it with love and kindness and then let it go. Sometimes it is difficult to discern which type of fear you are feeling. I find when I decide to honor instinctual fear, I experience a sense of peace, and when I decide to honor anxious fear, I feel more fear and anxiety. The truth is, the goal isn't to live fearlessly but instead to be wise and discerning in your relationship to fear.

January 10

Connect with Your Heart

If you have lived all your life hearing another voice in your heart, maybe it's time to channel her.
~ Sarah Ban Breathnach

Your heart center is the seat of love and compassion.

It can be challenging to stay connected to our hearts as we move through our daily lives.

Today, pause and place your hand on your heart. Close your eyes and take three deep breaths. Notice how taking this minute or two to turn inward and drop your awareness into your heart shifts your energy and brings you back to your center.

january 11

How Are You? (Really)

What would happen if one woman told the truth about her life?
The world would split open.
~ Muriel Rukeyser

"How are you?"

We ask and answer this question multiple times a day, usually responding with a quick, "I'm fine." Or, "Things are good."

But how are you, *really*?
How is your heart, your mind, your body, your soul?
What is true for you, right now in this moment?
Let yourself name it, even if only to yourself.

january 12

Sometimes You Will Forget

I am a planner. A list maker. A lover of structure.

I plan my self-care just like I plan my work schedule. I make a list and schedule my self-care activities into my week, giving them as much priority as other appointments and tasks. It all works beautifully. *Except when it doesn't.* At times I have crossed from structure into rigidity and let my plan supersede the wisdom of my body.

It was a Friday. I was working at the office even though Friday is my self-proclaimed day off. I had a massage first thing in the morning, treated myself to lunch after, and then headed to work. I meant to grab dinner somewhere between clients and meetings and picking up some much-needed new underwear, but I was running late. I had written in my planner that I would head to yoga at 7:30pm after my last meeting. I was tired. My body felt spent from acupuncture the day before and the massage that morning. I hadn't had enough water and I was hungry. I thought about not going. I thought about how I had another long day on Saturday. And I thought about how important my practice is to me and how there wasn't another time I could go to class that week. "*Stick to the plan,*" I told myself and I went to yoga class. Afterward I was so drained that having gone to yoga class felt more like self-sabotage than self-care. You see, I forgot.

I forgot that boundaries are to be held and rules are for breaking. I disregarded my boundaries by working on my day off, and I clung to my rules by going to yoga when I was exhausted. I forgot that self-care means listening to your body over your mind. I ignored the message that what I needed most at 7:30pm on Friday was a nourishing meal and some rest. I forgot that there is no prescription for self-care, that it is intuitive by nature. I lost sight of the fact that while a plan and a schedule are amazing support structures, there is no replacement for the wisdom of moment-to-moment awareness.

For a second I wanted to beat myself up about it. Judgments started running through my mind. I took myself to the mirror and looked into my own eyes. "*I forgive you,*" I said. "*I will learn from this and try my best not* to let it happen again," I promised. *"I love you even when you mess up,"* I reassured myself. I remembered that although I am a therapist, yoga teacher, and self-care badass, I am also an imperfect human being. Messing up sometimes is part of the deal.

Sometimes you will forget. You will wander off your path of self-care. It's okay. Be gentle with yourself. We are all in this together.

January 13

What Do You Need?

Like many women, I struggle to acknowledge my needs. Honestly, sometimes I still buy into patriarchal nonsense and struggle with the fact that I even *have* needs. I get caught up in thinking that I am simply here to take care of everyone else's needs while ignoring my own. For many years I delayed taking care of my needs until I had tended to everyone else.

I remember when I would not even pee when I had to pee. My worth was so wrapped up in checking things off of a to-do list that I would not honor my body on this most basic level. At the time, I thought sacrificing my most basic needs in service of getting shit done for other people meant that I was an amazing, hardworking woman. What I know now is that ignoring my own needs left me depleted and was a disservice to myself and others.

Now I have a practice of being in regular dialogue with myself about my needs. On Sundays, when I review my schedule and create my to-do lists for the week, I also make a self-care list based on what I feel I need that week. Most days I am engaged in a moment-to-moment practice of checking in with myself. On particularly difficult days, I invite myself to pause and make a list of what I need in my journal.

What do you need today? Take the time to pause and tune into yourself. You deserve your own love and attention. Your needs matter.

January 14

Live Your Days

It was the day before my daughter's prom, two days before we took nine teenagers (and one 5-year-old) camping. I had a full day of work and an appointment at the eye doctor afterwards; my husband had an overnight retreat for work. There were lunches to be packed and kids to be picked up and dropped off and so many lists: to-do lists, packing lists, shopping lists. And I realized I'd forgotten to pay the taxes, and then I remembered it was almost Father's Day.

And I woke up and thought, "I'm going to get through this day."

And immediately I felt an *ick*, a dread. An old feeling from long ago when I existed but did not live. When I disconnected from my body and my soul in order to function. And I told myself, "Oh, hell no!"

I did not want to "get through" the day. *I do not want to "get through" any of my days.*

Getting through is holding my breath, tensing up, smiling through discomfort, denying my truth, and numbing out to survive. I do not want to get through my days. I want to live each and every one. The beautiful, easy days and the gut-wrenchingly hard days. I want to be there, open-hearted and all in. Living is breathing with the discomfort, surrendering, crying, laughing, and everything in between. Living is being here, being present, feeling and experiencing all of it.

So, I committed to staying present, to finding the moments of joy and ease inside of a hectic day. I paused and listed five things I was grateful for in that moment. I asked for help, and I adjusted my expectations. It was a wildly busy day, but it was *my* day, and I was there inside of it, living it.

Spend some time with your journal today. Are you getting through your days or living them? What might help you shift into more presence inside of your days?

january 15

We Are One

So hum is an ancient mantra meaning, "I am that."

It reminds us of the interconnectedness of all beings and invites us to step outside of ego.

So hum. I am that.

How am I exactly like everyone who is hurting, aggravating, and angering me?

Mean, greedy, impatient, petty, jealous, fearful, insecure, arrogant.
I am that.

Going back for more when I'm no longer hungry.
I am that.

Sobbing because my heart hurts for them and I feel powerless.
I am that.

Yelling at her because I'm tired.
I am that.

Picking a fight with him just because I want his attention.
I am that.

Thinking I know better.
I am that.

How am I exactly like those I admire and adore?

Kind, nurturing, devoted, content, grounded, confident, humble.
I am that.

Inhaling so, exhaling hum on my meditation cushion.
I am that.

Laughing over tacos.
I am that.

Holding her while she cries.
I am that.

Breathing peace on my yoga mat.
I am that.

Hugging her tight, holding on a few seconds more.
I am that.

Breathing in so, breathing out hum. I am that. We are one.

Me and the haggard woman who wanders the street,
Me and the mom at school pick-up who seems so put together,
Me and that woman halfway across the world who has no rights,
Me and the teacher whose wise words soothe my soul,
Me and you.
We are one.
I am that.

Underneath it all, we are the same.
We are all connected.
I feel this truth deep in my bones.

Breathing into the responsibility to cultivate peace within in order to grow peace without. Returning to the prayer tattooed on my arm, *lokah samastah sukhino bhavantu*: May all beings everywhere be happy and free and may my words, thoughts, and actions in some way contribute to that happiness and freedom for all.

Who's Driving Your Bus?

We all have different parts inside of us. There's the inner critic, the inner child, the nurturer, the protector, our most wise self—just to name a few. I strongly believe in giving all the parts of myself a seat on the bus that is my life, meaning I work to not deny or reject any part of myself. I believe that all of me deserves to be seen and loved, even my darkest parts.

Depression rides on my bus and has since I was about 12 years old. Depression ignores every good, kind thing I've ever done while replaying every awful thing I've ever done over and over. Depression talks in absolutes: *no one cares, everything is awful.* Depression doesn't leave any room for change: *things will always be terrible, why are you even trying?* For many years, depression was driving my bus. She directed my actions and my life. We were not heading to a good place. Now, depression is like a kid on the back of the bus. Sometimes she's asleep and I forget she's there, and sometimes she's loud and annoying. *I'm not going to throw her off the bus, but there is no way I am letting her drive.*

What does this mean in my daily life? It means that I hear what depression has to say, but I don't let it dictate my day. Instead, I choose practices that help me quiet the voice of depression and activate the voice of my inner wise self, my bus driver of choice.

Who's driving your bus today? Know that you can acknowledge, love, and accept all the parts of yourself while also being purposeful about which part of you gets to be in charge of your daily life.

january 17

Silence

Silence introduced in a society that worships noise is like the Moon exposing the night. Behind darkness is our fear. Within silence our voice dwells. What is required from both is that we be still. We focus. We listen. We see and we hear. The unexpected emerges.
~ Terry Tempest Williams

I used to say so much, to really spell it all out. Now I have learned to leave some things unsaid, to allow for others to create their own meaning. I can be in the silence with you. I can be in the silence with myself. Even if only for a moment.

An invitation: Close your eyes. Commune with your breath. Be still. Listen.

january 18

Protect Your Emotional Energy

I am passionate about protecting my emotional energy. For me, it feels like a form of reclaiming my power. When I say "protecting my emotional energy," I mean honing my ability to stay inside of my own feelings despite what's going on around me. The image that comes to mind is me standing strong like a mountain while all kinds of weather swirls around me. I am steady and grounded no matter how much wind and rain (other people's emotions and behaviors) go on around me. *This is an aspirational image.*

The truth is I get caught up in other people's emotions and behaviors all the damn time.

Like most things in this book, protecting your emotional energy is a practice. Here are a few tools that help me:

Visualizing: I use imagery to help me stay inside of my own emotional energy. I like to imagine myself inside of a protective bubble that prevents other people's energy from reaching me. Another image I like is that of wearing a cloak that absorbs whatever energy comes my way that I don't want to take on.

Mantras: I choose a simple phrase to repeat to myself, such as "I am not responsible for other people's emotional experience," or "I am grounded in my own energy," or "That's not mine to take on."

Body Sensations: I come back into my own experience by connecting with my body. I use my breath by simply focusing on my inhales and exhales. I also bring awareness to my hands or feet; sometimes I even rub my fingertips together or wiggle my toes.

Energetic Cleansing: I have regular practices to cleanse my energy. My favorite is taking a salty bath. I like to add essential oils like lavender or frankincense. I also cleanse myself and my space by burning sage or incense. Plus, I see an energy healer as needed.

Today, observe your emotional energy. Notice how it varies depending on where you are or who you are around. Choose one of the tools listed above and practice in a situation that feels energetically draining. Notice any shifts that occur. Don't expect immediate results; remember that this is a lifelong process. Your ability to protect your emotional energy will increase with time and practice.

January 19

Nurture Your Relationship with Your Inner Self

Gather yourself.
Every morning.
As soon as you wake up.
Embrace who you are before the world can get in the way.
~ Chani Nicholas

I believe my relationship with my inner self directly informs how I show up in my life, personally and professionally. I feel it is imperative to take regular breaks from the tasks of daily life in order to devote time and energy to nurturing my relationship with myself. I spend time doing things such as being in solitude, practicing yoga, reading and writing, communing with nature, and meditating. Taking this time away allows me to return to my life feeling refreshed and reinvigorated.

Today, consider how you can nurture your relationship with your inner self. What helps you feel connected to yourself? What activities feel rejuvenating? What places soothe your soul? Make a plan to incorporate spending time with yourself into your regular routine. This could be a few minutes every day or a larger chunk of time weekly or monthly. Choose what feels right for you and commit to nourishing your relationship with yourself.

january 20

Acknowledge Your Achievements

So often we focus on getting to the next thing. We move from one goal or to-do list item to the next with barely a breath in between.

Today, pause and celebrate all that you have achieved.
Make a list of your accomplishments thus far in life. Give yourself credit for the challenges you have overcome. Acknowledge your hard work. You can go as far back as you'd like—the second grade spelling bee totally counts! Nothing is too big or too small. List everything from raising your children with love to that amazing cup of coffee you brewed this morning. Keep the list and add to it often.

Next time you set a big goal, plan your celebration ahead of time. How will you acknowledge your accomplishment? This could be something simple like taking yourself out for a meal or something bigger like throwing a party or taking a trip. There is no right or wrong, just what feels good for you. Take the time to celebrate your achievements and give yourself the recognition you deserve.

Everything You Need is Within You

One day in graduate school I forgot my planner. It was the same feeling you might have now if you left your smart phone at home, kind of like you are walking around naked and lost. As my heart started to race and I felt my throat closing with anxiety, a wise voice in my head whispered, "Everything you need is within you."

Everything I need is within me.
Everything I need is within me.
Everything I need is within me.

A mantra for my racing mind.
A balm for my worried heart.
A promise for my uncertain self.
Delivered straight from me to me.

Where do you call home?
What peaceful haven awaits you?
Have you rested in the sanctuary of your inner self?

So often we seek solace outside of ourselves when truly the refuge lies within.

Your breath.
Your pulse.
Your truth.
Your knowing.

Look within.
Breathe and feel your way into it, all of it.
The mess and the beauty, the questions and the answers.

You do not require fixing, for you are not broken.
Every answer that you yearn for is inside of you.
There is nothing outside of you that can deliver what you crave the way that turning toward yourself will.

Everything you need is already within you.

january 22

Your True Self

You are not your thoughts.
You are not your feelings.
You are not your body.

You are something more.
The *Something More* that exists beyond your thoughts, feelings, and body.

Awareness, consciousness, bliss.

Whenever we forget this truth, we suffer. Which is a lot of the time for most of us! We over-identify with our thoughts, our feelings, our bodies, our jobs, our kids, our stuff, our bank accounts, and the many other components of modern daily life. We live disconnected from our true selves—the divine spark within all of us.

Your true self is pure light, love, and beauty.
Your true self is whole. It's never been hurt or broken; it can't be.
Your true self is unconditional love and acceptance.

When you are connected with this place within yourself, grounded in the truth of your inherent worthiness, there is nothing to earn or prove. There is only divine connection, love, and peace.

January 23

Feel into The Goodness

By taking just a few extra seconds to stay with a positive experience—even the comfort in a single breath—you'll help turn a passing mental state into lasting neural structure. ~ Rick Hanson

Back when I worked in academia, I used to experience this awful anxiety on Sunday nights. I would be nauseous worrying about the week ahead and sad that the two enjoyable days of my week were coming to an end. I knew it wasn't right. I knew I didn't want to live a life that only felt good on the weekends.

Sunday is now my favorite day of the week. It is a true day of rest and relaxation. I usually sleep in. I might go to brunch or take a yoga class or make a pot of soup. I've come to take my peaceful, joyful Sundays for granted. They are my new normal. It is easy to ignore the goodness in our lives. Our brains are wired to look for the negative, which is great for survival, but not so great for happiness.

Today, pause and feel into the goodness in your life. Think of something or someone that you love and appreciate. Close your eyes and visualize. Notice the emotions and sensations that you feel in your body. Soak up the joy and gratitude. Let the goodness sink in; stay with the image and really let yourself feel the emotions and sensations that arise for at least 30 seconds. Research has demonstrated that our thoughts and experiences leave lasting marks on our brain. Pausing to really feel into the goodness in your life not only feels good, it also positively impacts your brain structure.

January 24

Your Inner Knowing

I believe we can trust ourselves.
I believe we each have a reservoir of untapped wisdom inside of us.
I believe that we simply need to re-learn how to tune into the knowing that resides within.

I am referring to wordless, visceral knowing: the way you just know something even if it doesn't make logical sense. The knowing is there; it has always been there inside of you. Sometimes it can be difficult to tap into because it's been buried beneath the layers of social expectations, cultural conditioning, our personal and collective traumas, and the overwhelming stimulation of modern life. Sometimes we are nervous or scared of our inner knowing because it is in conflict with the outer world. Sometimes we are driven by fear and we ignore our inner knowing. We worry about what people will think of us. We choose the rational and sensible over the intuitive and instinctive. We turn away from our knowing, our truth.

Spend some time with your journal today. What deep inner knowings do you have? Is there something that you know that you've been trying to ignore? What do you know to be true despite your fear of what it might mean?

Your inner knowings may not make logical sense. Listen anyway. You can trust yourself and your inner knowing.

January 25

Create a Vision Board

When I was a teenager I used to clip quotes and images from my favorite magazines, *Jane* and *Sassy*, and create collages to hang on my walls. I got away from this practice until I was in my thirties. At that time I learned about creating vision boards—collages of words and images that represent what you want to call forth in your life.

Now visioning is a regular part of my self-care practice. There is no right or wrong way to vision. Let this be fun! Grab some magazines, scissors, and glue. Cut out whatever calls to you, whether it makes sense or not, and then glue everything down into a collage. This is not about making art, though you may create something beautiful. This is about letting yourself dream and creating a concrete reminder of your hopes and wishes. You could create a vision board for the year or make a new one with each New Moon, which is a great time for planting wishes.

I don't believe that you can change your life just by making a vision board; you have to put some action behind your visions. I *do* believe that having a visual reminder of what you desire is powerful and will influence your choices and behaviors in a way that will help bring your dreams to fruition. Place your vision board in a spot where you will see it regularly. Let it be a daily reminder of what you are calling forth.

january 26

Peace in Found Moments

Modern life is busy and often moves at a frenetic pace. Many of us feel like there is no downtime in a day. Personally, I prefer to relax in long stretches of time because it takes me a bit to settle my mind and body. However, I know that it is challenging to find big chunks of time in daily life, so I have taught myself to relax in small increments—in the found moments during the day. Sitting at a red light, waiting in the doctor's office, the few minutes in between activities—these times offer a chance to pause and breathe, to practice relaxation in the midst of everyday life. I also carry my journal and the book I am reading with me as I go about my day. That way, I can write or read if I have a few spare minutes.

Today, look for found moments—tiny spaces within your day. Instead of picking up your phone and scrolling through social media, do something to support your self-care. Breathe consciously, read a book, or simply look out the window and be where you are. Allow yourself to cultivate peace amidst the hectic pace of modern life.

january 27

Reconnect with Your Child Self

*...[A]ge ten was probably the last time you trusted your instincts. . . . Try
to contact the girl you once were. She's all grown up now. She's your authentic
self and she's waiting to remind you how beautiful, accomplished,
and extraordinary you really are.*
~ Sarah Ban Breathnach

Who was your 10-year-old self?
What did she know for sure?
How are you still like her? How are you different?
What do you miss about her?

*Spend some time with your journal today. Reconnect with your child self. Be
open to the wisdom and gifts she has to share with you.*

january 28

Small Steps Can Lead to Big Changes

True life is lived when tiny changes occur. ~ Leo Tolstoy

So often when we think about making changes in our lives we think in big, broad terms.

I want to declutter my house!
I want to prioritize my health!
I want to start a business!

It can be easy to get overwhelmed by our aspirations and feeling overwhelmed typically leads to not taking action. Not taking action leads to feelings of defeat. Our dreams can feel impossible to achieve.

Think about a big change you'd like to make, such as feeling more centered, being more patient, or having more energy. What is one small step you can take toward your goal? Maybe you will commit to five minutes of meditation every morning, or taking one deep breath before you respond, or going to bed 15 minutes earlier. Pick one small thing and commit to doing it today. Small steps can lead to big changes!

You Can Find Peace Within the Life You Already Have

It's easy to get caught in the trap of thinking, "I'll relax when _____."

I'll relax when the kids are older.
I'll relax when the bills are paid off.
I'll relax when I get a promotion.
I'll relax when I get in shape.
I'll relax when the house is decluttered.

We can spend our entire lives working toward some nebulous moment when we will finally relax. Or we can choose to find peace right now within the life we already have by simply making up our mind to do so.

We will always be able to find a reason why we can't relax; that is the nature of life. There is no use in waiting for perfect circumstances in order to unwind. Instead, practice finding peace right here inside of your current life.

Roll out your yoga mat amidst the mess in your bedroom. Leave the dishes in the sink and have a dance party in the kitchen. Turn off your phone for 15 minutes even though you might miss a message. Go away by yourself and trust that everyone will be okay. Meditate even though there is still work to do.

There will always be a reason we think we can't take time to relax. Take the time anyway!

January 30

Remember to Breathe

Breathing in, I calm my body.
Breathing out, I smile.
Dwelling in the present moment,
I know this is a wonderful moment!
~ Thich Nhat Hanh

The breath is a powerful tool for regulating our emotions.

When we are stressed, we often hold our breath or breathe in a shallow manner. This in turn creates more stress in the nervous system and our heart rate goes up, our blood pressure rises, and we mentally and emotionally experience more stress. Consciously deepening the breath reverses these effects and helps to calm our bodies and minds.

Today, notice when you feel stressed or anxious. Consciously pause to take a few deep breaths and observe how this impacts you.

January 31

Pause and Check in with Yourself

Smile, breathe, and go slowly.
~ Thich Nhat Hanh

Life is busy. It's easy to go through the day and never pause to turn inward and check in with yourself.

Today, set an alarm or some other reminder for at least four points during your day (e.g., 9am, 12pm, 3pm, and 6pm). Each time the alarm goes off, close your eyes and tune into your breath, mind, emotions, energy, and physical body. This can be a one-minute check-in or a ten-minute check-in. Whatever fits inside of your day today is just right. Each time you turn inward, practice observing without any judgment. Just notice what comes up for you. Accept things as they are and release the need to change anything.

february

February 1

The State of Loving Ourselves

To love oneself is the beginning of a life-long romance.
~ Oscar Wilde

In my experience, we all crave self-love, but it feels difficult to articulate what that actually means or how it looks in everyday life.

So, what *does* it mean to love yourself?

I don't believe that we need to learn how to love ourselves. I believe we need to un-learn everything that keeps us from loving ourselves. I believe we came into this world loving ourselves. It is through experience that we learned to evaluate and judge ourselves, that we created conditions for our self-love. I also believe we came into this world more closely connected to the truth about ourselves and our souls: that we are divine love embodied. Modern life disconnects us from this truth, and we over-identify with our humanness.

So the work of self-love is an un-learning and de-conditioning of what keeps us separated from the truth of our inherent worthiness and lovability. There are many ways to reunite with the truth of our being: meditation, yoga, writing, time in nature, creating, and more. Choose what works for you and practice regularly.

February 2

The Work of Cultivating a Loving Relationship with Ourselves

There is the state of loving ourselves, the feeling, and then there is the work of being in a loving relationship with oneself. As with any relationship, it takes work to keep the connection with yourself healthy and vibrant. This is the work of mindfully choosing how you treat yourself and how you speak *to* and *about* yourself.

Here are a few concrete action steps you can take to cultivate a loving relationship with yourself:

1. *Act as if you do love yourself, even if it feels like you are faking it at first.* Choose behaviors aligned with self-love. Ask yourself, "If I truly loved myself, what would I do in a day?" Maybe you would prepare yourself a beautiful meal, spend time in nature, take a nap, move your body, or take an art class. There is no right or wrong answer, just what-ever feels true for you. Try to live every day from a place of self-love.

2. *Date yourself.* Schedule time to be with yourself. Take yourself to the thrift store or the art supply store. Go to a coffeeshop and read. Spend time wandering around a favorite city or town or go exploring out in nature. Do whatever it is you feel called to do.

3. *Keep your promises to yourself.* Stop compromising on your needs and letting yourself down. If you say you're going to do something for yourself, do it. This cultivates self-trust, a huge part of self-love. Be dependable for yourself, as you are for others.

4. *Learn to tune into your needs and wants.* Check in with yourself regularly. Ask yourself, "How am I feeling? What do I need?" Respond lovingly. Give yourself space for exploring what you want. I love to free write around this by simply writing "I want..." at least ten times in a row and just letting the words flow. You might want to take a vacation or buy new clothes or quit your job or learn to play the piano. Again, there is no right or wrong. This is about getting to know yourself.

5. *Observe your self-talk.* Most of us say horrible, mean things to ourselves that we would never say to another person. Do the work of unpacking your negative beliefs about yourself. I believe we deserve support as we do this. Invest in working with a therapist or a coach.

6. *Notice how you talk about yourself to other people.* What is your response when someone gives you a compliment? Do you brush it off or qualify it? What do you say about yourself to others when you make a mistake? Do you excessively apologize? Begin by just noticing, and then invite yourself to make adjustments so that you are speaking kindly about yourself when interacting with others.

{Side note: these strategies also work beautifully in relationships with others.}

Self-love can feel like an elusive ideal. It doesn't have to be this way. Underneath it all, you are pure love. Spend time deepening your relationship with your true nature (love). Devote energy to cultivating a loving relationship with yourself. And no matter what you do or don't experience, be gentle with yourself. You are doing the best you can and that is enough. You are enough.

February 3

Practice Self-Compassion

Do you consider yourself a compassionate person?

Most women I know and work with are very compassionate toward others. They are kind, understanding, gracious, and forgiving in their relationships. But these same women are incredibly hard on themselves. They say harsh, critical things to themselves that they would never say to another person. They have unrelenting standards for themselves. They beat themselves up when they make a mistake.

Today, practice giving yourself the same compassion that you give so freely to others.

Hold loving space for your feelings as they arise.
Say kind things to yourself when you look in the mirror.
Be mindful of the expectations you set for yourself.
If you mess up, forgive yourself.

Most of us were not taught to be kind to ourselves, so the practice of self-compassion may feel unnatural at first. That's okay, stick with it. You are worth the effort.

Write a Letter to Yourself for When You Are Triggered

Self-care includes planning ahead and preparing for difficult moments. One of the most challenging times to be kind and loving toward ourselves is when we are triggered. "Being triggered" is when old hurts are activated by present circumstances. We can be triggered by sights, sounds, smells, or sensations in our bodies. Our response can be cognitive (our thoughts), emotional (our feelings), physical (our body sensations), or behavioral (our actions). When we are triggered we respond from our hurt places, which are often our younger, unhealed selves. We do not think or act from our most wise, adult self. We often get stuck in a loop of negative thoughts, feelings, and behaviors.

For example, like many women, sometimes I struggle with feeling not good enough. One of my big triggers is making mistakes. When I make a mistake I have negative thoughts about myself, such as, *"I can't believe I did that! I'm so embarrassed. I always mess everything up. What is wrong with me?"* My emotions are usually fear or shame. The sensations in my body include my heart racing or feeling sick to my stomach. Behaviorally, I might cry or obsessively talk or think about the mistake I made. Then I start to think more negative thoughts and have more negative feelings, and the negative loop continues.

It can be hard to break out of this negative cycle because our emotional brain is intensely activated and our logical, thinking brain is offline when we are triggered. One of my favorite ways to practice self-care when triggered and to get my logical, thinking brain back online is to read or write. Specifically, I will write myself a compassionate letter to break the negative cycle.

Sometimes it can be challenging to access our tools when we are triggered. One way to address this is to write the letter ahead of time. This way you will have it on hand for when a trigger arises. Most of us get activated around the same stuff over and over; we can predict our triggers and therefore, we can proactively write ourselves a compassionate letter. I include three parts: I know... (acknowledging the facts of what is going on); I understand... (empathizing with my feelings); and lastly, imparting some advice from my most wise self.

Here is an example of a letter to myself to be read when I am feeling triggered because I made a mistake:

Dear Mindy,

I know you just made a mistake. It's okay. I understand that you are beating yourself up about it and feeling like you never do anything right. Maybe you are even falling into shame and self-loathing. You are probably trapped in all-or-nothing thinking, using words like "always" or "never." Take a few deep breaths. Mistakes are allowed. They are part of being human. You're okay. Take a few more deep breaths. Ground back into your center. Now that you are feeling calmer and thinking more clearly, ask yourself if there is any action you need to take to rectify your mistake. Was it a simple thing you can let go, such as forgetting to send sneakers to school on gym day? Forgive yourself and release it. Or was it something more serious, such as yelling at your kids or forgetting to pay a bill? If the mistake requires action (e.g., an apology to your daughter or a call to the bank), make a plan to do what you need to do. Then forgive yourself and let it go. I love you no matter what.

What triggers come up for you repeatedly? Write yourself a compassionate letter. The next time you are triggered, pull it out and read it. Let your wisest self take care of your struggling self. Give yourself the gift of your own words of comfort and care.

February 5

Practice Loving-kindness

Love creates a communion with life. Love expands us, connects us, sweetens us, ennobles us. Love springs up in tender concern, it blossoms into caring action. It makes beauty out of all we touch. In any moment we can step beyond our small self and embrace each other as beloved parts of a whole.
~ Jack Kornfield

Loving-kindness has the power to shift our inner state and our outer world. We can cultivate loving-kindness through both formal and informal practice.

Formal practice involves sitting in meditation, connecting with the feeling of loving-kindness, and sending well wishes to ourselves and others. I use the mantra, "May I/they be happy, May I/they be healthy, May I/they be free from suffering" and imagine wrapping a series of people in pure love and kindness, first myself, then a loved one, followed by a neutral person, then a person I am having negative feelings toward, and lastly all beings everywhere. I usually repeat the mantra three times for each person while imagining them in my mind.

There are many ways to informally practice loving-kindness. You can dedicate the energy of an activity to someone you love. The activity could be your first sun salutation of the day, your walk around the block, or even your meditation practice. You can connect with the feeling of loving-kindness before going out into public and then imagine sending out love beams to people you pass on the street or in the store. You can silently send compliments or positive wishes to people you interact with throughout your day. When I teach a yoga class, this is what I do while the students rest in final relaxation pose. Cultivating loving-kindness feels good, and I believe it is good for our world too!

Spend a few minutes today either formally or informally practicing loving-kindness. Notice how you feel afterwards and consider adding this practice to your daily or weekly routine.

February 6

Find Peace Amidst the Chaos

*To experience peace does not mean that your life is always blissful.
It means that you are capable of tapping into a blissful state of mind amidst the normal chaos of a hectic life.*
~ Jill Bolte Taylor

If we wait for life to be peaceful in order to feel peace, we might be waiting a long time.

If we want to feel peaceful, one of the most powerful things we can do is accept that there are things we do not have control over and focus our energy on that which we do have the ability to change, namely our inner experience. We can reclaim power over our internal state no matter what our outer circumstances may be. We can practice cultivating an inner state of peace that we can connect with regardless of what is happening around us. We can learn to find peace amidst the chaos.

What helps you connect with a peaceful feeling? I recommend using your breath and an image. I like to take deep belly breaths and imagine myself as a strong, steady mountain that remains grounded no matter what is going on around it. When I am inside the chaos of daily life, I invite in peace by pausing and breathing deeply while focusing on this image. It doesn't change my outer circumstances, but it does help shift my inner state of being. We can find peace inside of the lives we have right now.

Begin now by taking a few moments to breathe deeply and focus on an image that evokes peace for you. Today, practice pausing and connecting with your breath and the peaceful image throughout the day. Notice any shifts that occur as a result of this exercise.

february 7

Accept Yourself

*To be beautiful means to be yourself. You don't need to be accepted by others.
You need to accept yourself.*
~ Thich Nhat Hanh

We all want to feel accepted. Too often we look outside of ourselves for validation. Sometimes we may receive the affirmation we seek, sometimes not. The truth is, the acceptance we crave is always available to us because we can give it to ourselves.

You may find that it is easier to accept yourself when things are going well or you are performing at a certain level, but that it is harder to accept yourself when you are struggling or not performing so well. This is *conditional* acceptance: we accept ourselves as long as we meet certain criteria. I believe we deserve *unconditional* self-acceptance.

Accepting ourselves no matter what may sound difficult or even impossible. That's okay. Just start where you are. Practice saying, out loud or in your mind, "I accept myself exactly as I am." If that feels too far-fetched, try, "I am learning to accept myself exactly as I am."

February 8

Let Your Intuition Guide You

I believe the wisdom of our intuition lives inside of our bodies, not our minds. After years of practice, I am usually tuned into my intuition and can feel a clear yes or no when making a decision. However, this wasn't always the case. I used to make my decisions based on what I thought others expected of me or what I thought would please people or earn me recognition. It took me many years to unlearn these habits and relearn to connect with my most wise inner self.

Sometimes I still struggle with making decisions. My intuition can get clouded, usually by fear. When that happens I give myself space to sit with the decision. I might talk to people I trust, do my own research, or make a pro/con list. I almost always use my two most-trusted tools, meditation and journal writing. Ultimately, I decide by tuning into my body and seeing how the decision feels.

Because my intuition speaks to me through my body sensations.
Because I am the only one who knows what's best for me.
Because I trust my gut feeling over any logical list I might make.
Because my mind can keep going in circles for days, but once I tap into it, the wisdom of my body is visceral and clear.

Spend some time with your journal today. How do you make decisions? What helps you connect with your intuition? What role does your intuition play as you make decisions?

february 9

Work Toward Change from a Place of Love and Acceptance

I did then what I knew how to do. Now that I know better, I do better.
~ Maya Angelou

In this day and age it seems like we are on a never-ending quest to do more and be better: earn a promotion, buy a nicer car or a bigger house, organize the closets, learn another language, grow our own food, start meditating, take up knitting—there is always another goal to be reached. So often we try to motivate ourselves to change by being mean to ourselves. We judge and berate ourselves for not being who or where we want to be. I understand and agree with the desire to evolve. *And* I want us to work toward that change from a place of love and acceptance.

The psychologist Carl Rogers said, "The curious paradox is that when I accept myself just as I am, then I change." It certainly does sound paradoxical to accept yourself as a means to change, but I believe we can hold both things at once: a deep love and acceptance for who we are in the moment, and the desire to change.

Try saying this to yourself:

I love and accept myself.
My efforts toward change come from love.
I work toward change because I love myself.

Can you feel the difference in this approach to change?

Make Room for What Brings You Joy

Twinkle lights are the perfect metaphor for joy. Joy is not a constant. It comes to us in moments—often ordinary moments. Sometimes we miss out on the bursts of joy because we're too busy chasing down extraordinary moments. Other times we're so afraid of the dark that we don't dare let ourselves enjoy the light. A joyful life is not a floodlight of joy. That would eventually become unbearable. I believe a joyful life is made up of joyful moments gracefully strung together by trust, gratitude, inspiration, and faith.
~ Brené Brown

I need to tell you something: life isn't just about getting things done.

It took me a while to learn this. I spent many years hyper-focused on ticking things off a socially determined to-do list: finish the degree, get a job with benefits, find a partner, buy a house. Eventually I noticed that I felt miserable and exhausted even though I was "doing well" when it came to achieving these socially expected outcomes. I began to question these expectations and wonder what the point of it was if I wasn't feeling happy and content inside of my life.

I believe we are here on this planet to experience joy. Yes, there are many tasks of daily living that require our attention, but let's not sacrifice our happiness in the name of getting things done. Joy doesn't have to be expensive or complicated; there is no need to jet off to some exotic location to feel happy. Find what brings you joy where you are right now. I find joy in my dog, the nature right outside my door, a good book, spending time with friends, a hot cup of tea and warm chocolate chip cookies, hugs from my husband, fresh flowers from the grocery store, shopping for a new lipstick, going to a yoga class, and eating at my favorite restaurants.

Today, make a list of at least 10 things that bring you joy. Commit to doing something from the list every day—yes, every day. Because it feels good. Because you deserve it. Life is more fast-paced and stressful than ever; make room for what brings you joy.

February 11

Awaken Your Inner Truth

Something inside me has always been there, but now it's awake.
~ Rey, Star Wars: The Force Awakens

I love this quote because it reminds me that we all have divine wisdom inside us, just waiting to be awakened. In the moment when Rey says this line, she is feeling afraid and asking for help. It can be jarring to wake up to the force (the truth) within you. If you choose to tap into your inner truth, you might find that your life doesn't seem to make sense anymore. If you choose to tune into the wise voice inside you, you might start saying or doing things that other people don't like. If you choose to look within and honor the wisdom you find there, you might no longer be willing to tolerate people and situations that feel out of alignment with your soul.

And it will all be worth it.

Because living your life guided by your truth is freedom.

So much of modern society is set up to have us constantly searching outside ourselves. The truth is, everything that you need is already within you, including the answers to all of your questions. It is simply a matter of reconnecting with your truth, your divine inner self, and being willing to listen.

Connecting with your truth can feel scary, inconvenient, and confusing.
It can also feel amazing, inspiring, and exhilarating.
Often it is all of that and more.
And it is always, always, always worth it.

february 12

Practice Self-Trust

If braving relationships with other people is braving connection,
self-trust is braving self-love.
~ Brené Brown

We live inside of a society that tells women, implicitly and explicitly, that we cannot be trusted. We are culturally conditioned to second guess ourselves or to not value our own opinions while also being programmed to believe that the views, opinions, and experiences of men (white men in particular) are correct, best, and true.

Because we did not grow up knowing we are trustworthy, our default is self-doubt and uncertainty. We have to actively re-learn how to trust ourselves. We can consciously practice self-trust by affirming our innate trustworthiness, validating our lived experiences, and listening to our intuition. Trusting yourself helps you move from relying on external authority to honoring your own internal knowing; it profoundly changes how you move through the world.

Spend some time with your journal today. Do you trust yourself? When did you first learn to question your truth? What people or situations encourage your confidence, and what people or situations bring up self-doubt? Set the intention to cultivate self-trust and follow up with practices to support your intention such as introspection, meditation, or therapy.

Connect with Your Soul Self

Quiet the mind, and the soul will speak.
~ Ma Jaya Sati Bhagavati

I think of each of us as having a human self and a soul self. The human self is the part of us that is here on the physical plane, managing daily life. The soul self is the divine love inside each of us. There is an amazing complexity to the human self—thoughts, feelings, memories, relationships, responsibilities, and more. With so much to navigate, it is easy to over-identify with our human self and disconnect from our soul self. This can leave us feeling anxious, unfulfilled, and depleted. When we are connected with our soul self we feel peaceful, content, and free. The truth is that when we prioritize our connection with our soul self, it makes the human stuff more manageable because we are approaching our lives from a place of feeling grounded and centered.

What connects you to your soul self? Make a list. For me, it's time alone in nature, visioning, writing, meditating, yoga, and reading inspirational texts. Once you have your list, think about how you can spend time doing what connects you to your soul in your daily life. This doesn't have to be a big time commitment. You might schedule 15 minutes a day for contemplation, writing, praying, or whatever practice connects you with your soul. Create a routine that fosters your connection with your soul self and notice how this shifts your experience of daily life.

February 14

Fifty Simple Ways to Show Yourself Some Love

1. Wear fuzzy socks.
2. Take your vitamins.
3. Soak in the bathtub.
4. Take a nap.
5. Listen to your favorite music.
6. Listen to a podcast while driving.
7. Savor a cup of coffee or tea.
8. Unplug for 30 minutes.
9. Give yourself a foot massage with coconut oil.
10. Go outside and look up at the sky.
11. Go to bed early.
12. Go to the library and borrow a book.
13. Burn a candle or incense.
14. Close your eyes and breathe deeply for five minutes.
15. Take a day off from your to-do list.
16. Take a day off from social media.
17. Spend five minutes in Savasana or Crocodile Pose.
18. Stand in front of the mirror and say kind things to yourself.
19. Clear one small space (such as the top of your dresser or the front seat of your car).
20. Throw out all your socks and underwear that have holes in them.
21. Write down 10 things you are grateful for in this moment.
22. Read a poem.
23. Write a poem.
24. Say the thing you think you cannot say.

25. Do the thing you think you cannot do.

26. Ask for help.

27. Stay in your pj's all day.

28. Watch your favorite movie.

29. Take a selfie.

30. Watch the sunset.

31. Let yourself dream.

32. Take one small step toward a big dream.

33. Check in with your body and ask her what she needs.

34. Drink a glass of water.

35. Eat a meal by candlelight.

36. Write yourself a love note.

37. Pick out your clothes the night before.

38. Bake something yummy or cook yourself a nourishing meal.

39. Paint or draw.

40. Clip words and images out of magazines and make a collage.

41. Take yourself out to lunch.

42. Buy yourself a treat that you loved as a child.

43. Be gentle with yourself, remember mistakes are allowed.

44. Forgive yourself.

45. Get it out of your head and down onto paper: free write or make a list.

46. Ask for a hug from someone you love.

47. Snuggle your kid or your pet.

48. Stop comparing yourself to other people, especially on social media.

49. Say no when you want to say no.

50. Sweat: dance, run, shake it out.

I invite you to pick one thing from the list and do it today.
What will you choose?

february 15

I Hope You Know You're Not Alone

If you're feeling behind in life or like you're not good enough or that everyone else seems to have their shit together...

I hope you know you're not alone.

If you're feeling like you never measure up and there's always more to do...

I hope you know it's the system that's broken, not you.

If you're feeling like you're always working so hard to prove your worth...

I hope you know you are inherently worthy and you do not have to earn love.

If you're feeling like you need to change your body in any way to be acceptable...

I hope you know you are beautiful. And I hope you know that so much of our culture is set up to convince you otherwise. And I hope you know that you are worth the work of challenging the ubiquitous messages of the thin-ideal and diet culture.

If you're feeling like you are always in a rush and life is over-scheduled...

I hope you know you can opt out of the glorification of busy.

If you're feeling burnt out and exhausted...

I hope you know you can't care for everyone else if you're not caring for yourself first. I hope you know you deserve rest. I hope you know you can say no.

If you're feeling like you don't know what to believe or that everyone seems okay with certain things that just don't feel right to you...

I hope you know you can trust yourself. And I hope you know that those glimmers of self-doubt come from patriarchal messaging that's been ingrained in you from the start. And I hope you know that it is possible to de-condition yourself from that bullshit.

If you're uncomfortable with jokes, comments, or behaviors and you wonder if you're being too sensitive...

I hope you know micro-aggressions are real, pervasive, and completely unacceptable. I hope you know you have a right to call people out on their shitty behavior.

If something terrible happened to you once or many times and you're still trying to heal from it...

I hope you know you are not damaged or defective in any way. I hope you know you deserve safety and respect.

Wherever you are and whatever you're going through...

I hope you know you're not alone.

What If?

We make a contribution to the world just by being ourselves every moment.
~ Shakti Gawain

What if you didn't have to earn it?

The love you desire.
The acceptance you crave.

What if it was your birthright?

No conditions.
Nothing to prove.

What if you could trust that you deserve good things?

Peace, happiness, safety.
Love and abundance.

What if you could live your life from a deep knowing of your inherent worth?

Truly believing that you are already enough, exactly as you are right here, right now.

Today, I invite you to step inside of this truth.

february 17

Who Are You Underneath It All?

You are the sky. Everything else—it's just the weather.
~ Pema Chödrön

Who are you?

You are not your body.
You are not your thoughts.
You are not your feelings.
You are not your job.
You are not the many roles you play in this life.
You are not your degrees or your house or your car or the number in your bank account.

So who are you?
What is left when you peel all those layers away?

Close your eyes,
Steady your breath.

Can you sense that?

The space between your thoughts,
The pause after the exhale and before the inhale,
The moment of nothingness and everything all at once.
That is you. That is me. That is all of us.

Expand Your Definition of Epic Love

Close your eyes. Fall in love. Stay there. ~ Rumi

I want my life to be an epic love story.

Our culture prizes romantic love above all other types of love. Because of this messaging, so many people feel incomplete when they are not in a romantic relationship. Not only is this problematic, *it's just not true.* I think we need to expand our definition of love. When we open our awareness to love in its many forms, we can see that we are always surrounded by so much love. Sure, sometimes epic love might be the dramatic stuff we see in movies and on TV, but epic love can also be quiet and small; it can even appear boring.

Epic love might be making eye contact with the person cashing you out at the store.

Epic love might be holding her hand while she gives birth.

Epic love might be taking out the garbage or bringing home the milk.

Epic love might be your best friend checking in on you.

Epic love might be your puppy snuggling up against you.

Epic love might be making yourself your favorite chocolate chip cookies.

Epic love might be him being kind and forgiving when you take your own shit out on him.

Epic love might be buying coffee for the person behind you in line.

Epic love might be thinking about her every day even if you go for weeks without talking to her.

Epic love might be neither of you thinking twice about the time that's passed and instead just falling back in step.

Epic love might be how you feel when you look up at the stars in the sky.

Epic love might be the knowing that you would do anything for them.

Epic love might be not looking away, letting the other person be seen.

Epic love might be devotion to your career or a cause.

Epic love might be calling bullshit.

Epic love might be choosing not to have that person in your life anymore.

Epic love might be holding his hand while he takes his last breath.

Epic love might be how you feel when you sing or run or teach.

Epic love might be him playing with your hair while you watch Netflix.

Epic love might be laughing until you cry.

Epic love is connection, kindness, vulnerability, honesty. Epic love is friends and strangers, lovers and family, nature and spirit, ideas and inspirations. Epic love is our birthright and we can experience it in a multitude of ways.

Today, open yourself up to epic love in its many forms.

Feelings Are Not Facts

All feelings are real—valid and true for the one who feels them.

And feelings are *not* facts.

Feelings are by nature subjective and vary widely among people, even those having the same objective experience. *Feelings are not facts* is a mantra that I use frequently. It helps remind me that while everything I feel is worthy of my love and attention, it is not necessarily *accurate*.

For example, one afternoon I was feeling especially sexy. I was rocking a new outfit, heels, and lipstick. I was excited for my husband to come home from work, and I was looking forward to him noticing my hotness. Instead he walked in the door excited to give our daughter a treat he'd brought home from work for her. Sweet, but not what I was wanting in that moment. He barely glanced my way when I wanted so badly for him to notice me. I was immediately triggered and went upstairs to cry.

After a few minutes, I checked in with myself. What were my feelings? *I'm not good enough. I'm invisible. I'm not important. My husband doesn't care about me.* (Yes, all of that from a simple non-interaction.) What were the facts? *My husband loves me. I am important. He was excited to see our daughter and surprise her with a treat.* Sometimes I can have this conversation with myself in my mind, and other times I need to write it down in my journal so that I can see it more clearly. I feel more grounded and centered after I go through this simple exercise.

Please do not use this concept that feelings are not facts to make your feelings wrong. There is no such thing as a wrong feeling. Feelings are simply that—feelings! A subjective internal experience. And it is helpful to remember that our feelings are not an objective reflection of reality; that feelings are not facts. The aim is to welcome our feelings with love and acceptance while also checking in with ourselves around the accuracy behind our beliefs.

february 20

Know Your Love Language

In his book *The Five Love Languages*, Gary Chapman outlines five main ways that people express and receive love: words of affirmation, gifts, physical touch, quality time spent together, and acts of service. You might know what your top one or two are just from reading that sentence! If not, you can search for *The Five Love Languages* online and take the free quiz to find out.

This simple concept is very powerful when it comes to expressing love in our relationships. It is helpful to know your own love language, as well as that of your partner, friends, and family. Often there is a disconnect between how we show love and how others receive love.

For example, my top love language is *words of affirmation*, and my husband's is *acts of service*. This means I give and receive love through words, while he shows his love by doing things for me—making dinner, getting the groceries, folding the laundry, taking my car for an oil change. All of that stuff goes right over my head. And while I might tell him often how amazing I think he is and how much I love him, he feels my love the most when I take out the garbage. You can imagine how this disconnect could create hurt feelings inside of our relationship. The same thing can happen in relationships with friends and family, not just with romantic partners.

The good news is that once you know your love language you can start a dialogue with your loved ones to ensure that everyone is feeling loved and valued. Tell people what you need and ask them what they need. If your best friend receives love through gifts, take the time to occasionally pick up something small for them. If your child receives love through words, send a sweet note in their lunchbox from time to time. If your partner receives love through physical touch, offer them a foot massage or back rub. Be willing to have the conversation about love languages, to directly ask for what you want, and to give your loved ones what they need.

Connect with Your Inner Child

Caring for your inner child has a powerful and surprisingly quick result:
Do it and the child heals.
~ Martha Beck

We all have an inner child, and it is healing to spend time connecting with her. No matter how amazing our caregivers were (and many weren't), we are each left with some wounds from our developmental years. Connecting with your inner child can spark creativity, bring more fun into your life, and facilitate healing.

Find a picture of yourself at a younger age, preferably before age ten. Carve out some quiet time to intentionally connect with your inner child; 20 minutes is a good starting point. Begin by centering yourself with some deep breathing or a few minutes of meditation. Connect with your inner child by dialoguing with her through journal writing or meditation. You might ask your inner child what she needs. What does she want you to know? Perhaps your inner child would like you to take her on an adventure. What would she like to do?

Commit to checking in with your inner child as a regular practice. It might feel silly or awkward at first, but trust that there is healing to be found in your connection with your younger self.

february 22

Mirror Work

Perhaps
we should love ourselves
so fiercely,
that when others see us
they know exactly
how it should be done.
~ Rudy Francisco

When I am having a hard day, one of my practices is to look at myself in the mirror and say kind, encouraging things.

You're doing great!
You've got this!
I love you.

A few minutes of looking into my own eyes and giving myself support creates a shift.

We don't have to save this practice for hard days. There is no need to be stingy with our self-care! Take a few minutes today to look at yourself in the mirror and say whatever it is you need to hear.

February 23

Practice Radical Acceptance

There is something wonderfully bold and liberating about saying Yes
to our entire imperfect and messy life.
~ Tara Brach

We spend so much of our lives inside of resistance.

We want things to be a certain way. We think things *should* be a certain way. We each have our own ideas about how people should behave and how events should unfold. The truth is, we are setting ourselves up for disappointment, frustration, and resentment. Our expectations interfere with our ability to just be with what is, to accept reality.

It is important to note that acceptance is not the same as tolerance. Acceptance is surrendering to the truth. Tolerance is allowing something to occur or continue to occur. For example, let's say someone is being rude and disrespectful while talking to you. Resistance thinks, "I can't believe this is happening!" Acceptance thinks, "Okay, this person is being rude and disrespectful." Tolerance would be taking no action, passively allowing the behavior to continue. Acceptance acknowledges what is happening and allows for space to mindfully respond. Tolerance is poor boundaries; acceptance is self-care.

Today, release your expectations and approach people and situations with an open heart and curious mind. Practice accepting whatever arises. Remember to extend your radical acceptance to yourself as well.

Clean Pain vs. Dirty Pain

Emotional discomfort, when accepted, rises, crests, and falls in a series of waves. Each wave washes parts of us away and deposits treasures we never imagined.
~ Martha Beck

Clean pain is the pain of grief or loss. Feeling it is necessary and healing. Dirty pain is the pain of the stories we create around our circumstances. It is not useful.

Clean pain is the heartache of a relationship ending. Dirty pain is believing no one will ever love you again. Clean pain is the disappointment of not getting the job. Dirty pain is telling yourself you're a loser. Clean pain is feeling bad when you yell at your kids. Dirty pain is carrying shame around long after.

Are you currently inside of any clean pain? If so, let yourself feel your feelings. Write them out to help you process. Share what you're going through with a friend or therapist. Clean pain serves a purpose. You will emerge on the other side.

Where in your life are you inside of dirty pain? What stories are you telling yourself? Are they helpful or harmful? Dirty pain does not serve you. It creates a cycle of negative thoughts and emotions that keeps you stuck. Identify your dirty pain, the negative thoughts and stories you're telling yourself about your circumstances, and let it go.

February 25

Take a Baby Step Toward Your Dreams

As you move toward a dream, the dream moves toward you. ~ Julia Cameron

What would you do if you could do exactly what you want? Often we don't even let ourselves consider what we want. We are so focused on what we are "supposed to" or "have to" do that there isn't any space for our desires. What you want matters. Give yourself a few minutes today to consider what you would do if you could do exactly what you want. You might start small and think about what you would do today, or you might go big and think about what you would do with your life. For the sake of this exercise, let yourself dream! No restraints, no being reasonable. Put the whole truth down on the paper. Your wildest desires.

Once you have written down your vision, think about how you could incorporate some of your desires into your current life. If you dream of living in Paris, cook a French meal, start a vacation fund for a trip to France, or read a novel set in Paris. If you dream of owning a bakery, bake something beautiful, start a blog to share your creations, or research selling your stuff at a local market. If you dream of running a half marathon, research running trainer apps, browse sneakers online, or join a local running group.

Your dreams and desires are important. They deserve your time and attention. You don't have to turn your life upside down to honor them. Today, find a way to take a baby step toward your dreams.

February 26

See the Soul in Others

Just imagine becoming the way you used to be as a very young child, before you understood the meaning of any word, before opinions took over your mind. The real you is loving, joyful, and free. The real you is just like a flower, just like the wind, just like the ocean, just like the sun.
~ Don Miguel Ruiz

We all came into this world as babies.

I believe babies are inherently connected with the truth that we are all made of divine love.

You can almost see this fade as we grow and interact with the world. We become conditioned to believe that our value lies in our minds or our possessions or our accomplishments. We get further and further from the truth of our divinity, our soul. It is easy to see the soul of a baby. I think that is why many people love babies so much: they remind us of that divine part within ourselves; they elicit the unconditional love we all crave.

Today, try to see the soul in everyone you interact with. If it feels challenging, imagine people as they were when they were babies. Remind yourself that underneath it all, we are truly made of the same stuff—divine love. Observe how connecting with this divine part in people—seeing their soul—impacts your interactions today.

February 27

It's Okay to Turn Off the News

We are exposed to so much information on a regular basis. The world has always been full of tragedy and injustice, but now news about the state of things around the globe is more readily accessible than ever. There are upsides to carrying around a tiny computer (smartphone) in your pocket, but there are definite downsides, as well.

It is important to be informed. It is also important to take care of yourself. Overconsuming the news can lead to anxiety, depression, compassion fatigue, and feelings of hopelessness. Our job as adults is to know our own capacity for taking in information and to honor it. It can be helpful to notice when we have moved beyond learning and understanding and into overwhelm and despair. Being informed helps us to act as responsible citizens of the world, to be inspired to take action—to speak up, write letters, vote, donate money, go to a rally, etc. But when we move beyond this point and into feeling overwhelmed, we can become consumed with negativity and paralyzed by analysis of how awful things are.

Notice how your consumption of news and media impacts you physically, emotionally, mentally, and energetically. Remember it is okay to turn off the news and take a break. Being a good citizen of the world is a marathon, not a sprint, and we need to honor our capacity for taking in information so that we can be present for the long haul.

Just Do Nothing

If women were convinced that a day off or an hour of solitude was a reasonable ambition, they would find a way of attaining it. As it is, they feel so unjustified in their demand that they rarely make the attempt.
~ Anne Morrow Lindbergh

One of the best ways to connect with yourself is by doing nothing.

Truly, we don't have to "work" hard to hear our inner voice or sense our inner truth. It's quite the opposite; we need to *stop* working so hard. Once we quiet down and find some empty space, our inner self will begin communicating with us. The more regularly we take time for quiet and reflection, the easier it becomes to connect with ourselves. In the space of doing nothing, we learn about our inner thoughts, hopes, fears, and dreams.

Today, find some time to disconnect from your to-do list. Let go of trying to be productive. Find some room to simply be. If you'd like, you can close your eyes and take some deep breaths. Or maybe you'd prefer to sit outside and listen to the sounds of nature. Whatever you choose, give yourself space to feel into the quiet. Observe what happens when you do nothing for a few minutes. Let go of any expectations or judgment around your experience; just be with whatever arises for you. Consider building time into your daily or weekly routine to just do nothing.

February 29

Let Yourself Be Inside of the Truth of Your Life in this Moment

Don't wish me happiness—I don't expect to be happy,
but it's gotten beyond that somehow.
Wish me courage and strength and a sense of humor—I will need them all.
~ Anne Morrow Lindbergh

Today, I invite you to pause and ask yourself, *"What is true for me right now?"*

Your first answer might be, *"I don't know."* (I say that a lot too. My therapist often asks me if *"I don't know"* actually means *"I don't want to say."*) Sometimes it is hard to just be with ourselves, to acknowledge our truth. Sometimes we feel really far away from ourselves, kind of lost. Sometimes things are hard and it's challenging to lean into that. Sometimes things are good and it's hard to lean into that.

Mostly we seem to be focused on getting to the next thing. We want to skip over the in-between spaces, but life is made up of in-between spaces. This practice is about being where you are, living into whatever the truth of your life is at any given moment.

What's true for you today? Can you let yourself just be inside of it?

Drinking Water as a Self-Care Practice

Our bodies are truth-tellers; deep wisdom lies within our cells. Understanding that our bodies are the sacred home of our soul and treating them with care and kindness forms the foundation of our self-care practice. Tending to our basic physical needs facilitates our ability to tend to our higher needs. A key practice in physical self-care is drinking plenty of water and staying hydrated. What is your relationship to hydration?

I am blessed in that I have always loved to drink water. On the other side of this blessing is the truth that not being well-hydrated impacts me greatly. By the time I feel thirsty I am already anxious or irritated. Everywhere I go I carry my water bottle with me, knowing how much shifts for me when I am hydrated. The first thing I do when I am feeling out of sorts is drink a glass of water. It brings me back to center, over and over.

Today, aim to drink at least 64 ounces of water. Experiment with flavoring your water with a slice of fruit or try sparkling water. Notice what comes up for you throughout the day. Observe your mood, your energy, your concentration, and your hunger. How does this simple act of self-care impact your day?

Rest is a Necessity (Not an Indulgence)

It is so powerful to realize you are not a machine. You don't have to grind.
~ The Nap Ministry

We live in a society obsessed with getting things done. Some days it feels like we are all involved in some twisted contest to see whose life is the busiest. Let's opt out of that nonsense.

Let's allow ourselves to rest.

Resting does not come naturally to me. If I have a free moment, my first instinct is to turn to my to-do list and get something done. I am still working to untangle my sense of self-worth from my daily productivity. The truth is we cannot always be "on." Trying to be consistently alert and productive is how we burn out. Rest is essential.

Here are some ways I've learned to incorporate rest into my life: I've let go of the idea of getting up at 5am to have time to myself before the day starts. I plan for downtime when I know I will need it—after travel, post-parties, and the month of September (so much transition!). I put giant Xs in my planner to ensure I don't fill the time. I say no to fun stuff that I would love to do when I know that it will drain me rather than fill me up. I always carry my water bottle, tea bags, and a variety of essential oils in my purse. It's like a portable reset button. I schedule a monthly massage and acupuncture appointment. I don't bring my phone to the dinner table. I soak in a tub filled with Epsom salts and lavender oil at least once a week, every day when I am pre-menstrual. I watch hilarious sitcoms and laugh my ass off. When I am tired, I take a nap. I modify my physical activity and social plans based on where I am in my menstrual cycle. I take an hour lunch break. I limit the activities that my daughter participates in so that we have unscheduled time during the evenings. I schedule time off from work every quarter, even if I am not traveling.

Spend some time with your journal today. What does rest mean to you? How can you include more rest in your day, week, month, and year?

march 3

Food as Self-Care

From a young age, we receive mixed and confusing messages about what we eat. Next time you are in line at the grocery store take a look at the cover of a magazine targeted to women. It is not uncommon to see a headline like "ultimate brownie recipe" right next to "lose 10lbs in 3 days." So which one is it? Should we make amazing brownies or lose weight? Are we supposed to do both? Is that even possible? We are set up to do the wrong thing before we even begin; advertising truly creates an impossible set of rules for us to follow when it comes to food and our bodies.

Day after day we are bombarded with messages about what's wrong with our bodies. What begins as a fun and loving relationship with food transforms into fear and judgment, with girls as young as 5 reporting dieting behavior. So many of us have spent our lives battling our bodies, and that battle has been fought through our relationship with food. A woman's relationship with food is often complicated. We restrict, deny, and judge our eating in the name of trying to transform our bodies into something else. *What if you were to love your body exactly as it is in this moment?* Right here, right now. Not after you lose ten pounds or have your hair done or get a tan.

Take some time to think about your current relationship with food. Release any judgment that comes up and just observe. If there is anything you wish to change, let it come from a place of love and acceptance. Trying to change our relationship with food from a place of discontent with our body is punishment. Making changes in our choices from a place of love and acceptance is self-care. When we are in a place of acceptance, we choose from love, and love chooses in alignment with how we want to feel. There is no right or wrong here. There are no good or bad foods. There is simply how you want to feel in your body and what brings you there.

Today, invite yourself to think of food as self-care. Let go of any thoughts about needing to change your body. Release any comparing. What if you surrendered the fight with your body? What if you chose to love and accept yourself exactly as you are in this moment? How would this impact your relationship with food?

march 4

Choose Your Own Beliefs About Your Body

Today, let's consider the messages we've received from our community, friends, and family about food and our bodies.

Where and when did you first learn positive or dysfunctional messages about food? What is/was your mother's (or other primary caregiver's) relationship with food and her body? Who were the other influential figures in your childhood and what were their messages to you (implicit or explicit) about food, your body, or both?

This inquiry is not meant to place blame on our parents or anyone else. We are all adults now. We have the power to decide what we want to continue to believe and what we want to release. First comes awareness, then choice, and from there, change. We can't change what is not in our conscious awareness.

Like many girls, I learned from a young age that food and my weight were things to be controlled. I was a naturally thin girl, yet I remember hating my body and thinking I needed to restrict my food intake. When I was a teenager, most of my friends were focused on losing weight. It was just a given that everyone was dissatisfied with their body to one degree or another and wanted to change it.

I continued to live inside a negative body image until I was about 25 years old. I was in graduate school studying the sociocultural factors that influence body image and eating disorders. I watched Jean

Kilbourne's documentary *Killing Us Softly*, and I got pissed. I woke up to the reality of having a woman's body in this culture. I decided to opt out of the nonsense—to let go of the belief that my weight or size had anything to do with my worth as a person. I decided to put my time, energy, and money toward changing the world rather than my waistline. I also started teaching 10-year-old girls these same ideas, and I wanted to be an authentic, healthy role model for them. I am not saying that I never have a negative thought about my body. I absolutely do. But they are fewer and farther between than my younger self would've imagined possible. And when a negative thought comes in, I simply notice it and let it float by. I don't grab on and follow the train of thought. And I do not allow those negative thoughts to dictate my behavior. I make my choices about food from a place of self-love and body appreciation.

Today, consider what beliefs about food and your body are no longer serving you. Write them down and let them go. Consider writing a new set of beliefs to guide your relationship with food and your body.

march 5

The Care and Keeping of You

Society teaches us to view our bodies as objects to perfect and present for others' consumption. This is damaging and leads us to harm ourselves in ways big and small. My hope is that we can all shift how we view our bodies and recognize them as amazing temples that are worthy of love and care. Today, let's consider the care and keeping of our bodies.

Do you have a car? If so, you probably take care of your car by bringing it in for an oil change every so many miles. Maybe you take it to the car wash here and there. If your car makes a weird noise, you bring it to the mechanic for a check up. You take good care of your car because you want it to last, to stay in good shape. Maybe even because you love it.

How do these ideas apply to our bodies?

First, consider medical appointments. Are you up to date with your preventative care? When is the last time you had a physical? Gynecological exam? Skin check at the dermatologist? Cleaning at the dentist? What have you been avoiding? Make the call and schedule an appointment today. Second, what are you putting in and on your body? Are you taking any supplements? When is the last time you had your vitamin levels checked? What kind of beauty products do you use? Do they contain harmful chemicals? Third, what other kinds of care does your body need or enjoy? Are you bothered by pain or other issues? When is the last time you had a massage, a facial, or a manicure? What type of specialized care do you need or want to seek out? You deserve to have a team of medical and health professionals that you trust.

Who is on your team? Who needs to be fired and replaced? What referrals do you need? For example, my team includes a primary care doctor, a gynecologist, a dermatologist, a dentist, an acupuncturist, a massage therapist, an aesthetician, a chiropractor, an applied kinesiologist, and an energy healer. Let's give our bodies the exquisite care they deserve by enlisting the services of trusted, kind medical and health providers.

march 6

Allow Yourself Pleasure

Pleasure.
Ritualize it.
Be loyal to it.
Crave it.
Let it write your schedule.
Ask it to wander with you into creativity.
~ Hannah Marcotti

What is your relationship to pleasure?

Our bodies, the female body in particular, are designed for pleasure. In fact, unlike men, we have a body part that is entirely devoted to pleasure. Yes, I am talking about your clitoris! Did you know that it has no other function than to feel pleasure? Sex is an obvious (and lovely!) way to experience pleasure through the body. There are many other ways as well.

Today, let's make a list of ways we can experience pleasure through the body. I find it useful to keep the five senses in mind as I make this list. What sights, smells, sounds, tastes, and sensations bring you pleasure? Some ideas include massage, soft blankets, silk pajamas, walking, dancing, yoga, a hot shower or bath, fresh flowers, singing, listening to music, the smell of lavender, kissing, bare feet on the earth, petting a cat or dog, and drinking herbal tea. Make your own list and choose one thing from it to do today. Consider devoting time daily to pleasure.

Dear Body

Our body is the carrier of the stories
Of the world
Of the earth
Of the mother.
Our body is the mother.
Our body came from mother.
Our body is our home.
We are crying here
We are found
We are too much
We are empty
We are full
We live in a good body
We live in the good body
Good body
Good body
Good body.

~ Eve Ensler

Dear Body,

I forgive you for freezing when you were under attack,
I forgive you for the baby you could not sustain,

I forgive you for not going into labor naturally,
I forgive you for being so sensitive.

Please forgive me for not trusting you,
Please forgive me for all the years I hated you,
Please forgive me for believing them when they said you were dirty,
Please forgive me for every time you said *no* and I ignored you.

Thank you for your wisdom and all that you allow me to experience,
Thank you for growing and birthing my two amazing daughters,
Thank you for being trustworthy when my mind is in chaos,
Thank you for carrying me through this life.

I promise to keep you hydrated and happy with lots of water and salty
        baths and time by the sea,
I promise to nourish you with foods that make you sing,
I promise to dress you in the softest, flowing fabrics,
I promise to delight you with fresh flowers and sparkling water
        and dark chocolate with sea salt,
I promise to treat you like the sacred temple you are and take you for
        monthly massages and anoint you with precious oils and adorn
        you with gorgeous lacy things,
I promise to do the things that light you up and turn you on,
I promise to love and honor you in sickness and in health,
I promise to listen to you and respond to your needs.

Love,

Me

Today, write a letter to your body.
You can borrow my format or create your own.

Turn the Camera Around and See Yourself

You are beautiful and whole just as you are *in this very moment.*

Today, take a moment to really see yourself. Carve out a few minutes to play around with taking some self-portraits. This may feel like an edge for you. Or it might seem silly! I promise you that an intentional selfie can be transformative. When you turn the camera on yourself you are reclaiming your body and your sovereignty. You are sending the message, "I get to decide how I am presented and portrayed," and that is a powerful message.

I view selfies as part of my self-care practice. Something shifts for me when I look into my own eyes. Pairing a picture with a few words describing my truth is an act of self-validation and self-compassion. Sharing a picture of myself with another or on social media with many others reinforces the message that I deserve to be seen. This is huge for women. We are told to shrink and disappear and be small before we are even born. Showing up and sharing your truth is an act of rebellion against the system.

Take a picture of yourself today. There are no rules. You don't have to be or look a certain way. You sure as hell don't have to smile if you don't want to. Simply invite your truth in the moment to come through. Because you deserve to be seen in your joy, your sadness, your triumph, your mistakes, in all your beautiful messy truth. If you feel called, share your selfie with a friend or on social media.

Navigating the Dark

Someone I loved once gave me
A box full of darkness.
It took me years to understand
that this too, was a gift.
~ Mary Oliver

It has taken me many years, but I have learned to get comfortable in the dark—in the sad, the lonely, the messy, the scary, the shadow. It's still not easy, but I have learned to stay and mine the gifts.

Today, I offer you some instructions for navigating the dark:

1. *Don't drink alcohol.* It will interfere with your mood, your sleep, and your processing in general.

2. *Eat, even if you don't want to.* Your body needs nourishment, and food will keep you grounded. Tune in and see what you are craving. I like hot tea, spicy lentil soup, and warm chocolate chip cookies. Your list will be different.

3. *Stay hydrated.* Water is essential for helping things to flow.

4. *Move your body.* Run, dance, go to yoga, ride your bike, or do what feels good and is accessible to you. Physical movement helps with emotional movement.

5. *Connect with someone.* You don't have to go it alone. We deserve to be seen and loved inside of our dark places, too.

6. *Write in your journal.* I swear it changes your brain chemistry.

7. *Do something nice for someone else.* Buy coffee for the person behind you, send some words of affirmation, drop off a surprise gift. Get out of your own head for a bit.

8. *Is there a trigger? Deconstruct it.* See what you can learn about yourself.

9. *Make a gratitude list.* Aim for 50 things. It helps to remember the goodness that is there, right beside the not-so-goodness.

10. *Remember that you and your emotions are not problems to be fixed.* Practice simply witnessing yourself and your experience with compassion.

11. *Breathe.* It's going to be okay. The light will return. It always does.

Be with yourself in the dark and the light.
Practice welcoming all the parts of you.

Relaxation vs. Restoration

What's the difference between relaxation and restoration? For me, relaxing is about releasing and chilling out, while restoring is about rejuvenating and refilling our inner well.

I believe we need both. I have observed that many people's self-care is missing restorative practices.

Relaxing is watching television, having a glass of wine, scrolling through social media (although sometimes that can be anything but relaxing). Relaxing is about releasing stress—it takes away something negative.

Restoring is meditating, writing in your journal, spending time in nature. Restoring is about replenishing your inner resources—it adds something positive to your inner life.

I think most things that are restorative are also relaxing, but most things that are relaxing are not necessarily restorative. If our self-care behavior consists only of relaxing activities, we will continue to feel tapped out.

Self-care is about so much more than behaviors; it is an embodied knowing of one's worth that creates a mindset that shapes daily life. But behaviors are a beautiful starting point and a grounding touchstone inside of our daily lives.

Today, I offer you five ways to restore your mind, body, and soul:

1. Practice conscious breath work such as alternate nostril breathing.
2. Put on your favorite song and dance it out.
3. Spend 5 minutes in crocodile pose.
4. Write down 25 things you are grateful for.
5. Sit outside in nature and just be (leave your devices inside).

What would you add to the list? How do you restore and refill your inner well?

march 11

When It Feels Impossible

If it's out of your hands, it deserves freedom from your mind too. ~ Ivan Nuru

When it feels impossible, just do the next right thing.

Drink a glass of water.
Empty the dishwasher.
Make a list.
Take a shower.
Breathe.
Make a cup of tea.
Go outside.
Take a nap.
Ask for help.

Just do something, love.

Pace Your Life

Running is one of my self-care practices. It clears my head and boosts my mood. One day I realized I have two speeds when I run: going as fast as I can for as far as I can, or walking. All or nothing. It occurred to me that I often run my life this way, too. I posted about this on social media and ended up connecting with an avid runner who is also a personal trainer. She gave me some advice on pacing that not only helped me with running, but also with life.

She said, "I like to use a 1-10 scale, 1 being basically not moving and 10 being absolutely maximum effort."

I played with this scale as I ran: *Here's what a 2 feels like, walking slowly. Here's a 4, a light jog. Here's a 5 or 6, a medium jog. Here's a 7 or 8, running faster, but it feels manageable. Here's a 9 or 10, it's hard to breathe and I could not run any faster even if I wanted to.*

I started to think about my life. What does a 1 feel like in life? *When I'm not feeling well and can't do much else besides sleep.* What about a 2, 3, and 4? *A lazy day at home, a mellow day with a few tasks to complete, and working from home.* And an 8, 9, and 10? *Twenty-five clients in a week, lots of appointments or social events, working at home until 10pm, and working six days a week and not having time to exercise or unwind.*

"If you're trying to increase mileage and do longer runs," the trainer said, "I'd recommend trying to stick to a 5 or 6."

I'm definitely trying to do a long run of this thing called life. So why was I trying to run my life at an 8 or 9? I started to think about what it would take to bring all of my days into the 5 or 6 zone. I let myself get specific: *exercise first thing in the morning followed by journal writing and meditation, four clients, plenty of time to cook a healthy dinner for my family, no working after 9pm.*

"After a while, you'll learn what feels 'comfortable' for longer distances," she said. *"It's the pace where you could just go forever."* This is where I want to be living my life: "the pace where you could just go forever." A life that feels sustainable. A life that feels full of joyful effort *and* beautiful ease.

I realized that when I paced myself, I actually ended up running faster overall. I'm still letting that powerful observation sink in.

Think about the pace of your life. Write out what each number on the scale of 1-10 looks and feels like. Where are you in this moment? What does a typical day feel like? Are you at a 10 and finding it hard to breathe? At what pace do you feel best?

Are You Paying Attention?

I don't know exactly what a prayer is.
I do know how to pay attention, how to fall down
into the grass, how to kneel down in the grass,
how to be idle and blessed, how to stroll through the fields,
which is what I have been doing all day.
Tell me, what else should I have done?
Doesn't everything die at last, and too soon?
Tell me, what is it you plan to do
with your one wild and precious life?
~ Mary Oliver

Pause. Close your eyes and breathe deeply. Let your breath carry you home to who you are, to that place of inner stillness that lies beneath it all. Are you paying attention?

When is the last time you really tasted a strawberry? I mean looked at it and saw the sun, the soil, and the rain that grew it, as well as the hands that picked it, and then smelled it and inhaled the whole universe before gratefully taking a bite.

When is the last time you saw the sunset? I mean *really* took it in, your eyes welling up with tears as you not so much saw, but really felt with your heart, the glory of the sun setting in the sky.

When is the last time you watched her while she slept? I am talking about letting yourself feel that scary vulnerable feeling of complete and unconditional love, the kind that catches in your throat and makes you want to run away, but you stay and it is amazing and frightening all at once.

Are you paying attention? Life is beautiful and hard and really fucking painful sometimes. Yet there is ease and joy to be found even on the most gut-wrenching of days.

Breathe. You are here. You are alive.

Trillions of cells are working together to make that happen. You are a miracle. So is that person next to you and that one over there, even that person who you really can't stand. Miracles. All of us. And we run around frustrated by the smallest things. We lack perspective.

Are you paying attention?
Do you see what's going on here?

Once I was lost and upset while driving in the car with my (then) three-year-old. She said, *"Don't worry, Mommy. I know where we are. This is just a playground where we come to dream our dreams."* My tiny spirit guide.

I don't know where we come from and I don't know where we go from here, but I'm guessing it all has something to do with love—and that we most certainly are here to dream our dreams.

This is your one wild and precious life.

Pause. Breathe. Are you paying attention?

Practice Staying with Yourself

*The good did not outweigh the bad but it accompanied the bad,
and I am grateful for that unexpected companionship.*
~ Mari Andrew

Checking out can look like anything from simply choosing to ignore or deny a feeling, situation, or need, to going somewhere else in our minds to dissociating. Checking out can be very helpful, adaptive really, when we are in the midst of a trauma. But it often hangs around long past the point of utility. I lived with checking out as my default for a long time. I have checked out by overachieving, overworking, shopping, drinking, eating, sleeping, and a whole other host of behaviors. I used to spend so much of my time checked out that once I learned to stay present, *to really be here now*, I vowed to never (consciously) check out again. I don't live inside trauma anymore and yet there are still plenty of opportunities to check out, anything from a hard day at work to a challenging yoga pose can trigger the urge. I choose to stay present. I want to be here, in this body, in this moment. I want to stay with myself, during the joyful times and the challenging times.

In what ways do you check out? How can you practice staying?

Discipline Equals Freedom

I used to think discipline meant punishment and restriction, and that freedom meant doing whatever you wanted. I was confusing self-indulgence with self-care. By drinking too much wine, overeating, and mindlessly watching television, I was preventing myself from realizing my true desires under the guise of "being good" to myself. Eventually I realized that my behaviors were not generating the feelings I craved: aliveness, joy, inspiration. In fact, they were dulling me down.

Now I know that freedom does mean doing whatever you want; it just depends which "you" you are listening to—ego or spirit. Ego promotes separateness, scarcity, and grasping. There is never enough for ego. Spirit believes in connection, love, and abundance. She moves toward clarity, peace, and joy.

Discipline feeds my spirit.

Discipline gets me out of bed for yoga on Sunday morning.
Discipline reminds me to take a deep breath before I respond.
Discipline leaves my phone in the other room so I can be fully present.
Discipline tells me to go to bed early and read a book.
Discipline packs my lunch the night before.
Discipline brings my water bottle with me wherever I go.
Discipline reminds me the to-do list can wait while I write my morning pages.

Discipline plants my ass in front of the blank screen to write.

Discipline asks me, "Do you really need that?" as I fill my cart at Target.

Discipline knows how I want to feel and helps me to choose accordingly.

Discipline has my back.

Discipline equals freedom because it honors the longings of my spirit and helps me align my choices with my values and priorities.

Check in with yourself today. Are you acting from a space of ego or spirit? How can discipline support you?

march 16

Set Yourself Up for Success

We each have the things in life that seem to trigger our struggles over and over. Once we can identify what they are, we can prepare in advance and practice setting ourselves up for success.

Traveling is challenging for me. I find it very un-grounding, and it is one of my top anxiety triggers. But I have learned that travel—like anything else—can be filled with joy and ease. I just have to set myself up for success.

Here are a few ways I prepare to travel:

1. *I allow myself to receive.* I open up to receive support from my husband, friends, and colleagues. It might be a ride to the airport, help with my kids or pets, or coverage at the studio or office. I have learned that people are happy to help, we just have to ask.

2. *I make a shit ton of lists.* They comfort me.

3. *I consciously craft the story in my head.* My old story about travel is this: *I hate traveling. Flying un-grounds me. I won't be able to sleep. I will have crazy anxiety.* My new story: *Traveling can be fun. Life can be easy. It's okay to ask for help. I know how to take care of myself. Any stress I feel will be far outweighed by the amazing experiences I am going to have. I deserve this time away.*

4. *I visualize.* Every day I devote a few minutes to imagining myself wherever I'm going. I see myself wearing my favorite clothes, surrounded by kindred spirits, soaking up the amazing views. These images evoke joy and relaxation, and I take the time to allow myself to really feel the feelings so they have a chance to sink in and soothe my spirit.

5. *I plan ahead to create a peaceful space for myself, physically and mentally.* I bring a travel altar and my yoga mat. My phone is loaded with relaxing music and guided meditations. I pack my purse with oils and teas. I make sure to drink plenty of water and take time for journaling, reading, meditating, and practicing yoga.

The thing that feels challenging for you may not be travel—it could be social functions, tests, interviews, or holidays. Whatever it is, take some time to think about how you can set yourself up for success.

You Can't Outrun Anxiety

to heal
you have to
get to the root
of the wound
and kiss it all the way up.
~ rupi kaur

You can't outrun anxiety—believe me, I have tried! I spent years fighting my anxiety and panic, seeing it as an opponent to be bested. When my anxiety was really high, the energy of resisting it left me exhausted, physically ill, and mentally beaten down.

I have learned that the most effective way to soothe myself when I am feeling anxious is to pause and give some love and attention to my fear and worry. Instead of running away or trying to make it go away, I turn *toward* my fear and anxiety and just notice. I take some deep, conscious breaths. I practice being with myself inside of the discomfort. I remind myself that I am okay, that I can handle whatever feelings are arising inside of me, and eventually the anxiety passes. When I fight and try to change the anxiety, it grows stronger. When I surrender and turn toward the anxiety, I find the peace that I have been seeking.

Are there feelings that you are trying to outrun? What would it be like to pause and sit with whatever is arising for you today?

march 18

Exercise as Pleasure

i will dance a little. i will move with the wind. i will give my body to my love and celebrate that we have substance beyond the idea of ourselves. we can move. we can touch. this is my physical exclamation point. this is how I can awaken my mind to the possibilities in the day.
~ mary anne radmacher

How do you currently think about exercise?

Is it an obligation? A method for changing your body? A form of punishment? A way to burn calories? Is it something you do for fun? Does it feel like a way to burn off stress? There are no right or wrong answers, just allow yourself to notice your current thoughts about exercise.

Today, I invite you to think about exercise as pleasure.

What type of movement feels amazing in your body? How can you do more of that? This has nothing to do with losing weight or changing your body. Instead, think about what would feel enjoyable for you. What helps you feel full of vitality? What physical movement feels like pure fun for you? Can you find a way to do it today?

Managing Overwhelm

Feeling overwhelmed is part of the human experience at times. Honestly, most of us do more than any one person should be expected to do, and we definitely handle more stress than is reasonable. I think of overwhelm as our nervous systems being over-activated. If you find yourself feeling overwhelmed, try this: pause, acknowledge how you are feeling, and take some first-aid action such as drinking a glass of water, taking some deep breaths, or writing in your journal. Often we only need a few brief moments to re-regulate our nervous systems.

If the thing creating overwhelm is going to be long-term (such as taking care of a sick or elderly relative), create a more comprehensive coping plan using the steps below.

1. *Begin by thinking about how you can take exquisite care of your body.* Overwhelm taxes the nervous system, so it is vital to get proper sleep, regular exercise, and nourishment through food and water.

2. *Next, think about who you can reach out to for support.* Most of us are not great at asking for help. Different people are equipped to help in different ways. Think about who you can lean on for emotional support (things like talking stuff out or just being witnessed inside of your feelings), physical support (things like helping with meals, transportation, or babysitting), or financial support.

3. *Finally, acknowledge and accept that you may have to let some things slide while you are inside of the overwhelming situation.* Your house may not be as clean as you'd like it to be, or you might give only 80% at work, or you might miss work more often than usual. Know that this is okay. Our capacity shifts during times of intense change, work, or caregiving.

When you find yourself inside of overwhelm, take steps to care for yourself. Remember that everything is temporary and this too shall pass.

march 20

Evolution and Expansion Cannot Be Rushed

When you plant seeds in the garden, you don't dig them up every day to see if they have sprouted yet. You simply water them and clear away the weeds; you know that the seeds will grow in time. Similarly, just do your daily practice and cultivate a kind heart. Abandon impatience and instead be content creating the causes for goodness; the results will come when they're ready.
~ Thubten Chodron

I have a vision of the woman I want to be, the woman I am becoming.

I want to be a woman so grounded in love that her kindness can be felt when she walks into a room. I want to be a woman who confidently takes up space, who believes so much in abundance that she feels only inspired by other women, never threatened. I want to be a woman who creates strong, safe containers for bravery and healing. I want to be a woman who approaches her work with ease, who gives from a place of overflow, whose work nourishes herself and others. I want to be a woman who is strikingly clear in her boundaries; a woman whose "no" feels as good as her "yes." I want to be a woman steeped in self-trust and self-love. I want to be a woman who is unapologetic about her needs. I want to be a woman who speaks her truth with a strong, steady voice. I want to be a woman who fearlessly advocates for others.

Can you picture her?

I am imagining myself as this woman, calling her forth. There is a lot of work involved in stepping into her. There are layers of pain, hurt, and shame to be named and healed. There are practices to commit to at a deeper level. There are things asking to be left behind. The truth is I am not yet who I want to be, and that is totally okay. Evolution and expansion cannot be rushed; they *can* be supported and encouraged—and that is my work in this life. So I move my body, I spend time in nature, I write in my journal, I meditate, I practice, I see my therapist, I read, I study, I let go, I surrender, and I trust that she is on her way to me.

Who is the woman you want to be? How can you support her evolution?

march 21

A Ceremony for Releasing What No Longer Serves You

We hold on to so much—physically, mentally, and emotionally. It can be healing to have regular rituals and practices for letting go. Today I offer you a simple ceremony for releasing what no longer serves you.

1. *Carve out some quiet time for yourself.* Gather your journal and a glass of water or a hot cup of tea.

2. *Begin by cleansing your space.* You could use palo santo, incense, or an aromatherapy spray.

3. *Center yourself with a few deep breaths followed by some time in meditation.* If you're not sure where to begin with meditation, there are many free guided meditations on the internet, as well as many apps with a variety of options.

4. *Spend some time writing in your journal.* Note any insights from your meditation, and then reflect on the following prompts: *What do you want to invite into your life? What is preventing you from moving forward? What is weighing you down? What is asking to be shed?*

5. *Write down everything you want to let go of on a separate piece of paper.* Fold it up and hold it close to your heart. Close your eyes and set your intention to release that which no longer serves you. If it resonates for you, you can ask the Universe, Creative Source, God, or whatever you call the divine to support you in your intention.

6. *Release your words.* Rip them up, burn them, bury them, or toss them in the sea—whatever feels good to you.

Observe how you feel after completing the above steps. Come back to this releasing ceremony as often as you'd like. It can also be powerful to be witnessed inside of this practice. Consider gathering with a group of friends and going through the releasing ceremony together.

Sometimes You Need a Chart

There are days I drop words of comfort on myself like falling rain and
remember that it is enough to be taken care of by myself.
~ Brian Andreas

I have struggled with depression off and on since I was a teenager. Sometimes I go for years without any symptoms, but there are still times when I struggle with a consistently low mood and my thoughts get dark and scary. One of my tools when I am inside of depression is to use a chart to keep myself accountable to the choices that support my mental health. During my most recent depressive episode, every day for seven months I tracked whether or not I exercised, meditated, wrote in my journal, drank alcohol, or ate refined sugar. I picked those five things because I know they are what impact my mood the most.

The chart helped me immensely. I felt accomplished when I colored in those little squares every night before bed. I loved adding up the number of days I'd stuck to my goals at the end of every month. The (mostly) daily exercise, meditation, and writing was the boost I needed to come out of the funk I was in. Seven months after I started the chart, I woke up and felt like I didn't need it anymore. I knew in my heart that I no longer needed a tool to keep me accountable. I felt like I had internalized the benefits of my practices. I felt like I could trust myself to take care of myself without an outside reminder.

Sometimes we need structure before we can move to a more intuitively-guided place.

When I was inside of depression, I couldn't practice self-care intuitively. I needed the structured plan in order to recalibrate my system. Once I was on the other side, I could intuitively choose my self-care. One way is not better than the other. There are times that call for structured practice and times that call for intuitive practice. The wisdom lies in discerning what you need given the season of your life. The two types of practice are also not mutually exclusive. For example, when I was charting my exercise I would still intuitively choose what physical activity to do that day based on how my body was feeling. One day I might need yoga, another day a long walk in nature, another day strength training.

I believe structure can support our relationship with our intuition. Having structures and rituals in place serves as a reminder to tune into ourselves. Our relationship with our intuition deserves and requires attention and tending just like any other relationship. My deepest intention is to live an intuitively-guided life, and I appreciate and honor that structure supports me on that path.

When You Want to Cut Off All Your Hair and You Hate All Your Clothes

Find out who you are and do it on purpose. ~ Dolly Parton

Do you know that feeling like you are floating around in liminal space? It happens to me when I am uncertain about what comes next. I usually feel like I am kind of a mess. When I am inside this space, I want to cut off all my hair and I hate all my clothes.

For me, that is a sure sign that I am on the edge of something new. I've been inside of this space many times now, and I've learned to follow the clues, the little nudges from my intuition that guide me toward my next becoming. I spend a lot of time alone so that I can hear my inner self more clearly. I tune into my body and nourish her in whatever ways she is craving. I step away from technology and spend more time in nature. I let go of my focus on *doing* in order to give more space to *being*. When I create conditions that support connection with my intuition, the ideas come as downloads directly from my higher self. I leave myself notes in my phone, my journal, and on random scraps of paper. I follow these bits as I know they are clues leading me on my path. They don't always make much sense individually, but I have learned to trust that together they will add up to my next iteration.

Spend some time with your journal today. Have you had your own "I want to cut off all my hair and I hate all my clothes" times in life? What did you find on the other side? Who are you becoming now?

march 24

Get Off the Scale

Dieting is the most potent political sedative in women's history; a quietly mad population is a tractable one. ~ Naomi Wolf

Convincing girls and women that their bodies need improving is big business. The "health and beauty" industry makes billions of dollars from us each year as we buy up their creams, shapewear, diet pills, and all kinds of other products designed to help women achieve some impossible thin-ideal. *This is by design.* Did you know that as women have achieved more freedom and independence in society, the ideal body size put forward (by men in power) has decreased? Again, this is not a coincidence. As long as women's minds are preoccupied with thoughts about their weight, they will be more easily controlled. Imagine if we directed the time, energy, and money we spend trying to change our bodies toward trying to change the world. We would be a powerful force.

This focus on women as objects prevents us from stepping into our full feminine power and keeps the patriarchal status quo afloat. *Trust me when I say transforming your relationship with your body has the power to change the world.* Get off the scale. Opt out of the thin-ideal and all the bullshit that comes with it. Eat in a way that feels nourishing for your body. Move in a way that helps you feel vibrant and energized. *Or don't.* Health is not a moral imperative. It's your body and you get to choose. Whatever you choose, don't hook your worth up to a number on the scale. You are so much more than that.

You Deserve Clothes That Fit Your Body Comfortably

My body changed as I neared 40. I could still wear my clothes, but they were tight and uncomfortable. I didn't want to buy new clothes because I was holding on to the idea that my body could go back to its previous version. I wore those too-tight clothes for an entire year. I was resisting the changes that were happening in my body. My closet and drawers reflected a stuckness, the clothes a constant reminder that I was holding on to the idea of going back to a previous version of myself. To buy new clothes would mean I was letting go of the idea of going back to who I was before. When I finally took myself on a shopping trip, it was about so much more than the clothes. It meant I was fully embracing moving forward, accepting that my body was not the same as it had been. Wearing clothes that fit comfortably made a huge difference for me; it truly felt like an act of self-love.

Spend some time with your journal today. Are you holding on to clothes that don't fit? Are you resisting changes in your body? How can your clothing choices be an act of self-love?

PSA: No One Has Their Shit Together

"When am I going to get my shit together?!" This was a regular refrain in my mind for the first twenty years of my adult life. *Okay, it still pops into my mind sometimes now.* What does it even mean?

When I really dig into this idea of "having my shit together," I find it's another form of perfectionism. One more ideal to try to live up to. I imagine "having my shit together" would mean that my house is clean and organized, I am a superstar at work, I'm an amazing mom, my marriage is thriving, and I have plenty of time for socializing and exercising and volunteering. *I'm tired just reading that sentence.* No one has their shit together. Or if they do, it's not a permanent state and it probably doesn't stretch across situations. Maybe you're having a stellar day at work but you forgot to pack your kid's gym clothes. Maybe you baked some epic cupcakes for the school fundraiser but you're still wearing yesterday's makeup and you forgot to pay the electric bill.

Here's what I know: I'm a full-grown adult in her forties and my house is messy most days of the week. Nearly every day I wish I had been more patient and present with the people I love. And at the end of most days I feel like I should have done at least three more things than I did. I think it's just called being a woman inside of patriarchy. We will never live up to their standards, so why keep trying? Create your own idea about what it means to have your shit together or just let go of the idea altogether. Love yourself the way you are and trust me, *you've done enough today.*

march 27

Going Backward is Part of Moving Forward

Say it with me, "I am a work in progress AND a work of art."
~ Elizabeth DiAlto

Patterns of behavior are associated with neural pathways in the brain. As we work to change our habits, we are literally rewiring our brains. It can be helpful to remember that over time we have established well-worn neural pathways, and that just like water flows through the path of least resistance, we are pulled toward our old habits and ways of being. Know that when you are creating change in your life you are creating change in your brain. It takes time. Be patient and kind with yourself. Remember that change is not a linear process. We move forward toward what we want, and then we take a step backward toward what is comfortable. *It's okay.* This truly is part of change—an expected step on the path of evolution.

Spend some time with your journal today. Have you had the experience of feeling like you were moving backward? How did you respond? How can you treat yourself with patience and kindness as you move toward change in the future?

Reclaim Pussy and Tune into Your Yoni

It's our wholeness, our intuition, our magic, and our power – the power that lies between our thighs – that will truly change the world.
~ Lisa Lister

How do you refer to your genitals?

Many people say *vagina*, but that only describes one part of the whole. I feel like *pussy* is the most accurate, all-encompassing term for what lies between my thighs. It's a word we need to reclaim because it's been turned into a slur. I invite you to take it back and say it proudly. Pussies truly are amazing and powerful. Another option is *yoni*, a Sanskrit word that means sacred womb and also refers to the whole of our lady parts.

Whatever you want to call your pussy, I invite you to practice tuning into her. There is a lot of wisdom between your legs. Notice how your yoni feels in different situations and around different people. Take note and act accordingly; she will not lead you astray.

Make the Mundane Sacred

This mind is an amazing thing. It can conjure love from the scent of orange blossoms, peace from a dry breeze, and joy from a patch of grass on a summer day.~ Karen Maezen Miller

I love to infuse a bit of the sacred into my everyday routines. One of my favorite ways to do this is by tapping into my senses in order to add something beautiful to a task or routine that is otherwise boring or mundane.

A few ideas:

Play music while cooking.
Light candles while taking a bath or eating a meal.
Listen to an inspiring podcast while folding the laundry.
Have fresh flowers in areas of the house where you spend a lot of time.
Place something beautiful (such as a plant, feather, or stone) above the sink where you wash dishes.
Diffuse essential oils: lavender for relaxation or something citrus to brighten your mood.
Set up tiny altars throughout your living space using items you already have such as pictures, candles, rocks, and plants.

Little things can make a big difference. When we add a bit of the sacred to our everyday life, we bring together our physical and spiritual selves. By releasing the separation of our daily life and our spiritual life, our mundane routines become sacred rituals.

Abundance is More Than Money

Often people attempt to live their lives backwards: they try to have more things,
or more money, in order to do more of what they want so that they will be
happier. The way it actually works is the reverse. You must first be who you
really are, then, do what you need to do, in order to have what you want.
~ Margaret Young

We live inside of a capitalist culture, and while there are some things we
can do to step out of that system, the effects on us are very real. Money is
important, especially when you don't have enough of it, and I do not want
to deny the significant impact of poverty. Many of us are (understandably)
fixated on earning money, saving money, and spending money or not
spending money. It's exhausting and it plays right into capitalism. Our
culture wants us to devote our lives to earning money and buying things;
it's what makes our society function.

Today, I invite you to step outside of the produce/earn/spend cycle and find
abundance in something non-monetary. Love, nature, health, curiosity, time,
space, art, compassion, magic, your breath—count the ways you are rich that
have nothing to do with money.

march 31

Let Your Breath Be Your Guide

The quality of our breath is extremely important because it expresses our inner feelings. ~ TKV Desikachar

When I teach yoga I encourage my students to let their breath be their guide. Throughout class I remind them to tune into their breath and make adjustments accordingly. If one finds that they are holding their breath or that the breath has become shallow, it's an indicator to back off from the pose or pause and take a break. Like everything in yoga, this translates to life.

Today, notice your breath as you go about your day. When is it deep and slow? When do you notice yourself holding your breath? When does it feel hard to breathe? Notice how you feel around different situations and people, as well as during different times of day and throughout your various activities. For now, just take note without any judgment. Over time you can use this information to determine if you'd like to make any adjustments.

Create Rituals to Mark Time

It is easy to feel as if time is passing us by more quickly than ever in this modern world. Have you ever had the experience of thinking, *"What did I even do today / this week / this month / this year?"* We can go through the motions of daily life or we can choose to pause and take the time to live our lives with purpose and intention. As I've deepened my connection to my feminine self I have come to honor the importance of ritual to help mark time. Taking time to capture the moments that make up my life has become a sacred celebration of my journey.

We can create rituals around a variety of markers. There is no right or wrong way. Here are a few ideas to get you started:

Seasonally: Use the solstice and equinox as guides. With every change of season make a list of things you'd like to experience or create a photo book to capture your memories of the season.

Monthly: Use the New Moon and Full Moon as guides. On the New Moon set intentions for the upcoming month; spend some time dreaming about how you want to feel and what you want to experience. Write a list or create a collage of images as a reminder. On the Full Moon think about what is asking to be released. Write a list and burn it, perhaps even gathering with friends around a fire.

Weekly: Choose a day of the week for reflection, maybe Sunday if that is the day you prepare for the week ahead, or Friday if that feels like a good place to pause. Carve out some quiet time for yourself or gather with others in reflection at church, a yoga class, or women's group.

Daily: Pick a time of day to devote to your practice, perhaps first thing in the morning or at the end of your day before bed. Keep a gratitude journal or take one photo a day to help capture the moments that make up your life.

Other ideas: Write your children a letter every year. Light a candle and set your intention for the week. Take a self-portrait every Sunday.

Choose what moves your soul. Experiment until you find what feels right. Allow your rituals to be an anchor helping you to mark time.

april 2

Let's Not Talk About Each Other's Bodies, Ever

Our culture is loaded with messages about women's bodies.

She looks like she lost weight.
She looks like she gained weight.
She's so skinny—I just want to feed her a burger!
I can't believe she is eating that—doesn't she care about her health?!
You look amazing—have you lost weight?

Fat shaming and skinny shaming are different sides of the same bullshit coin. Giving body-based compliments feeds into diet culture. Any discussion about a woman's body shape and size plays into patriarchy in some way because it keeps the focus on how we look; it perpetuates the idea of women as objects.

Let's not talk about each other's bodies, *ever.*

There are so many more interesting things to talk about: our hopes and dreams, our struggles and celebrations, our longings and knowings. Women are amazing and complex creatures. Let's not reduce each other to our body shape and size.

april 3

Have Done List

You are enough,
You have enough,
You do enough.
~ SARK

Inside of our modern world, we all do so much in a day. Yet at the end of the day, we tend to focus on what we *didn't* accomplish.

Today I invite you to make a Have Done List— a list of the things you did today. You could keep a running list as the day goes on or take a few minutes at the end of your day to write your list.

Here's an example from a typical day in my own life:

Made breakfast and packed lunches
Took child to school and walked the dog
Meditated and wrote in my journal
Saw six therapy clients
Picked child up from school and helped with homework
Returned voicemails and emails
Connected with friends by text and/or social media

Give yourself credit for all that you do in a day. Instead of focusing on what you didn't do (there will always be something), think about all the things you did do. Let that be enough.

If You Don't Get on a Bandwagon, You Can't Fall Off

If you don't get on a bandwagon, you can't fall off.

This is one of my favorite reminders. I started saying this to clients in relation to dieting. All of the research on dieting shows that diets do not work. One of two things happen when people lose weight by dieting: they either gain back all the weight they lost (and often a bit more) or they develop an eating disorder. The problem with a diet is that it involves restriction, and anytime we are restricting ourselves we will inevitably veer off and eat what we were restricting. You get on the bandwagon (diet) and eventually you will fall off, likely right into a binge of whatever you've been depriving yourself of. Don't get on the bandwagon and you can't fall off.

I can hear you now: *but I want to eat healthier!* So go ahead and eat healthier. Add in more fruits and veggies or drink more water or prepare more meals at home—just don't think of it as a diet because diets are temporary and they have rules that automatically set you up for failure. Instead of dieting consider your relationship with food as just that—a relationship. Relationships ebb and flow; they are constantly in flux. There is permission to change.

I now see how this idea of not getting on any bandwagons applies to so much more than food. If you tell yourself you're going to meditate every day for 21 days (bandwagon!) and you miss day four, what do you do? You probably quit because you've already failed by missing just one day. Same idea for exercise, creating art, decluttering, marketing your business, etc. Anytime we set ourselves up with strict rules and expectations, we set ourselves up to fail.

So don't get on any bandwagons. Instead, set your intention for whatever it is you want to change and allow it to be a process. Be gentle and forgiving with yourself. Remember you can begin again at anytime. Allow change to be a process and let go of perfectionism.

april 5

You Don't Have to Fit Inside a Box

For most of my adult life I was a vegetarian. As I neared 40, I started to feel hungry all the time. Intuitively I knew I needed to add some meat back into my diet. I resisted this truth for a while because I identified so strongly with not eating animals. Eventually I realized I had a choice—stick to my vegetarian diet simply because I had put myself inside that box for so many years, or listen to my body and make the adjustments that I needed, labels be damned. I moved just outside the box of vegetarian and began eating organic, free-range chicken a few times a week. My body felt better and my mind was able to accept this shift as well.

Is there a box you've put yourself in? Does it feel like freedom or something else? Are there adjustments asking to be made? Set the intention today to open up and consider other possibilities. Be flexible and creative as you allow yourself to explore any labels you've put on yourself and the resultant impact. You have permission to change—always and in all ways.

april 6

Be Honest with Yourself

It always comes back to the same necessity:
go deep enough and there is a bedrock of truth, however hard.
~ May Sarton

Sometimes we mistake self-indulgence for self-care. Take some time today to reflect on your behaviors and choices. Be honest with yourself. Are there things you are doing that are out of alignment with how you want to feel? For example, I went through a period where I considered a nightly glass of wine an act of self-care. The truth is I was using that glass of wine to numb out my feelings, and drinking it seriously interfered with my sleep. Shifting my relationship to alcohol was an act of self-care that improved my mood and my energy.

We want to approach ourselves with unconditional acceptance and kindness. That doesn't mean we bullshit ourselves or let ourselves off the hook about unhealthy behaviors or choices that no longer serve us. True self-love and self-care include being real with ourselves, taking responsibility for our actions, and making adjustments as needed.

Don't Should on Yourself

I should be more patient,
I should be more like her,
I should have my life together by now,
I should have said something different,
I should have done something different,
I should drink more water,
I should stop caring what people think,
I should be grateful I have a job,
I should watch less television,
I should start meditating.

Pause and check in with your body right now. How do you feel after reading that list of shoulds? I'm guessing at least a few of them resonated for you because they are statements I consistently hear women say. Personally, I feel a tightness in my chest and tension in my shoulders when I consider that list. My body contracts in response to the word should. For me, "should" holds so much expectation and judgment. It feels like something I can never live up to, a constant reminder of my shortcomings.

Words are powerful. Pay attention to your use of the word should today. Notice how you feel when it finds its way into your thoughts. Consider shifting your "shoulds" into more self-acceptance and compassion by choosing phrases like "I am working on..." or "I am learning to...."

april 8

Create a Traveling Altar

Even though I live in a relatively big house with only a few other people, I often feel like there is not a space just for me. I crave a corner where I can set up an altar and sit to meditate. I would love a room of my own to lounge in and journal. I have spent a fair amount of time (internally) whining about my lack of sacred space and not taking much action because it felt impossible.

Then one of my teachers, Melinda Alexander, suggested we use a tray and create a traveling altar that can be moved from room to room. This was a game-changing idea for me! I bought myself a gorgeous gold tray and gathered some sacred objects to place on it (a candle, some stones, and tarot cards). It's visually appealing and effective. I can easily carry the tray from room to room and have an instant sacred space for meditation or journaling.

Do you have altars in your home? An altar is a visual reminder to connect with your higher self. You can create one with objects you already have on hand. I love feathers, rocks, candles, pictures, cards, and books. An altar can be as simple or as complicated as you'd like. You might simply have a statue of the Buddha or Mother Mary. Or you could have a more elaborate altar with pictures, flowers, and other sacred items. There is no right or wrong, just what feels good for you. If you don't have a space for a permanent altar, look around and see if you have a tray you can use. If not, invest in one so that you can create an altar that you can carry from room to room.

april 9

Connect with Other Women

I define connection as the energy that exists between people when they feel seen, heard, and valued; when they can give and receive without judgment; and when they derive sustenance and strength from the relationship.
~ Brené Brown

There is a special kind of loneliness that comes with being a woman in our modern world.

The loneliness comes from comparing and striving.
The loneliness comes from our disconnection with nature.
The loneliness comes from the overwhelm of social media and technology.
The loneliness comes from the multiple roles we play inside of our lives.
The loneliness comes from our culture and the constant exposure to impossible ideals.

Our culture tells us that we are supposed to be perfect women. We have been taught that we can have it all, and that has somehow translated into the idea that we can *do it all*. Oh, and we are supposed to do it all on our own.

Women have internalized these ideals, and we hesitate to share our truth for fear of judgment. We each think that we are the only one who is struggling. We hide because we are afraid that others will find out the truth—that we aren't perfect women. This leads us further into isolation. So many of us carry so much alone.

The antidote to loneliness is community.

I crave the connection of women, the magic that occurs when another says, "yes, I feel that way too." For me, this is part of the beauty of writing—that you might read these words and feel a little less alone. *Just writing the words helps me feel a little less alone.* I think books are wonderful places for connecting with kindred spirits. Reading and writing have saved me many times. I also know that we need more than the written word to counteract the special loneliness of being a woman inside of our culture. It is important to find your people. This connection can happen online or in person. One of the amazing things about technology is how we can connect with people all over the world from the comfort of our homes. I adore online communities and have many meaningful and fulfilling online friendships. As an introvert, I love connecting online. I also appreciate being face-to-face with my soul friends, sharing a cup of tea and a hug.

Consider how you can connect with other women. What would feel nourishing? Do you already have women in your life who witness you with compassion and non-judgment? Schedule a date to get together. If you're looking to connect with like-minded women and aren't sure where to start, research women's circles either locally or online. We are each deserving of love and support. Moreover, I believe it is necessary for our healing and growth. Take a step toward connection today.

april 10

Release, Respond, Receive

Journal writing is one of my go-to self-care practices. Writing helps me center myself, process my emotions, and problem solve stressors. In my experience many people want to have a journal writing practice, but they are not sure where to begin. Today I would like to offer you a structured journal writing practice that you can use daily or whenever you need it. The practice has three parts: release, respond, receive. It is based on a technique I learned from the author SARK during a writing retreat years ago.

Release: Do a brain dump. Write whatever is on your mind in a stream of consciousness. Don't worry about spelling or grammar. Just let everything you're thinking out onto the page. You can set a timer for five or ten minutes or just write until you feel complete.

Respond: Pause and take a moment to connect with your wise inner self. Take a few deep breaths and drop into your body. From this place of wisdom, respond to what you wrote above. For example, if you wrote about being stressed because there is so much on your plate right now, your wise inner self might respond with advice on letting some things go to create more space in your life; or she may respond with reassurance, such as: *You've got this! Everything will be okay.* There aren't any right or wrong answers. This is a place for you to trust yourself and your inner knowing.

Receive: End your journal writing practice by listing everything you are grateful for in the moment. This could be anything from the specific to the general, the small to the big. List whatever comes to mind: the coffee that your colleague brought you this morning or the fact that you love the people you work with. The sun peaking out from behind the clouds or that you have a safe place to live. Aim for at least ten things, but feel free to list many more. If you're struggling to make a list, think of the non-toothache that Thich Nhat Hahn talks about. The idea is that we forget to be thankful for not having a toothache until we have a toothache, and then we are very much aware of how we took feeling well for granted. There are many things we take for granted in this life—our health, clean water coming out of our faucets, our cars starting, or arriving safely at our destinations throughout the day. Let these things make their way onto your gratitude list too.

Notice how you feel after completing your journal practice.
Consider adding Release, Respond, Receive to your self-care routine.

.

Get Out of Your Element

Novelty is the great parent of pleasure.
~ Robert South

It's easy to fall into monotony inside of our daily routines—to drive the same way to work, to eat at the same restaurants, to go to the same exercise class. I love routine; I find it comforting. I also value having new experiences, even if it pushes me out of my comfort zone. Trying something new or different can spark my creativity or pull me out of a rut that I didn't even know I was in. Plus, it's just fun!

How can you invite a sense of adventure into your day today? Switching up your routine doesn't have to be complicated. You might take a different path on your morning walk, try a new recipe, or go to a new class at the yoga studio. Choose something that feels fun and playful. Practice getting out of your element and notice how it impacts you.

april 12

A Simple Practice to Brighten Your Day

We are all in the gutter but some of us are looking at the stars.
~ Oscar Wilde

Do you ever have one of those days when your mood is in a funk?
Often a simple shift can move us in a more positive direction. One of
my favorite practices when I'm feeling a bit down is to list things that
I am looking forward to in the future. I also love sharing this practice
on social media and inviting others to join me. It's fun to celebrate
the positive things that people are looking forward to, and it
brightens the day of everyone who participates.

*Think about one thing you are looking forward to today, this week, this
month, and this year. Write your list in your journal. If you feel called to,
share it with others on social media and invite them to join you in this
practice. Pay attention to how you feel after creating your list. File this
strategy away in your mind for whenever your mood needs a bit of a boost.*

april 13

Sometimes the Healthiest Choice is Letting Go

Once my therapist gave me an assignment to identify my internal working model. It's an idea from attachment theory, a sort of mindset you view the world through. It only took me three sentences to get to mine: *If you want people to love you, give them what they want even if it hurts you.* It's an old idea, and I couldn't believe that it was right there, still impacting my life. I immediately got defensive. *But I am amazing at self-care! But I set boundaries! But I make myself a priority!*

Then I thought about the conversation that sparked her giving me this assignment. I was explaining how it feels like someone always needs something from me and that I have to accommodate those needs whether I want to or not. I was feeling burnt out and powerless. I was feeling like I couldn't say no to the people I care about. *If you want people to love you, give them what they want even if it hurts you.* This is an idea I learned from my father, a man who was entrusted with the task of loving and protecting me, and instead hurt and traumatized me. His lessons in love led me to a decade of abusive relationships, crippling anxiety, and deep depression. And still all I wanted was his love and approval. That's why it took me nearly 30 years to cut him out of my life.

Today is his birthday and it always brings my grief to the surface. I will probably cry for the father I never had, for the hurt little girl inside, and for what will never be. Not having a relationship with my father is hard but having a relationship with him was harder. It's an awful position to be in, to have to weigh the pain of being in relationship with a parent against the pain of not, and I hope you can't relate to this essay at all, but if you can, know that I am sending you so much love.

april 14

What's the Worst That Could Happen?

One of my practices when I am inside of fear is to pause and ask myself, "*What's the worst that could happen?*" Often I have to follow it up quite a few times with, "*And then what would happen?*" Eventually one of two things happens—the question helps me get to the root of my fear, or I realize my fear is irrational and I am able to release it.

For example, let's say I am worried that I said something hurtful to someone I love. (When you have anxiety this happens all the time.)

I ask myself, "*What's the worst that could happen?*"
They might be angry with me.

"*And then what would happen?*"
They might cut me out of their life.

"*Is that something that could really happen?*"
Probably not.

"*And if it did, what is the worst that could happen?*"
I would be really sad.

"And then what would happen?"
I would probably try to make amends.

"And then what would happen?"
They would forgive me or maybe they wouldn't.

"And if the worst thing happened and they wouldn't forgive and you lost the relationship?"
I would be really sad but eventually I would be okay.

Often when we are inside of fear our nervous system and emotional brain are highly activated. Writing or talking (even to yourself in your mind) helps to bring our thinking brain back online and to soothe our nervous system. Next time you find yourself inside of fear, pause and have a dialogue with yourself, either mentally or in your journal. Notice how this helps to shift your internal experience.

april 15

Ask Before You Unload

Imagine this: While you are in an important meeting, a friend sends you a long text message about a struggle they are having. Or you are in the middle of a project and your co-worker walks up to your desk and begins a long diatribe about an issue with your boss. Or you are figuring out what to make for dinner when your partner walks in the door and immediately starts ranting about their day. You have likely experienced these or similar scenarios. These kinds of interactions can leave us feeling unprepared or even resentful. If you are highly sensitive, it might take a bit for your nervous system to recalibrate.

Unloading on people without first asking permission is a common and problematic boundary issue. Most people don't realize the impact of their behavior; honestly, they are just trying to get their needs met. A beautiful practice that gives people permission to honor their capacity is to simply ask before you unload. Here are some ways to do that:

"Hey, I've got something on my mind. Do you have a few minutes to talk? I had a terrible day today. Would you be willing to listen to me vent for a bit? I am so worried about XYZ. Can I talk it through with you?"

As you begin to use this language with others, you may notice that they start to do the same. Asking before you unload is a beautiful way to communicate clearly and give people a choice. It's okay for someone to say, *"No, I can't do that for you right now"* or *"I would love to talk, but right now isn't a good time. Can you call me at 7pm?"* And it's okay for you to do the same, even if someone didn't ask before they started unloading. You can pause the conversation and say something like, *"You are important to me and I want to have this conversation with you. Now is not a good time. Can we talk again later?"*

Today, pay attention to your interactions with others. Are you unloading on them without asking first? Are they doing that to you? Notice how you feel when it happens. Practice healthy communication and boundaries by asking permission before you share something emotionally charged and observe how this impacts your relationships. Don't stress out if you forget and revert back to old habits. It takes time to shift our communication patterns. Be gentle with yourself and others.

april 16

You Don't Need Anyone Else's Participation in Order to Heal

You may not control all the events that happen to you,
but you can decide not to be reduced by them.
~ Maya Angelou

We each have our own wounds to heal in this lifetime.
We have all been hurt by someone.
We crave healing; we deserve peace.

I want you to know that you don't need anyone else's participation in order to heal. Healing is an inside job. You don't need anyone to validate your experience; you can give that to yourself. You don't need the person who hurt you to understand or apologize. You might *want* those things, and that is totally understandable. However, when we wait on someone else to acknowledge our pain or take accountability for how their actions impacted us, we can get stuck.

Witness and validate your own experiences.
Take exquisite care of your feelings and needs.
Give yourself the gift of healing.

Unhook Your Worth

You are worthy.
Period. End of story. No qualifiers.

You are worthy.
Of love, kindness, joy, appreciation.
Simply because you exist.

In our culture we are encouraged to hook our worth up to external factors such as appearances and material objects. We believe we will be worthy when we achieve certain socially defined goals related to our bodies (e.g., lose five pounds), our careers (e.g., get a promotion), and our belongings (e.g., live in a big house). These are lies. You don't have to earn your worth. You can sink into your worthiness right now in this moment. You are worthy, you are deserving, just as you are today. Simply because you exist.

Spend some time in meditation or with your journal today. Do you feel worthy? If not, what is standing between you and your worthiness? Where did you learn that you had to earn your worth? Who would you be without those beliefs?

Is It the Thing or My Reaction to the Thing?

Let everything happen to you: beauty and terror.
Just keep going. No feeling is final.
~ Rainer Maria Rilke

Sometimes I notice myself having big reactions to small things. Everyday stressors like traffic, technology moving slower than I'd like, and my dog acting like a dog or my kid acting like a kid can all bring up intense emotions of anger or frustration and I find myself overreacting. When this happens I have a process I use to bring myself back to center. First, I invite myself to notice what is going on within and around me. I try to observe without any judgment. I practice self-forgiveness. Then I invite in some perspective by asking myself, "*What are the things that truly matter in this life?*" Finally, when I am inside of stress I ask myself, "*Is it the stressors that are creating my feelings or my reaction to the stressors?*" Usually I am making small things into big things. Sometimes I am making big things into even bigger things. Either way, my negative reaction—my resistance—to what is occurring creates more struggle than the actual thing that is happening.

"*Let everything happen to you: beauty and terror. / Just keep going. No feeling is final.*"

I love these lines from Rilke.

"Let everything happen to you."
Surrender to what is.
Let go of trying to control the uncontrollable.

"Just keep going."
Do the best that you can.
One foot in front of the other.

"No feeling is final."
Everything is temporary.
Find the place within that is beyond feelings and thoughts.

Today, let Rilke's words be a mantra as you go about your day. Observe your reactions to things and work to keep stressors in perspective. Know that you will forget, you will falter. That's okay. Forgive yourself and begin again.

april 19

You Can Take Up Space in Your Life

i am mine.
before i am ever anyone else's.
~ Nayyirah Waheed

One of my self-care practices is to attend a retreat by myself once a year. Because I hold so much space as a therapist and teacher, I have to continuously remind myself that I am allowed to just be a participant and not think about other people's needs during the retreat.

I use the mantra "*I can take up space*" to remind myself about this.

The year I turned 40 I realized I could carry the mantra out of the retreat and into my life.

I began writing in my journal, "*I can take up space in my life.*"

Sometimes it can feel like there is no room for me inside of my own life; I could easily give myself over to my roles and forget to think about my own needs. I know that a lot of women feel this way. It has taken years, but I have learned that I can have needs, ask for help, say no, hold my boundaries, go to yoga, stick to my meditation practice, take long baths, talk about how I am feeling, see my friends, go on dates with my husband, and do my daily journal writing no matter what is going on around me.

Sometimes it is still a struggle. I think, "*Am I really allowed to do that?*"

The idea that I have to sacrifice myself to care for those around me is still my default programing, even after years of unpacking my internalized patriarchy and teaching others to do the same. It's understandable. The messages of patriarchy are all around us, and the current system benefits from us buying into them. We have to actively work to de-condition our minds and to create new belief systems that support us as we center ourselves inside of our own lives.

Spend some time in meditation or with your journal. How does this idea of "taking up space in your life" land for you? What would it look like to allow yourself to take up space inside of your life?

april 20

Finding Steadiness Amidst the Ever-Changing Nature of Life

Feelings come and go like clouds in a windy sky.
Conscious breathing is my anchor.
~ Thich Nhat Hanh

Life is constantly in flux. One moment we feel like we are on top of the world, and the next we are inside of fear and anxiety. Situations, thoughts, feelings—things around us and even inside of us are always changing, but we can learn to find steadiness amidst the ever-changing nature of life as a human.

When we peel away our situations, our thoughts, our feelings, our bodies—what is left?

Something.
Can you sense it?
Awareness, consciousness, soul—call it what you will.

When we can remember that there is *something more* beneath our current situation or mood, that in fact we *are* the *Something More*, we can connect with the ground of our being—the divine, peaceful essence that is within all of us. When we are connected with this place inside of us, it is easier to navigate the ups and downs of life. The *Something More* is a touchstone we can return to for comfort no matter what is happening in our lives.

It can be challenging to nurture our connection with the *Something More* because of the over-scheduled nature and constant stimulation of our modern world. Natural moments of quiet and reflection have been erased by technology. Thus, we have to consciously carve out time to be with this divine, peaceful place within ourselves. Once you connect with this place within yourself, you will be changed.

Of course, it's not a thing we do once. Connecting with the *Something More* is a process; you are forming a relationship with this divine part of yourself. It takes time, attention, and commitment. Sometimes our connection will feel strong, and sometimes it will feel strained, as with any long-term relationship. The important thing is to find your way in—to discover the tools and strategies that help you connect with the *Something More* that has been inside of you all along.

april 21

We Deserve to Flourish

Fine is never good enough. ~ Zuyapa Jackson

I love plants, but the truth is I am not great at taking care of them. When it comes to my plants I usually just do what I can and hope for the best. Sometimes they thrive, sometimes they wither. I don't change my behavior. Mostly because plants, as much as I love and appreciate them, have not been a priority in my life.

What if they were? What if I took the time to research what each plant needed? What if I invested the energy to really care for each plant in the way that it needs to be tended to?

They would probably flourish.

Where else might I be doing this in my life? Claiming to love and appreciate something but not taking the time to learn how to really care for it?

Plants and humans can survive on so little, but is this how we want to live? Getting by on crumbs?

I think we have learned to settle for "fine" in so many ways. The truth is we deserve to flourish. We deserve the care and attention that will allow us to fully bloom. What would that look like for you? Can you take a step toward it today?

Self-Care is More Than Pedicures and Brunching with Your Girlfriends

I practice yoga every day. Do I do asana (the physical postures of yoga) every day? *No.* Sometimes I will go more than a week without an asana practice; there have been times in my life when I have not done the physical postures of yoga for weeks or even months. Yet, I have practiced yoga every day. Because yoga is more than physical postures. Yoga is breath work, meditation, and ethical principles such as nonviolence and self-study.

Yoga is taking a few deep breaths.
Yoga is being mindful of my self-talk.
Yoga is reading an inspiring book.
Yoga is turning off my phone and sitting quietly in the dark.
Yoga is walking among the trees and saying thank you for all the goodness in my life.

Many people think yoga is only physical postures, especially before they have tried yoga.

Similarly, many people think self-care is only physical actions like getting your nails done or going to brunch with your girlfriends or taking a nap. I love (and do) all of those things, but they are not the entirety of self-care. Much as the images or ideas about the physical postures of yoga can keep people from trying yoga, this idea of self-care being only physical actions might prevent people from exploring self-care. They might think,

"*Who has time (or money) for that?*" With this limited view, one might even think that self-care "isn't for me."

The truth is that just like yoga, self-care is about so much more than physical actions. True self-care is about mindset:

Being gentle with yourself.
Practicing self-compassion.
Being on your own side.
Allowing yourself to want.
Speaking your truth, even if it's only in your journal.
Letting yourself feel your feelings.
Loving yourself no matter what.

Yes, pedicures, dates with your friends, and naps are lovely and important. And they are just the way into the deeper layers of self-care.

If you don't know where to start with self-care, try a physical action—whatever kind of behavior feels like self-care for you.

Put on your favorite song and dance.
Leave work early and take a nap.
Go to the library and check out a book.
Sign up for a retreat or workshop.
Clean out your closet.
Go to bed early.
Try a yoga class.
Schedule a date with your best friend.
Go for a massage or acupuncture treatment.
Paint, draw, color.
Browse the thrift store for treasures.

Soak in the bathtub.
Plan a weekend away with your beloved.
Start a meditation practice.

If you feel overwhelmed with the idea of finding time for self-care actions, work with the mental, emotional, or spiritual aspects of self-care.

Every time you look in the mirror, say something kind to yourself.
Forgive yourself; remember that mistakes are allowed.
Practice conscious breathing—you can do this during any of your daily activities.
Disconnect from technology—try setting a specific phone-free window of time (e.g., 9pm-8am).
When you wake up, set an intention for your day.
When you get into bed at night, name five things you are grateful for.
Practice tuning into your body throughout the day.
Connect with the idea that there is something bigger than you (God, Source, nature, whatever resonates for you).
Allow yourself to feel your feelings, and practice accepting whatever arises for you.
Spend time building awareness of your thoughts and beliefs. Notice how you talk to yourself.
Listen to a podcast while you drive.
Stand up for yourself.
Celebrate your strengths and accomplishments.

There is no prescription, no 10-Step Plan to Self-Care Land. There is not even any arriving. There is just the journey, the practice, the commitment to yourself. And that can look different every single day. What's important is to engage with the work in some way. Don't wait for perfect conditions to arrive. (They won't.) Just decide today that you love yourself enough to start or continue your self-care practice.

april 23

Self-Care in 10 Minutes or Less

I understand that you have so much on your plate. I know that some days it can feel impossible to pause and take time for yourself. I believe that self-care is vital to our lives—not a luxury for some, but a necessity for all.

Today, I offer you some self-care actions you can take in one minute, five minutes, or ten minutes.

One minute:

1. Practice conscious, deep breathing.
2. Inhale lavender essential oil or put a few drops on your wrists.
3. Place your hand over your heart and say one kind thing to yourself.
4. Rub lotion or warm oil on your feet.
5. Stand in Mountain Pose. Feel your feet connecting you with the earth.
6. Light a candle or some incense.
7. Roll your shoulders up, back, and down a few times.
8. Look out the window and just notice the world around you.

Five minutes:

1. Do any of the one-minute practices for five minutes.
2. Do a mindful check in of your breath, body, thoughts, and emotions.
3. Practice Crocodile Pose or Legs Up the Wall.
4. Step outside and look up at the sky.

5. Make a list of five things you are grateful for.

6. Take a selfie. Look into your own eyes with compassion.

7. Put on your favorite song and dance it out.

8. Read a poem. (My favorite poets are Nayyirah Wayeed & Mary Oliver.)

Ten minutes:

1. Do any of the one-minute or five-minute practices for ten minutes.

2. Do some stream-of-consciousness writing.

3. Call or text someone you love.

4. Practice loving-kindness meditation.

5. Do two or three Sun Salutations.

6. Make a list of ten things you appreciate about yourself.

7. Make a cup of tea and drink it mindfully.

8. Talk a short walk outside.

Grab a sticky note and jot down your favorite ideas from the lists above. Feel free to add your own practices as well. Put the sticky note somewhere you will see it every day. Commit to doing one thing on your list every day for a week. Observe what shifts for you as a result of these brief self-care practices.

The Radical Act of Resting Before You're Completely Wiped Out

Ask yourself how you can go gentler with this next path. Sometimes you have to learn that you don't need to be so sharply stung before you feel the flowers.
~ Victoria Erickson

At what point do you rest when you're not feeling well?

I typically only pause my life as scheduled when I absolutely cannot keep going; sometimes I don't even stop then, I just keep pushing through. I once read about a woman who takes herself to bed for the day as soon as other people around her are sick, a sort of preemptive sick day. She reported that she rarely fell ill. If one end of the spectrum is continuing to push through illness, I think what she described might be the other end of the continuum. At this point in my life, I'm just hoping to land somewhere in the middle. I call it the radical act of resting before you're completely wiped out. I do think it is radical because it runs counter to our go-do-produce capitalist society.

Next time you are feeling a bit run down, try going to bed early, taking a nap, or soaking in the tub—even if you feel like you can push through. It might feel self-indulgent or lazy but know that this is just your capitalist conditioning. The truth is, allowing yourself to rest is part of being a responsible and loving steward of your health and energy.

april 25

You Are Not a Mess; You Are Actually Quite Incredible

I want to unfold. Let no place in me hold itself closed,
for where I am closed I am false.
~ Rainer Maria Rilke

One of the refrains in my mind throughout adulthood has been, *"My life is a mess."* If I pause and think about what makes me feel this way, it boils down to this: there never seems to be enough time in the day to do all the things that are "supposed" to be done. I feel like I am chronically behind and that I am alone in this struggle to manage the many moving parts that make up life. Each time I catch a glimpse of the stacks of paper on my dining room table or the mess on the floor of my car, it feeds my fear that I suck at adulthood.

At some point, *"My life is a mess"* translated into *"I am a mess."*

I think so many of us feel like we don't have our shit together, but what does that even mean? We are comparing our very real lives to the idealized images of life we see portrayed in the media. It's not fair, and it plays into patriarchal nonsense. Let's opt out. The truth is, I am not a mess and neither are you; life is messy and we are actually quite incredible.

april 26

The Power of Ten Minutes

I have this habit of going in and out of attending spinning classes. I'll go to class for a few weeks, maybe even months, and then life happens and I drop off. Each time I go back after not having been there for a while, I want to quit during the first few minutes of class. It feels hard because I'm out of practice. But when I stick with it, I end up feeling great just a few minutes later.

I've noticed that I experience this snag at the beginning of a lot of things—and that if I can sit with it, or move with it, it takes care of itself. The first ten minutes of writing, doing accounting work, speaking in front of a group, and cleaning my house all feel hard, and I want to give up; but when I stick with the task, it gets easier just a few minutes later.

Now I play a game with myself when something feels hard or overwhelming. I tell myself I just have to do the thing for ten minutes. One of two things happens after those ten minutes: either I realize the thing is not so bad and I keep going, or I decide I've had enough and I stop, having at least made a dent in the thing I was avoiding. I feel good either way and it gets me unstuck.

Is there something that you've been avoiding? Spend ten minutes on it today and see what shifts.

april 27

It's Okay to Rest

Almost everything will work again if you unplug it for a few minutes, including you. ~ Anne Lamott

It's okay to rest.

We are humans, not machines. I don't believe that we exist simply to produce and achieve. I know it can feel like the whole world will crumble if you sit down for a few quiet minutes. But is it true? Does everything fall to pieces if you allow yourself to rest?

The idea of rest might conjure visions of taking a nap or getting a good night's sleep, but not much else easily comes to mind for most people. When I think of resting, I think of restoration. Restoring oneself—mind, body, and soul. Rest can include anything that helps you restore – breath work, meeting a friend for tea, pulling tarot cards, doing yoga, walking in nature, meditating, reading, writing, wandering through the thrift store, taking a bath, snuggling your pet, or taking a break from the to-do list to just be.

Let's expand our definition of rest.
Let's honor the role of rest in our lives.
Let's prioritize restoring ourselves—mind, body, and soul.

How can you rest today?

april 28

What Matters Most is What You Do the Most

If your compassion does not include yourself, it is incomplete.
~ Jack Kornfield

I have this habit of beating myself up when I act in a way that I don't like. If I yell at my kids or engage in gossip, I hang on to it and keep replaying it in my mind. I start to question what kind of a person I am based on one tiny behavior, and I ignore or forget the 95% of the time when I act in alignment with my values.

I remember crying to my therapist one day about how I lost my shit and yelled at my daughter. I was swimming in guilt and self-loathing. She said something that has stuck with me all these years later, "What matters most is what you do the most." This sentence is a mantra I return to, over and over. Not to excuse my behavior, but to help me with self-compassion and self-forgiveness. We're human and we will make mistakes. Those once-in-a-while, every-so-often exceptions to our behavior do not define us. It's how we usually show up that makes us who we are.

april 29

Changing One Thing Changes Everything

Everything is connected, and this is good news.

So often we feel overwhelmed by all the changes we want to make in our lives. I want my home to feel like a sanctuary and I want to focus more on my health and I want to grow my business. Maybe you want to devote yourself more deeply to your spiritual practices, to feel more connected in your relationships, and to spend more time creating. It can be hard to know where to start or how to divide your time and attention. I have found that making a change in one area of my life affects all the other areas too. Tidying my house helps me feel peaceful, which helps me communicate more clearly with my loved ones. Exercising more regularly improves my concentration at work. Getting consistent, quality sleep makes it easier to connect with my creativity. Changing one thing changes everything.

Today, start with one step toward where you want to be, knowing that taking action in one area of your life will impact all the other parts too.

april 30

A Poem About Fear & Shame and Peace & Hope

Feeling not thin enough, pretty enough, smart enough,
Never enough.
Feeling too loud, too sexy, too smart,
Always too much.
What's wrong with me?
If people really knew me they wouldn't love me.

Hiding.
Feeling alone in a room full of people who love me.
Shame.
More hiding.
Striving to appear perfect in order to feel safe.

Being a survivor of sexual abuse,
Being in a physically abusive relationship,
What's wrong with me?
If people really knew me they wouldn't love me.

Hiding.
Confusing something horrible happening to me with me being something
horrible.
Shame.
More hiding.
Striving to appear perfect in order to feel safe.

Depression, anxiety, panic attacks, suicidal thoughts,
Self-loathing, self-medicating,
Therapy, antidepressants, Xanax,
How hard it can be to just carry on,
What's wrong with me?
If people really knew me they wouldn't love me.

Hiding.
Shoving it all down until I can pretend it doesn't even exist.
Shame.
More hiding.
Striving to appear perfect in order to feel safe.

Having a miscarriage,
Feeling unfulfilled with the "good" job.
What's wrong with me?
If people really knew me they wouldn't love me.

Hiding.
Throwing myself into my work, creating an armor of accomplishments.
Shame.
More hiding.
Striving to appear perfect in order to feel safe.

Breastfeeding a baby, raising a teenager, caring for an elder,
Unable to find myself inside all the roles I play,
Why does life feel so hard?
What's wrong with me?
If people really knew me they wouldn't love me.

Hiding.
Feeling broken and sad and lonely.
Shame.
More hiding.
Striving to appear perfect in order to feel safe.

Until slowly and yet somehow all at once,
Something shifts.
And I believe in the possibility of change.

Breathing, walking, reading, writing, meditating,
Finding my way home to myself.
Seeing the larger forces at play,
Understanding my experience of being a mother, a wife, a woman is impacted by the context I live inside of,
And that that context does not honor, support, or celebrate me as a woman; in fact it seems to hate women—to treat us like we need to be controlled and contained.

Finally understanding,
Nothing is wrong with me,
I am not damaged,
It is the system that is broken.

Knowing—deep in my belly, my heart, my bones,
All women feel some version of this not enough/too muchness,
We all fear that we will be rejected if we let people see our truth.

Committing—devoting myself to healing,
Myself,
Others,

So that we may all know our inherent worth,
So that we may collectively shift our world toward love and justice.

I believe in you,
I believe in me,
Our beauty, our worth, our knowing,
Let's heal together.

Take Stock of Your Life

It is important to regularly check in with ourselves, to identify where things are going well and where they are in need of attention. Today, take some time to reflect on the various areas of your life. *What are the main components that make up your life? Rate each area from 0 (not going well) to 10 (going very well). Create your own categories or choose from those below.*

Family
Home
Leisure / Travel
Relationships
Finances
Marriage / Partnership
Career
Health
Spirituality
Creativity
Self-Care
Service

Optional: *I like to create a visual image by drawing a flower with each petal representing one area of life. I draw the length of the petals to represent the number rating I gave each area (i.e., a shorter petal for a 3 and a longer petal for an 8). Look over your responses. What area did you rate the lowest? What is one step you can take toward creating change in that area?*

Know and Honor Your Priorities

We can't do it all.

This is one of the things that I have the hardest time accepting. Over and over again I fall into unrealistic expectations of myself. I buy into the lie that I *can* do it all if I *just try hard enough.*

It's bullshit.

The truth is we can only do so much. We have to choose where to direct our time and energy, letting go of some things and holding on to others. Before we can decide what to release, we need to know what is most important to us. I once heard someone say that if you want to know what your priorities are, just look around you. I love this idea that it is not so much what we *say* our priorities are but instead our *actions* that truly demonstrate what matters most to us. If we look around we will see the results of our time and energy in the life that we have created.

Spend some time with your journal today, using these prompts: When I look around me I see... Set aside judgment and take note of what you see around you. When I look around me I don't see... What's missing? What feels out of alignment? Getting clear on our priorities helps us set boundaries and protect our time and energy. As you look at your two lists, what adjustments are asking to be made? Keeping your priorities in mind, consider how you can begin to create some shifts in your life to honor what is most important. What can you take off your plate? What are you ready to release?

may 3

Let Go of Complaining

If you don't like something change it; if you can't change it,
change the way you think about it.
~ Mary Engelbreit

I am not of the "good vibes only" camp. Negative thoughts, feelings, and experiences are part of life, and I believe in being open to the full range of being human, not just the good stuff. However, there is a difference between acknowledging what is wrong or difficult and complaining. It feels hard to articulate this difference; it's something I mostly feel. There is a different energy behind stating a problem so that you can connect with someone or problem-solve and expressing dissatisfaction simply for the sake of complaining. The hard truth is that complaining is an energy drainer that serves no purpose.

For today, observe when you feel the urge to complain. What situation are you in? Who are you with? Notice how often the people around you complain. Observe how you feel in your skin when you are listening to complaints (either your own or someone else's).

may 4

Clear Space

The best way to find out what we really need is to get rid of what we don't.
~ Marie Kondo

Our physical surroundings impact us mentally, emotionally, and energetically. I crave being surrounded by order and beauty, yet I have struggled with clutter for as long as I can remember. When I think about releasing all of the clutter in my house and decorating every room beautifully, I feel totally overwhelmed. *And then I do nothing.* When I think about sprucing up one corner or sorting through one dresser, it feels doable—and then I take action. The action comes from a place of self-love, a knowing that I deserve to be surrounded by beautiful spaces that feed my soul.

For today, pick one small area to clear. This could be your desk, the front seat of your car, your underwear drawer, or the top of your dresser. Take note of how you feel on the inside after clearing on the outside.

may 5

Be Mindful of Your Thoughts

Our thoughts are powerful; they influence our feelings and behaviors and, ultimately, our lives. Most of us are not consciously aware of the thoughts that go through our mind on a daily basis. Research shows that 80% of our thoughts are negative and 95% are repetitive. This means that we tend to think the same negative things over and over again. Bringing awareness to our thoughts and consciously shifting them is a powerful practice.

As an example, when I was struggling with burnout at work, some of my thoughts were *"It is impossible for me to take care of myself"* and *"Everyone needs me all the time"* and *"I can't get a break."* These thoughts were not serving me. While I was stuck in them I felt overwhelmed, anxious, and depressed. After we identify our thoughts, we can begin the work of changing them. This is how I chose to shift my thoughts from the above example:

Original thought: It is impossible for me to take care of myself.
Shifted thoughts: I now choose to prioritize my self-care. I am allowed to take care of myself. It is safe for me to take care of myself. I am allowed to set healthy boundaries. Healthy boundaries are good for me and for my clients.

Original thought: Everyone needs me all the time.
Shifted thoughts: I hold a lot inside of my work. Ultimately, I am only responsible for myself. I cannot take care of my client's needs; they have to be responsible for their own self-care.

Original thought: I can't get a break.
Shifted thoughts: I will no longer compromise my schedule. I will block out days and times where I can take breaks. I will fiercely protect this time.

Once we have articulated new thoughts we need to *actively* work with them. There are several ways to do this: write or say the thoughts daily, put them on sticky notes around your house, program them into your phone as reminders to pop up on the hour, or create a piece of art around them. Many of our default thoughts are automatic and have been with us for a long time; they aren't simply going to shift or go away. We are reprogramming our minds, which takes regular effort.

Think of a situation that feels challenging in your life at that moment. What are your thoughts around it? Take a few minutes to free write in your journal or sit with yourself in meditation to help you identify your thoughts. Once you've identified your thoughts, notice if they are serving you. If there are thoughts you would like to change, write out what you would like to believe instead. Choose at least one idea from the list above to work with your new thoughts. Stay committed to being aware of your thoughts and notice how this practice impacts your life.

may 6

Releasing Our Old Stories

Today, I invite you to consider an old story that is no longer serving you.

Perhaps something comes to mind right away. If not, here are a few journal prompts to get you started on this contemplation. Free write around as few or as many of them as feels right for you.

I don't deserve...
I'm not good enough because...
The thing I don't like about myself is...
The hardest part of life is...
Other people...
I can't...
The way the world works is...
Thoughts that I notice myself having over and over...

And a few prompts to consider after your free writing:

What did you learn about the stories in your mind?
What would you like to release?
Where did these ideas come from? Family, friends, school, community, the media?

No one is born with negative thoughts about herself. We learn and internalize beliefs from our interactions with the world. One of my oldest stories is that if I want people to love me I have to give them what they want, even if it hurts me. I have been working on releasing this old story for 20 years. There are a lot of layers. Some of the layers are as thick and heavy as concrete, and I have found the courage to just cut them off completely, like leaving an abusive boyfriend and quitting a job I hated. Other layers are more complex and subtle and seem to come and go, like my fear of saying no and my people-pleasing.

This learning about our stories and shifting them is a process, maybe even a life-long process. For today, just practice bringing awareness to your old stories. Also, I want you to know that you don't have to do this work alone. We all deserve a safe space to process. Many of us need help excavating and working with our old stories and their origins. I highly recommend giving yourself the gift of working with a professional therapist.

may 7

Fostering a Healthier Relationship with Guilt

Guilt is for when you have done something wrong. Guilty feelings provide us with data on behaviors that we would like to change. For example, I feel guilty when I yell at my daughter. This type of guilt can be useful because it motivates me to change my behavior, to take a deep breath or walk away when I am frustrated with her rather than start screaming. However, I have noticed, personally and professionally, that women tend to spend an excessive amount of time inside of guilt. Many of us are mentally beating ourselves up day in and day out, and oftentimes we feel guilty when we haven't done anything wrong. We feel bad about things like taking time for ourselves, setting boundaries, and having needs. This type of guilt is a result of our social conditioning and serves no purpose other than to maintain patriarchal norms.

For today, notice when guilt comes up for you. When you observe it, ask yourself if you have done something wrong. Is the guilt providing you with useful feedback about a behavior you would like to change? If so, great! Thank the guilt for the useful information, take note of what you would like to change, and release the guilt. It has served its purpose. There is nothing to be gained from staying inside of guilt for more than the few moments it takes to receive the information about what you would like to change. If you find yourself feeling guilty when you haven't done anything wrong, notice that with curiosity and compassion and invite yourself to let go of unnecessary and unproductive guilt.

may 8

You Have the Right to Choose the People You Spend Time With

Relationships can be nourishing or depleting. Sometimes we forget that we get to choose the people who we spend our time with. We deserve to be surrounded by people who lift us up. If there are people in your life that make you feel small or unimportant or judged, consider limiting or ending the time you spend with them. Keep in mind that if your life is filled with unhealthy or depleting relationships there will not be room for new relationships to enter.

Relationships generally fall into three categories: acquaintances, friends, and inner circle (the people closest to our hearts). Sometimes we have placed a person closer to the heart than makes sense, and we can shift them out into the friend or acquaintance category. It's also okay to have different friends for different things. You may have friends that are fun to hang out with but that you wouldn't lean on for emotional support. What's most important is to bring mindful awareness to your relationships and how they impact you while remembering that you have the right to make adjustments at any time. Invest your time and energy into supportive and reciprocal relationships that feed your soul.

Spend some time with your journal today. Who are the five people you spend the most time with? How do you feel when you are around them? How do their values and priorities align with your own? As you consider your relationships, notice any parts that feel unhealthy or in need of change. What shifts can you make to bring things into alignment?

Create Space to Breathe Inside of Your Life

It was Primary Day. I had exactly 15 minutes between mothering and working to go and vote. I was rushing, worrying that I'd be late for my first client. I was already tired and only felt more exhausted as I thought about working until 8:30 that night. I was sad that my husband and I had only a five-minute overlap to connect as he came home from work and I left for work. At my polling place, I didn't even look up to make eye contact as I was signing my name. The truth is I was barely aware there was another human across the table from me. My breath was short and my heart was beating too fast as my mind raced with worry.

Then I heard a voice say, *"Are you a psychologist?"*
"Ugh," I thought. *"I don't have time for this right now."*

But the question put me into work mode so I lifted my head, smiled, and said, *"Yes, I am."*

I didn't recognize the man speaking to me; we had never met before. But he recognized me. *"You helped my daughter so much,"* he said. *"Thank you. She is in college now and doing well."* He went on to talk about her many accomplishments, how wonderful she was doing, and how grateful he was for the work I did with her years ago.

I instantly felt like an asshole. Here I was internally groaning about this guy slowing me down while I was trying to vote, and here he was opening his heart and genuinely thanking me for helping his child. Once I was done feeling like an asshole, I felt thankful. Thankful to this man for reminding me that my work is important and impactful. Thankful to the Universe for sending me this message at a moment when I had been feeling sad, hurried, and frustrated. Thankful for the reminder to slow down and be present—to be here, now.

Not long after that interaction, I made some significant adjustments to my life. I realized that it felt like there was no room to breathe inside of my life. All the bouncing from one thing to another was leaving me exhausted, unwell, and anxious. I chose to slow down so that I could reevaluate and recalibrate my life, and I adjusted my schedule to allow for more space so I was not rushing around with my head down.

Often we have more flexibility and freedom inside of our lives than we realize. What choices can you make to create more space in your life? Can you sit in your car and take three deep breaths in between appointments? Can you ask for help? Can you block out two hours a week for yourself, no exceptions? Can you take something off your plate? Spend a few minutes today thinking about how you can create space to breathe inside of your life.

I've Seen the Future and You Are Healed

Things feel hard right now. *I get it.* You are in a period of intense growth and change. You are peeling back so much, so quickly. It's painful and beautiful all at once. And so worth it, I promise. I'm here on the other side, enjoying the fruits of your labor. Thank you. Thank you for doing this work now so that we can grow into this next version of ourselves. It can feel so lonely and yet, you are never alone. I am here with you always. The times and trials you are navigating now are going to propel you further and higher than you can imagine.

Oh love, if you could see what you are going to create! Powerful, raw, honest, and impactful. Everything you dream of is coming, I promise. And after all this you will be able to feel it, *really feel* its goodness deep in your bones. Please keep showing up—creating, loving, making your art, caring for your people, for *yourself*. We need you—your voice, your story, your truth. It is all coming together now.

I've seen the future and you are healed. If you could only see who you are going to become. You will move through the world confidently, radiating your powerful energy, making no apologies for your intensity and the way you take up space. Healing others with your very presence. You will know how much you have to give and you won't hesitate to receive. You will understand that you are a gift to this world, love embodied.

For now, my love, patience + trust + surrender.
All is coming. You are amazing.

Love,

Your future self

may 11

Nothing is Wasted

One day I was driving home after a particularly tough session with my therapist. I felt like we had spent an hour going in circles, getting nowhere. As I replayed the session in my mind, I felt the anger rising. I have been working on healing my childhood wounds for 20 years. TWENTY YEARS!!! I have been in active therapy for ten of those years and practicing yoga for 15 of them. I have taken dozens of classes and workshops and probably read 100 self-help/ personal growth books. And the same shit keeps popping up in different ways.

I was pissed and a bit despondent. *What's the point? Am I here to spend whole life trying to heal? Why can't I just feel better?* I let myself be angry for a bit and then I invited the wisest part of myself to give her opinion on the matter.

She said that I am not always suffering. *True.* I don't feel terrible all the time. *Not even close.* I am healed in so many ways. *Fair point.* I have a beautiful life that I love, and I have some things I am still working on. *Not either or, both.*

A few days later I was watching a training on somatic experiencing and yoga. The teacher, Mariana Caplan, was telling a story about her Sufi mentor. She said she went to him after a year and said, *"I've been practicing so hard and still I am suffering so much."* And he replied, *"Nothing really happens for the first twenty years."* I laughed and remembered I'm not alone. I recalled what I often say during yoga class while we are teetering around in tree pose, *"Let's breathe with the wobbles and practice patience with the process."*

It doesn't bother me that I wobble in tree pose after 15 years of practice. Why does it bother me that I wobble in life after 20 years of practice?

In this thing called life there is no destination. We will never arrive. *And yet we are already there.* It is so hard for me to release the idea of a goal, an objective, a check box I can tick off at the end of the day. Mariana said something else during that training: *"Yoga is the union with all that is—right here, right now. Not the union with some ideal you have in your mind."*

Whoa. Yes.

Yoga is my path and this life is my practice.

To join with myself as I am right here, right now, moment to moment.
To be in union with myself when I am happy and when I am angry.
To be in union with my wounded, imperfect heart. Even if it never heals all the way.

To let that be enough.

To be here, to be human, to be able to practice, to be able to mess up and forget and start over and remember and do it all again the next hour or the next day. That is my practice, our practice. And in this thing called life, nothing is wasted. It is all part of the practice.

Being All In

Swim inside the ocean of tenderness yet build boundaries on the sand.
An open heart is a paradise to protect. ~ Victoria Erickson

How open is your heart? I spent many years with walls around mine. When I decided to be all in on my life, to stop holding back emotionally and really let people in, the walls came tumbling down. It was wildly intense. The whole experience was kind of terrifying but also really beautiful. Some days it was disconcerting, like I was walking around all raw and new. I felt things I had not felt in a very long time—fiery rage, brutal insecurity, love so strong that I felt frighteningly vulnerable.

Being all in is a serious practice in devotion.
Devotion to willingness, growth, love, heartache, *wholeness*.
Feeling it all, all the way.

The walls I had built were there for a good reason—to protect me and my heart. They served me until I didn't need them anymore. Letting those walls come down felt disorienting at first. The shedding of old stories and old identities happened so quickly and seemingly all at once. I wasn't sure who I would be on the other side, but now that I am here, I know that it was so worth it to do the work and find out.

Spend some time with your journal today. What walls have you built up around your heart? Are they still serving you? What would it be like to be all in on your life?

With Each New Layer, An Opportunity for Healing and Growth

Resistance is experienced as fear; the degree of fear equates to the strength of Resistance. Therefore the more fear we feel about a specific enterprise, the more certain we can be that that enterprise is important to us and to the growth of our soul. That's why we feel so much Resistance. If it meant nothing to us, there'd be no Resistance. ~ Steven Pressfield

Have you had the experience of bumping into stuff that you thought you had already worked through? I see this in my own life and in the lives of my clients. We think we have healed a certain wound, and then it shows up again. The truth is there are many layers to our fears, past hurts, and negative beliefs. Each time a layer is revealed, we tend to resist. *What? This again? No way! Been there, done that. Leave me alone.*

Fear can be a powerful force. In this liminal space we might feel like we don't know much of anything. Places that were settled are being shaken up. We suddenly feel like we don't fit—inside our hair, our bodies, our homes. We resist both the peeling away of these layers and what lies in wait behind them. We might find ourselves acting out of character—skipping our practices, mindlessly watching television or scrolling social media, blocking our connection with our higher self. When we find ourselves at this point, we have a choice: stay where we are by continuing to engage in these avoidant behaviors or be brave and up-level our lives.

We can stay with comfort and familiarity or move to the edge and step into the next evolution of ourselves, even if we have very little idea of what that might look like. I believe that bumping into old stuff is an invitation to heal and grow. Listen for the soft whispers of your intuition, calling you toward this path. She will have instructions for you. She will encourage you to breathe and practice trust. She will reassure you that all will be revealed in perfect timing. She will ask you to stop trying to figure everything out.

Remember that change, growth, and life are like spirals. It can feel like we are back where we started or in a place we've already passed, but really that is impossible. Even when we bump up against our old issues, it can't be exactly the same because *we* are different. We have had new experiences, learned things, grown. Each layer is an opportunity for healing and growth. I invite you to walk forward on the spiral. This very moment is a good time to begin (again). Breathe and practice trust. Know that resistance will return and you will bump into more layers of old stuff. Hold the image of the spiral close to your heart and choose to show up anyway.

may 14

Mistakes Are Allowed

Perfectionism discourages creativity, risk-taking, and trying new things. It fuels the hustle behind the endless striving to be "good enough." I spent much of my life as a child and young adult trying to be perfect. My version of perfectionism looked like earning perfect grades, being nice and accommodating to everyone all the time, arriving wherever I had to be at least ten minutes early, and trying to be thin and pretty. Just writing that sentence makes it hard to breathe. Thankfully, I have released most of my perfectionistic ways. Now when perfectionism arises, I have a simple mantra that I repeat: *mistakes are allowed*. These three little words help me shift in big ways. They remind me that it's okay to mess up. They encourage me to not berate myself for my mistakes. They allow me to move on from my missteps with kindness and grace.

How does perfectionism show up in your life? What would it be like to affirm for yourself that mistakes are allowed?

may 15

Practice for the Sake of Practice

Sweat is dripping off my forehead as I bow toward the earth. The familiar bliss of joyful effort washes over me, and it feels like every cell in my body is smiling. And then the teacher calls for crow pose. A slight tightness creeps in as I hear the faint chorus of familiar thoughts espousing my weaknesses. You see, I've been practicing yoga for years and I still can't do crow pose.

I think, "*What if this is it? What if I never master crow pose?*" The idea feels equal parts defeatist and freeing. Mastering postures is definitely not the point of yoga, and yet sometimes it sure feels like the postures are a measuring stick of my progress. We have to be headed somewhere, right?

Maybe not.

What if we exchange our goals for intentions?
What if we let go of any ideas about the outcome of our practice?
What if we release striving toward the promised fruits of our labor and instead focus on the process itself?

Practice for the sake of practice.
Yes, that feels true and holy as I type it.

And I don't think this applies to yoga alone. Whether it is yoga, writing, parenting, running, painting, loving, or *living*, our job is to show up and do our work, put in our joyful effort, and release the rest. Especially the expectations. Do our work, our practice, simply for the sake of doing it. Live our lives simply for the sake of savoring this moment and the next and the next. Practice as an end in and of itself, rather than a means to an end.

What if I never master crow pose? What if my hamstrings stay tight and my mind stays busy and my judgment keeps returning? Would I still be committed to my practice?

Would I keep trying, even knowing things will not change?
Would I do yoga just to do yoga, not for the sake of getting anywhere different than exactly where I am?

My answer is a resounding *yes, yes I will*. Even if this is it, even if it never goes any further than this, I will keep showing up on the mat and in my life. (Because really my life is my yoga practice.) I will continue with the practices that bring me closer to my highest self, not because I am trying to get anywhere or achieve anything, but simply for the sake of showing up for myself and my life.

may 16

Welcome All of Your Feelings as Valuable Information

Anger is meant to be respected. Why? Because anger is a map.
Anger shows us what our boundaries are. Anger shows us where we want to go.
It lets us see where we've been and lets us know when we haven't liked it.
Anger points the way, not just the finger.
~ Julia Cameron

Learn to welcome all of your feelings as valuable information. Our so-called negative emotions have the potential to reveal so much.

I try to practice nonjudgmental curiosity of my internal and external responses. I pay special attention to reactions that seem to be out of proportion with what is going on in the present moment; this is how I know past stuff is being triggered. There is so much beautiful information to be found within our emotional experiences. How do you respond to your feelings? Can you let go of ideas about right and wrong and approach your feelings with gentle curiosity?

Think of a recent time when you felt sad, anxious, jealous, angry, or any other feeling you view as negative. Spend some time with your journal today and explore the wisdom underlying your feelings. Sadness reveals what we are missing, anxiety what we fear. Jealousy often tells us what we desire to bring into our own lives. Anger can hold information about where we need to set boundaries. Allow your feelings to be what they are and approach them with gentle curiosity. What messages do your feelings have for you? The wisdom of our feelings, coupled with the power of curiosity, leads us toward who we want to be.

may 17

Letting Our Bodies Be Our Guides

One of my biggest challenges in this life has been learning to slow down.

My body has been my guide through the many layers of my journey to creating a breathable life. When I do too much, I get sick. When I try to push through not feeling well and just keep going, I end up in burnout.

It has literally felt hard to breathe at times. There was a period of time when I was sick with allergies and asthma for nearly a year. My western medicine doctor told me that my immune system was especially sensitive and that sometimes women develop asthma as they age due to hormonal shifts. I remember telling this doctor that I was frustrated that I had to take a nap nearly every day, to which she replied, "*Okay, so take a nap. You have to listen to your body. That's what you would tell your patients, right?*"

The truth is I was angry with my body. I felt betrayed. I was fed up with being highly sensitive in all the damn ways. I didn't want to have to work so hard (or rest so hard?) to feel okay. There was a lot of crying in frustration and even some screaming in anger during this time period. Eventually I ended up at an applied kinesiologist who diagnosed me with a candida infection and adrenal fatigue. I was able to heal my body with food, supplements, and a ton of rest. I learned that tuning into my body every day and giving her what she needs in terms of nourishment, movement, and rest is non-negotiable. I am still integrating the lessons from this period, but here is what I know for sure: our bodies are wise and listening to them holds the potential for healing and growth on a physical, emotional, and energetic level.

Spend some time with your journal today. What is your body trying to tell you?

may 18

Some Advice for the Space Between

I am learning every day to allow the space between where I am and where I want to be to inspire me and not terrify me.
~ Tracee Ellis Ross

The space between who you used to be and who you are becoming— it can be scary and unsettling. I don't think there is a way to avoid it. It is a necessary part of the process, maybe it can even be beautiful. *Maybe.*

Some days you will feel like you have no idea what you are doing. Some days things you thought were healed will come back up and rock you to your core. Some days you might want to run away. Some days you will swear you can feel your cells rearranging themselves. Some days you will feel afraid and lonely. You might not know how to talk about it. Words fail in times like these.

You are the goo inside the cocoon right now, in between caterpillar and butterfly.

Have faith in yourself and trust your process. This space is leading you toward your next becoming. You will come out the other side and it will all be worth it.

Try to see yourself with compassionate eyes. Take some time to be with yourself in front of the mirror or turn your camera around and capture your own gaze. Say kind things to yourself; give yourself the unconditional love and acceptance you deserve.

Be like a detective and search for clues about your becoming. Let your intuition guide you. What are you being pulled toward? What feels like you? What lights you up? Follow the clues even if they don't make rational sense.

Some days what you are yearning for will feel so damn far away. You will want your old self back. But you can't go back to her. Because that was before and this is now.

Pray in whatever way you pray.
Ask—please, please, please.
Receive—thank you, thank you, thank you.

Try to lean into the beauty of this liminal space.
Let go of trying to rush the process and get to somewhere else.
Practice being where you are— in the space between who you used to be and who you are becoming.

Practice Receiving

Until we can receive with an open heart, we're never really giving with an open heart. When we attach judgment to receiving help, we knowingly or unknowingly attach judgment to giving help.
~ Brené Brown

Like many women, I am a giver. I put a lot of energy out into the world through my relationships and my work. It is challenging for me to receive. I have a hard time asking for help, and I sometimes still believe that I should be able to do everything on my own. I am reminded of that saying about how if you don't learn the lesson from the tap on the shoulder you will get hit on the head with a brick. Burnout was the brick that taught me how to receive. I was forced to stop giving because I physically and emotionally could not keep going. Recovering from burnout demanded that I ask for help. I received help financially, physically, and emotionally. I received the gifts of time, patience, and love. I received physical and energetic healing from a variety of practitioners. I became new in so many ways after navigating the process of healing from burnout. I can now (mostly) receive with grace.

Today, practice receiving. If someone gives you a compliment, simply say a heartfelt thank-you. When you need help, ask for it and let go of any judgment about yourself that arises. State your wants and needs clearly and unapologetically and allow the people around you to give what they can. Receive with a thankful and open heart and observe how this impacts your experience.

may 20

You Don't Have to Hold Your Tears In

Remember you are water.
Of course you leave salt trails.
Of course you are crying. Flow.
~ adrienne maree brown

Nearly every day someone sits on the couch in my therapy office and apologizes for crying. *In a therapy office.* Beautiful, brave humans doing the hard work of therapy say *"I'm sorry"* for expressing their feelings in a space specifically designed for expressing feelings. The notion that we should hide our feelings is so deeply ingrained in our society.

Personally, I cry a lot. I cry when I am happy, sad, scared, angry, or confused. I cry when I am moved by beauty or deep in gratitude. Sometimes I cry during yoga. I cry when I am tired or overwhelmed. I cry when I am proud of my kids. I cry during live music and when I hear children sing. It doesn't take much to move me to tears. Sometimes I fall into feeling embarrassed about this, but mostly I welcome my tears as a sign of my superpower—feeling and expressing my emotions.

The truth is, expressing your feelings is natural and healthy. You don't have to hold your tears in. It's okay to cry.

may 21

Releasing Nice, Shiny Me

I used to hold my tears back. I remember being the person on the couch in the therapy office trying not to cry. For so long I shoved my tears, my sadness, my anger, and so many of my other feelings down, down, down. When I did let myself cry, I did so silently. I worked so hard to be who I thought I was supposed to be—quiet, composed, "strong"—that I had no idea who I really was. All I wanted, and what I think most of us want, was to be loved and accepted; and I was so afraid I would be rejected if I showed people the real me. So I held in the tears and so much more. I created a version of myself that I thought would earn me the love and acceptance I craved—an overachieving, self-deprecating, people-pleasing, really nice and shiny version of myself.

Nice, shiny me got me so far in life. She secured my place in my family as the smart, sweet girl with no common sense. She hid my depression and anxiety. She kept my buried traumas safe. She earned me a Ph.D. while being a single mother. She landed me a respectable job with great benefits. What she couldn't give me was true emotional intimacy, the feeling that comes from being seen and known and loved inside of my imperfect, messy truth. And that is the thing I crave most in this life.

So I had to let her go. I quit the job. I learned to set boundaries in my relationships. I stopped putting myself down to try to make other people comfortable. I started telling the truth about my life. I became less nice and shiny and more raw and real.

And the most beautiful thing happened—I found my people, or maybe they found me. We found each other. Some of them had been there all along. And I learned the truth about love and acceptance and feeling seen: we can only experience that amazing feeling of being loved for who we are if we let others see us in our naked truth. We must risk the vulnerability in order to get to the connection. It's scary and it's the only way.

Holding back our tears is only one of the many ways we hide our true selves from each other. Hiding our feelings, trying to be nice, shiny versions of ourselves, keeps us isolated and feeling alone. I want to feel connected. I want to know I am not the only one who feels what I feel. So I choose to share the raw and real version of myself and I hope that when I show up as her, it gives you permission to do the same.

may 22

Shine a Light on the Dark Places Within Yourself

Go out in the woods, go out. If you don't go out in the woods, nothing will ever happen and your life will never begin. ~ Clarissa Pinkola Estés

As soul nourishing as it is to walk through the woods, I think that when Clarissa Pinkola Estés tells us to "go out in the woods" she isn't just talking about spending some time in nature. I believe she is referring to our inner wilderness—the dense, dark places within us. We evolve by turning toward our shadows, fear, and resistance. I invite you to look inward, to shine a light on the dark places within yourself and look deeply and lovingly at what you may have been avoiding. Own what longs to be integrated and release what no longer serves you.

Spend some time in meditation or with your journal today. What parts of you are in need of love and attention? Is there a truth that you have been resisting? Be your own guide as you explore the wilderness of your heart. Approach the dark places with unconditional love and acceptance and remember that there are gifts to be mined from our pain and struggles.

may 23

Just Keep Going, No Matter How Slowly

Running is one of my forms of meditation; it helps me clear my head. Usually I love how I feel while I am running—strong and free—but I have had some awful runs too. During one particularly hard run, I was physically dragging. It felt like I was pushing a giant weight. It was no better mentally. My mind was filled with negativity and self-criticism. Since running is like meditation for me, I tried to approach these physical and mental challenges as I would during meditation by simply observing them without judgment and letting them come and go. I continued running, moving alongside the dragging feeling and the negative thoughts. Not trying to change anything, just being with things as they were in the moment.

Then I heard it.
The tender voice of my soul, the me underneath all the noise.
And she said, "*I know it's hard. Just keep going, no matter how slowly.*"

This piece of wisdom has stayed with me. It's a mantra I use often, and not just when I am running. It helped me write this book! I invite you to borrow it whenever you find yourself wanting to give up.

may 24

An Invitation to Slow Down

Every breath we take, every step we make, can be filled with peace, joy and serenity. ~ Thich Nhat Hanh

Modern life is busy. Many of us live at a frenetic pace, running from one thing to the next. It seems like we are always in a rush. Our minds race, our breath is in our chests, our shoulders are tight, our stomachs are in knots. *We are not meant to live like this.* I invite you to try another way. It doesn't require you to change anything about the details of your daily life. Instead, you are simply invited to slow down as you go about your day. Don't wait for things to be different or easier or less busy. Just create some change now by slowing down. Deepen your breath, slow the pace of your walking or driving. Do one thing at a time. Be where you are.

When you choose to slow down, nothing will really change except for you. *And that changes everything.* You will still be doing all the things inside of your life but instead of being up in your head about it all, you will be down in your body. You will still be holding space for so much but instead of doing it all at once, you will be where you are in the moment. You will become more in tune with what really matters to you. It will be easier to hold your intentions close to your heart. You will find peace and calm within the life you already have. How can you slow down today?

may 25

Do Your Part and Let Go of the Rest

Patience is a form of wisdom. It demonstrates that we understand and accept the fact that sometimes things must unfold in their own time.
~ Jon Kabat-Zinn

We all have dreams and goals we are working toward. Sometimes our big dreams can feel overwhelming. We're not quite sure how to get from where we are to where we want to be. The truth is, the best way to support our dreams and goals is to do what we can and let go of the rest. Take action toward what you want and trust that things will manifest in their own way, at their own time. Know that if you show up and take a step toward your dream, it will come back to you many times over. Let go of trying to control everything and focus instead on what you can do to support your dreams and goals.

Spend some time with your journal today. Name one of your current dreams or goals. What can you do to make it a reality? What parts are out of your control? Commit to taking action on what you can and letting go of the rest.

may 26

Be Willing to Do Things Poorly

Sometimes we hesitate to try new things or take up new pursuits because we are worried about the quality of our performance. The truth is, we have to be willing to do something poorly before we can do it well. No one's first soufflé or painting or short story is amazing. It takes a lot of practice to master things, and the only way to master something is by practicing, by doing it poorly for a while. Letting go of the outcome of our efforts opens up a whole new world of possibility.

Is there something that you are interested in but haven't pursued because you are afraid you won't be good at it? Give yourself permission to try it. Be willing to do things poorly and see how the world opens up for you.

may 27

Let Go of All-or-Nothing Thinking

We all fall into distorted thinking at times. One of the most common errors in our thoughts is all-or-nothing thinking. When we hear ourselves using words like *never*, *always*, *everyone*, *everything*, *nothing*, or *all the time*, it is a clue that we are stuck in this cognitive error. All-or-nothing thinking doesn't leave any room for growth or change. It assumes that things are stuck as they are, and this can lead to feelings of sadness or hopelessness.

Today, pay attention to when you think or talk about things in absolute terms. Notice how you feel. Write your all-or-nothing thoughts out so that you can look for exceptions and rephrase what you are telling yourself. For example, if one of your thoughts was, "*Nothing ever works out for me,*" make a list of times when things did work out for you. You might re-write that thought as, "*Sometimes things work out for me and sometimes they don't.*" Can you feel the difference between those two statements? The idea is not to lie to ourselves; we wouldn't want to shift the thought into, "*Everything always works out for me,*" because that is just as problematic. Instead, the goal is to be more realistic and balanced in our thinking.

May 28

Each Moment, We Choose

Today, I invite you to ask yourself, "*How can I be inside of my own energy today? How can I create the feelings I am craving?*"

I want to feel peaceful, present, and grounded in love. Life does not always support these emotions. It is easy to feel frustrated, disconnected, and impatient. I believe we have a choice inside of every moment and that we can come back to how we want to feel no matter what is going on around us. Here are some of the things I do to choose peace, presence, and love:

Meditate
Write in my journal
Go outside

Pray
Invite myself back to the present moment
Place my hand on my heart and take a deep breath
Drink a glass of water
Floss my teeth (big energy shifter, I swear)
Visualize
Repeat to myself, "Be here now"
Do things I have been avoiding that are creating stress
Make a list
Remember what really matters
Forgive myself and begin again
Share my truth
Ask for help
Release resistance and let things be
Allow my emotions to arise and watch as they shift

By reminding myself that I have a choice inside of each moment, I am able to return to peace, presence, and love.

How do you want to feel today? What are some things you can do to create those feelings?

may 29

Evaluating Our Habits

Any activity you engage in regularly is a habit. Some habits are supportive, and others do not serve us. Examples of habits include exercising, gossiping, reading, watching television, interrupting, skipping meals, watching the news, writing, spending time on social media, and meditating. We have habits around when we go to bed and when we wake up, as well as our hygienic care (brushing our teeth, washing our face). We have habits around how we interact with other people, such as overextending ourselves or not speaking up for ourselves. Often we engage in our habits without thinking much about them; we do what feels familiar. It is important to bring mindful awareness to our habits and recognize that we can change.

Today, I invite you to consider your habitual behaviors. Make two lists: one for habits that you want to continue and one for habits you wish to release. Approach this activity with kindness and non-judgment.

My Mind Lags Behind

The inner critic is always loudest right before the breakthrough.
~ Chani Nicholas

When I began my self-care journey I was very focused on behaviors—going to yoga, scheduling a monthly massage, meeting up with friends regularly, writing in my journal, and spending time in nature. I did a lot of work to align my behaviors with my beliefs about the importance of taking time for myself. After a few years of actively focusing on self-care, I realized that self-care is about so much more than behaviors. I began to understand the importance of mindset.

My journey with shifting my thoughts about self-care continues to this day. I sometimes still feel guilty when I take time for myself. Some days I still beat myself up in my mind, and it still creates mental discomfort when I take time to rest. I am able to follow through on the actions of self-care, but my mind lags behind, continuing to create stories about my worthiness. I am not sure if my mind will ever catch up with my actions, and I've decided that this is okay. I believe that the work of self-care is not to eliminate negative thoughts or self-judgment, but instead to shift my reaction to them. To lean into love and acceptance for all the parts of me, including my sometimes negative and judgmental mind.

Discern Between Real and Perceived Threats

Once I had a dream that my daughter Lainey and I were at a performance of some sort in a small auditorium. The place was packed with adults and children. Suddenly a tiger entered the space. I felt my heart beating in my chest and my mind began to jump from idea to idea as I thought about how I could protect my young child from this ferocious beast. All of the adults were quietly alarmed in the way that adults get scared but don't want to show it in front of children. I knew running was useless. So I sat there next to Lainey, trying to breathe. She was delighted at the sight of a real live tiger, right there roaming through the aisles of the auditorium. In her innocence, she showed no fear. In an instant, the tiger was right there, right next to us. I was so afraid I thought I would die. Lainey wanted to pet the tiger and before I could shriek in terror to stop her, there she was, petting this tiger and laughing. The tiger was licking her face and purring. I had been terrified for no reason.

How many things do we assume to be ferocious tigers when really there is nothing to be afraid of?

Did you know our nervous systems can't tell the difference between a real and perceived threat? This means that your body has the same reaction to an unfamiliar dog lunging toward you and you imagining that someone is mad at you. What are you currently afraid of? Is it a real threat or is the danger in your mind? If you find yourself making up stories about something being dangerous when it isn't, try to release your fear and stay open to the possibility that what you thought was a ferocious tiger might actually be a friendly and tame animal.

June 1

Use Your Breath to Create Space and Calm

The practice is simply this: keep coming back to your breath during the day.
Just take a moment.
This will give your mind a steadiness and your breath a gracefulness. . . .
There's so much to let go of, isn't there? Your nostalgia and your regrets.
Your fantasies and your fears. What you think you want instead of what is
happening right now. Breathe.
~Rodney Yee

I believe in doing what we can to find space within the reality of our lives. I believe we can choose an experience of stress or an experience of calm, moment to moment. I believe we can learn to create a restful feeling inside of our busy lives. My favorite tool for creating space and calm while going about my daily activities is breathing. Your breath is always with you, it doesn't cost you anything, and you can use this tool without anyone else even knowing. There are many types of breathing exercises; entire books and courses are dedicated to breathwork. For today, let's use a simple deep, diaphragmatic breath.

Here, right now, find space. Take a few deep breaths. If it feels supportive, close your eyes. Feel into the present moment. Practice resting, not on a beach somewhere far away, but right where you are inside of your life now. Use your breath to help you create space and calm as you go about your day. Whenever you feel your stress level rising, pause and take a few deep breaths. Notice how this practice impacts your day.

June 2

Walk Your Own Path and Let Others Do the Same

One truth, many paths. ~ Swami Satchidananda

I have a tendency to be self-righteous. I have worked hard to overcome this, but I used to think there was one right way to parent, take care of your body, interact with your fellow humans, and generally live your life. The truth is, my beliefs about the "right way" were fueled by my studies of self-improvement and spirituality. I came to a point where I had to ask myself what it meant if my self-improvement and spiritual paths were leading me to judge others. In my mind, the purpose of self-improvement is to be a better person, and part of that is releasing judgment. In my understanding, the core purpose of all spiritual paths is to understand that we are all one—none of us above the other. In order for me to progress on my path, I had to learn to release the idea of one right way. I had to learn to commit to my practices and walk my path without projecting it onto other people as the one right way. This is an area that I still struggle with at times. I am a work in progress, learning to walk my path and lovingly gaze over at you as you walk yours.

Spend some time with your journal today. What comes up for you as you consider this idea of walking your own path and letting others do the same?

June 3

Let Others Take Care of You

Once I was asked to teach a workshop at an amazing retreat led by a woman I deeply admired. I was honored to be invited and also very nervous to attend. I questioned what I had to offer and worried that I wouldn't fit in, but when I arrived I was welcomed with so much love that I almost forgot about my fears.

And then I got sick. I was angry and also very afraid. I felt like I was letting everyone down. I felt useless. I felt like my magical mentor friend would regret asking me to be a part of her team. I worried that everyone was judging me. I worried that I wouldn't be able to teach my workshop. I kept apologizing for being sick and needing to rest. The women around me kept picking up my slack and telling me to honor my body. There was no disappointment, no judgment. I felt like it was the end of the world that I was sick and couldn't contribute in the way I was supposed to, but they all acted like it was nothing to be concerned about. I allowed myself to receive their kindness even as I felt undeserving, even as I was terrified of failing. Letting those women take care of me was a powerful practice in surrender and receptivity, and I felt the impact of their tenderness deep in my heart. My prayer as I flew home from the retreat was to carry their love and support with me so that I could learn to create it inside of my own life.

Spend some time with your journal today. Are you able to allow others to take care of you? What stories do you have about receiving help? Are they serving you? What would it take for you to feel supported inside of your life?

june 4

How Much Good Can You Stand?

People who have experienced developmental trauma often have to build their tolerance for positive experiences, such as feelings of ease, calm, and joy, because their nervous systems were wired inside of fear and uncertainty. It is not uncommon for trauma survivors to feel uncomfortable when things are going well or even to seek relief from the discomfort of positive feelings by (subconsciously) creating difficulties.

Letting things be easy is one of my lessons in this life. I am more comfortable inside of chaos and struggle than peace and calm. My anxiety often spikes when things feel relaxed for me. My mind races and I have trouble sleeping. I start to have thoughts about not being worthy, and fears come up about the good things in my life being taken from me. Sometimes I revert to overcommitting and overscheduling myself.

The good news is we can learn to recognize our patterns and respond in different ways. I have a practice that I turn to now when I find myself slipping into discomfort around things feeling easy or going well. I take a few deep breaths and acknowledge how I am feeling without any judgment. I affirm to myself that I deserve good things and that it's safe to be happy. I lovingly notice my drive toward creating chaos and struggle, and then I invite myself to try another way. I practice staying with the discomfort of things going well so that I can build my tolerance for ease, calm, and joy.

Spend some time with your journal today. How much good can you stand? What lessons did you learn as a child about ease, calm, and joy? Do you recognize any of the patterns I described above about creating chaos and struggle? Just notice whatever arises for you without judgment or expectation. Send love to the part of you that feels uncomfortable inside of things going well. Know that you can learn to shift your patterns.

June 5

Let Your Feminine Energy Lead

Your life is much more than a calendar of events and a list of to dos. I hope part of your "hustle" includes breathing and feeling and loving and soaking in the precious moments, too. ~ Elizabeth DiAlto

We all have masculine and feminine energy inside of us. The masculine inside of me is strong. I love to accomplish things, am achievement-oriented, and feel a bit odd when I'm not working. I love and appreciate my masculine drive to *do, do, do*, but living too heavily from that energy is what led me into burnout. Part of my healing journey has been connecting with and living from my feminine energy. Honoring my feminine energy has taught me to rest, play, and simply be. My feminine energy guides me to spending time in nature and connecting with friends and family. She invites me to let go of having an agenda or task list and just be in the moment.

What is your connection with your feminine energy? Can you let her lead as you go about your day today? What would she have you wear, say, and do (or not do)? Let this be a playful experiment. The goal is not to live entirely from one energy or the other. Our masculine and feminine energies work together, and we need both for different aspects of our lives.

June 6

On Not Knowing What's Next

I have spent so much of my life focused on finding clarity, wanting to get to the other side of where I was in the moment, and resisting the space between. For years, I was stuck in a state of trying to figure things out so that I could get to where I wanted to be. *Until the moment when I realized all of that had fallen away.* Nothing really changed, and yet everything felt so different.

I remember the moment clearly. One night as I climbed into bed my mind was chanting, *"This is my life, this is my life"* in awe. There was nothing extraordinary about the day, and yet my heart was overflowing with gratitude. I was able to see the mundane pieces of my day, *my life*, as beautiful and filled with miracles, even the hard parts like my anxiety, frustration with my kids, the messy living room, and the never-ending to-do lists. In that moment I was able to lean into the unknown, to relax into the space between where I was and where I wanted to be. I was filled with fierce trust that everything would be okay, that really it already was. I lay in bed marveling at my messy, beautiful life, feeling like I had expanded and was able to hold the whole truth of my existence. My cells filled with a deep peace even though I hadn't gained clarity on so many of the things that were pulling on my heart. In that moment, I let go of needing anything to change, and I felt complete in a way I had never experienced before.

I did not stay in that state of trust and gratitude. Instead, I flow in and out of it all the time. Sometimes I am okay with not knowing what's next and can relax into where I am. Sometimes I am frustrated and grasping for answers. When I don't know what's next I try to embody the feeling of deep trust and tap into the place within me that doesn't need to know. I invite myself to surrender to the truth of my current reality. I remind myself of that moment when I climbed into bed with a grateful heart and a feeling of wholeness, and I take a deep breath and trust that it will return once again.

June 7

Come to the Fire

Fire is the element of action, discipline, and transformation. It is associated with the third chakra, which is located at the solar plexus, the home of our personal power and self-esteem. Tapping into our inner fire helps us to define ourselves and create change. *What is your relationship to the fiery power of your third chakra?*

I spent much of my life trying to survive off a single spark. That tiny ember carried me so far that I became fearful of tending to my inner fire. I believed that I didn't deserve more than that single spark. I felt at home in the dark and wary of the light. I feared what the fire wanted me to know, to say, to write, to do. I was worried that I would be abandoned if I let myself burn bright. I was afraid of my inner power and did things like overeating, drinking alcohol, and overworking to dampen it. Then I began to crave fire, even as I felt so full of earth. I felt called to my next evolution. I felt safe to burn more brightly, and my life transformed as I stoked my inner fire and began to step more fully into my power.

We come to the fire to sweat, to release what no longer serves.
We come to the fire to cleanse that which the water can't wash away.
We come to the fire to burn away our fears.
We come to the fire to activate our personal power.
We come to the fire for transformation.

Can you commune with fire today? This could be as simple as lighting a candle. What are you ready to release? What is asking to be alchemized? How can the heat support you in your transformation?

june 8

You Don't Have to Earn Your Rest

Aren't you fed up with internalizing shame and guilt about resting and sleeping? It is one of our most ancient and primal needs to rest and listen to our bodies. ~ The Nap Ministry

We have been programmed to believe that rest is for the end of the day after everything else has been taken care of or for when we are just too exhausted to keep going. Who benefits from this idea? The systems of capitalism, white supremacy, and patriarchy. The truth is we don't have to earn our rest. Resting is a natural and necessary part of life that we each deserve simply because we exist.

Let's let go of feeling like we have to earn our rest. Today, I invite you to play with the idea that you can rest whenever you need to, regardless of what you have or haven't done in a day. If you were able to believe that, what would you do today?

Your Appearance, Your Choice

Beauty begins the moment you decide to be yourself. ~ Coco Chanel

Patriarchy views women as objects to be put on display. The culture we live inside of prescribes specific beauty ideals for women. Because we are steeped in these messages, we have to de-condition ourselves from these beliefs and remember that there is so much more to us than how we look. When it comes to our appearance, we get to choose. Some women prefer to think as little as possible about things like clothing and makeup, while others truly enjoy these things. There is no right or wrong answer here. It can be hard to identify our own preferences when so much noise surrounds how we present ourselves to the world. How you dress and do your hair, what you put or don't put on your body, whether or not you shave—these are choices for you to make. There is nothing wrong with wanting to wear makeup or shave your legs, just as there is nothing wrong with *not* wanting to do those things. Just check in with yourself on whether you are doing it for you or because you are trying to live up to some socially-defined ideal.

June 10

Are You Being Self-Aware or Self-Critical?

Self-awareness is about knowing and understanding ourselves. I believe it is a critical component of a life well lived. The habit of analysis and striving toward positive change is deeply rooted within me. I have always been a person who values reflecting on who I am and how I am showing up in my life. When I was younger I used to make lists of all the things that were wrong with me. I was my own favorite improvement project, constantly deconstructing my faults and planning how I could better myself. I took self-awareness to the level of self-criticism.

Now I understand the difference between being self-aware and self-critical. To me, self-critical is self-awareness plus judgment. I aim to be fair and honest in my self-awareness while setting aside any judgments that arise. It is still important to me to spend time reflecting on my thoughts and behaviors. There continue to be areas where I would like to change and grow, but now I've learned to exist in a space where I can be accountable to myself while also being unconditionally loving. I can approach the changes that I am working on from a place of kindness.

Spend some time with your journal today. How do you feel about self-awareness? It is important to you? Why or why not? Are you able to approach the things you'd like to change about yourself with love and kindness, or do you move into being self-critical?

What Are You Carrying?

I wonder how much of what weighs me down is not mine to carry.
- Aditi

There is a story about a Zen master and his student who were taking a journey by foot and came upon a muddy passage in the road. As they approached the passage they saw a woman on the edge of the muck complaining loudly about the condition of the road: *"How am I supposed to get to my destination? It is unacceptable that the road is in this state!"* The Zen master offered to carry the woman through the muddy passage, and she grudgingly accepted. The woman continued her complaints as the Zen master carried her through the mud. Once through the mess he set her down and she was on her way without a word of thanks. The Zen master and his student continued silently on their path. As they walked the student appeared increasingly agitated. Finally, the student could not hold it in any longer and burst out, *"Why are you not bothered by that woman? She was rude and ungrateful in the face of your kindness!"* The Zen master turned to the student and said, *"Why are you still carrying that woman? I set her down miles ago."*

I can relate to the student in this story. I hold on to things. I keep score. I replay things in my head. I demand retribution. I want other people to admit I am right. The trouble with doing this is that I rob myself of peace in the moment by reliving the past. The truth is, holding on to anger, resentment, and frustration doesn't serve any purpose. I am not saying that we should simply let hurtful things go; I do believe that our feelings deserve to be voiced and taken care of. If there is something we can do, we should certainly do it. And then the work is about setting it down and not continuing to carry the feelings. We don't want to hook our peace or happiness to other people behaving in a certain way. It's a recipe for suffering.

If I was writing the story about the Zen master and his student, I would have liked the Zen master to say to the woman, *"It frustrates me that I am doing a kind thing for you and you are continuing to complain"* and then move on. Maybe that's not the most evolved suggestion, but I see so many women who don't speak up for themselves that I can't advocate us moving right into setting things down when we're the ones doing the carrying. The importance piece is letting go of expectations about how other people will behave in response to you speaking up for yourself.

What are you carrying in this moment? Is there something you can say or do about it? If so, make a plan to do just that. If not, I invite you to set it down and move on with your day.

june 12

Lost and Found

Promise to stay wild with me.
We'll seek and return and stay
and find beauty and the extraordinary
in all the spaces we can claim.
We'll know how to live.
How to breathe magic
into the mundane.
~ Victoria Erickson

In order to be found, we must first get lost.

Lose yourself in the fear of uncertainty,
Float in the sea of unnamed possibilities,
Surrender to the beautiful mess of the space between.

And then allow yourself to be found. *You will know when the time is right.*

Rather than crying into your pillow, let him hold you while you sob. Instead of smiling and saying *fine* when she asks how you are, share your truth. When your gut tells you the story of your next iteration, open up and listen hard.

In this life, there is nothing to be mastered, only cycles to be lived.

june 13

Leave Some Space for Possibility

*It is a paradox that by emptying our lives of distractions
we are actually filling the well.*
~ Julia Cameron

Life today is busier than it's ever been. Our calendars are packed. Our devices are always on. We rush from one place to the next. Instead of looking out the window and daydreaming while we're stopped in traffic, we check our phones. It's easy to feel like there is never a free moment to *just be*. I believe possibility lives in the empty spaces, that moments of doing nothing encourage reflection and inspire our creativity. We don't leave space for possibility when we schedule every moment of our day or fill all of our time with stimulation.

Today, I invite you to leave some space for possibility.

Space for not knowing, not needing to know.
Space for breathing, dreaming, and wondering.
Space to hear what's next.
Blank space on your calendar.
Free moments in your day.
Time to linger, to just be with yourself.

From Fuck You to Thank You

Life doesn't happen to you; it happens for you. ~ Jim Carrey

Wake up to a 48-degree house.
Discover the washing machine has broken.
Find water pouring in because the brand-new roof started leaking.

Swear. A lot. In your head and out loud.
Curse the Universe.
Worry that your husband might have a nervous breakdown.

Breathe. Trust. Take action.

Fix the boiler.
Order a new washing machine.
Place a bucket to catch the indoor rain.

Invite yourself to list all of the things that are working in the house.
Thank you, dryer.
Thank you, electricity.
Thank you, running water.
Thank you, stove.
Thank you, refrigerator.

Allow all of the chaos to spark something important and overdue.
See the larger plan at work.
Thank the Universe.
Feel so enlightened.

Until...

Wake up to find there is no hot water.
And the dishwasher is broken.
And the freaking roof is leaking again.
Throw a speeding ticket in for good measure.

Swear. A lot. In your head and out loud.
Curse the Universe.
Worry that you might have a nervous breakdown.

Breathe. Trust. Take action.

Drive to Mom's to shower.
Order a new dishwasher.
Leave a strongly worded voice mail for the roofer.
Cry. Explain to your toddler why the police are talking to Mommy.

Invite yourself to come back to gratitude.
Thank you broken boiler for reminding me of our abundance.
Thank you broken dishwasher for reminding me control is an illusion.
Thank you leaking roof for reminding me of the freedom in surrendering to what is.
Thank you Mr. State Trooper for reminding me to slow down.
Thank you life for clearing the way for something deeper and more beautiful.

Allow the chaos to work its magic.
See the larger plan at work.
Thank the Universe.
Know better than to feel so enlightened.

June 15

The Unnamed Evolution

Think you don't know what you are doing? There are seeds within you that know how to blossom. You don't need a manual or a tutor. You need your water and sun. Everything is designed to prosper and burst into its own song.
~ Tama Kieves

Sometimes when we are in the space between *here*—where we are—and *there*—where we are going to be—we have no idea what *there* looks like. You might be able to feel that you are on the cusp of an evolution, and you may even see shifts in your thoughts or behaviors, but you can't quite find the words to describe what's happening. It's not uncommon to feel uncertain, anxious, and confused. If you're like me, you will try really hard to figure everything out; you'll want to clearly see where you are going. The truth is this is the time to let go and trust yourself and your process.

Say this prayer to yourself today: "I am in the space between. I trust that shifts are occurring and magic is happening even if I can't name them. I am learning to let go and relax into where I am. I am learning that there is nothing to figure out, that my job is simply to show up and follow the clues on my path. It's okay if my truth is a feeling and not something I can articulate." Close your eyes and take a few deep breaths as you allow these words to sink into your heart space.

june 16

What Makes You Come Alive?

Don't ask what the world needs. Ask what makes you come alive and go do it.
Because what the world needs is people who have come alive.
~ Howard Thurman

This quote has been a guiding force in my life since I first discovered it when I was 29. If something makes me feel alive—excited, inspired, energized—I do it. If something feels draining—heavy, icky, gross—I don't. *It truly is that simple, and it definitely is not at all easy.* Let me pause here and say that the ability to make choices based on how you feel is a privilege that I know many people do not have. You might have to go to your job that feels draining because you have to pay your bills, interact with your ex who makes you feel icky because you have a child together, or live in a place that doesn't light you up because of familial or financial constraints. I do not want to discount whatever reality you may be living inside of. Instead, I invite you to allow this idea of doing what makes you come alive in whatever way *does* fit inside of your current life.

Today, notice how you feel inside your body as you go about your day. What activities, people, places, and situations make you come alive?

June 17

Let Go of Trying to Make Everyone Happy

The only thing wrong with trying to please everyone is that there's always at least one person who will remain unhappy. You.
~ Elizabeth Parker

Somewhere along the way I got the idea that I am responsible for making everyone happy. I know I'm not alone in this, as many women have told me they feel the same way. The problem with trying to make everyone happy is that *it is impossible*, not to mention physically and emotionally exhausting. Oh, and it's a never-ending endeavor. One could spend her whole life trying to make everyone happy, never pausing to think about making herself happy.

The truth is there is only one person whose happiness you are responsible for—your own! Read that again: you are not responsible for the happiness of other people, not even your family and friends. Don't try to change yourself to please others; be who you are. Don't give until you reach the point of resentment; give only what you can with an open heart. Don't push yourself to do more; honor your capacity and say no when needed. Yes, some people around you might be disappointed, particularly if you have been over-functioning and over-giving and you begin to shift away from that. It's okay. It's not your job to make everyone happy.

june 18

We Are Responsible for Meeting Our Own Needs

We all come into this world with needs for safety, belonging, love, self-expression, joy, and more. Many of us did not have our needs met when we were children, simply because our parents are human and imperfect. Sometimes this leaves us seeking out others to meet our needs when we are adults; we want others to care for us in ways that our parents did not or could not. The truth is that as adults we are responsible for meeting our own needs. This can feel hard to accept. It can also be an empowering truth. We now have power and freedom that we did not have as children. We can learn to meet our own needs with love and kindness.

This doesn't mean that we don't rely on other people. We can and should lean on others for help and support, but, ultimately, the responsibility rests with us for meeting our needs. If we need something from another, we need to directly ask that person. It's not fair to expect other people to read our minds or know what we need. For example, let's say you are overwhelmed and need some time to yourself today. You could meet your own needs by taking the day off from work, asking a friend to bring you dinner so you don't have to cook, planning a few hours alone for yourself in the evening, or reaching out for help with childcare to give you some self-care time.

How can you meet your own needs today?

June 19

Advice for When You've Slipped Back into Old Habits or Ways of Coping

As we try to create change in our patterns, we will sometimes revert to old habits and ways of coping. This is an expected part of the process when learning new ways of being. Here is some advice for when you've slipped back into an old habit or way of coping.

1. *Be kind and gentle with yourself.* Judging yourself and beating yourself up will not help. Greet your feelings with acceptance and compassion. So often we think we can create change within ourselves through internal reprimands and criticism. It's just not true. If you want to change, give yourself love and acceptance. I like to tell myself, *"It's okay, honey. This is the best you can do right now and that is enough."*

2. *Take some time to deconstruct what happened.* What was the trigger for your behavior? What was happening right before you engaged in the behavior? Where were you? Who was around? How were you feeling? What were you thinking? What did you notice in your body?

3. *Consider alternative behaviors that will meet your needs and help you feel the way you want to feel.* There are many ways to take care of our feelings. I am not here to judge how other people meet their needs. I truly believe that we are all doing the best we can with the resources (internal and external) that we have in the moment. Be honest with yourself: does your coping tool serve your highest good? Does it leave you feeling the way you want to feel?

4. *Plan ahead for next time.* Because there will be a next time. In the future, can you avoid whatever triggered you? If so, make a plan to do just that! If not, how can you plan ahead to support yourself? None of us can avoid stress, but we can set up some structures to support ourselves.

5. *Repeat as needed.* Changing our ways of coping is not a simple matter. We will fall back into our old ways over and over again. This is part of the process. Each time this happens, invite yourself to observe without judgment. Release any guilt that arises. Give yourself credit for doing the hard work of bringing awareness to your coping strategies and working to change your thoughts, feelings, and behaviors. You are amazing— just the way you are, right here in this moment.

June 20

Is It Worth It?

We humans often want to do what feels good now, not necessarily what will help us meet our long-term goals. A few ways this shows up in my life: I set my alarm to get up early and exercise, but I end up hitting snooze because I want to sleep in. I intend to spend focused time cleaning out my closet, but I end up lying down and watching Netflix. I want to be a more responsible steward of my money, but I go to Target and buy a bunch of things I don't really need. If these things happened once in a while they probably wouldn't be noteworthy, but these are regular occurrences for me. There is nothing wrong with any of the behaviors I listed, but they take me away from my long-term goals of taking good care of my health, home, and finances.

One way to help us bring our behaviors into better alignment with our goals is to imagine the long-term consequences of our actions. One day of skipping exercise to sleep in isn't going to have an effect on my health. But if it becomes a pattern and I continue to choose sleeping in over exercise, where will I be in six months, a year, or five years from now? If we can imagine the consequences that might come from our long-term behavior, we can more easily see that it's not worth skipping the workout.

If you have a behavior you are struggling to change, try this exercise. Imagine what life will be like and how you will feel if you continue with the behavior. Imagine yourself in six months, a year, five years, even 10 or 20 years. Ask yourself if it's worth it. Let this exercise be a motivator to help you choose in alignment with your long-term goals.

June 21

No More Whack-a-Mole

Don't chew your worries, your suffering, or your projects. That's not good for your health. Just chew the string bean.
~ Thich Nhat Hanh

I stopped drinking alcohol regularly the year I turned 40. It wasn't a big decision; it just sort of happened. I had been drinking less and less as I became more aware of how alcohol impacts my mood and my energy. It got to the point where even one glass of wine increased my anxiety and interfered with my sleep. It just became not worth it. When I stopped drinking alcohol regularly, I put sugar in the space where alcohol once lived. I didn't miss wine, but my stomach hurt from the mindless handfuls of dark chocolate chips I was eating instead. Some nights I went to bed with an ache in my belly, a fullness that hurt.

Do you remember the whack-a-mole arcade game? The one where you use a big mallet to whack the moles as they randomly pop up from different holes? I often use this analogy with my therapy clients: as long as we address only the *symptoms* of a deeper issue, it's like playing a game of whack-a-mole. You hit one thing down and another thing pops up. Let go of alcohol, grab on to sugar. I was tired of this game of whack-a-mole so I dug in a little deeper and realized that all the sugar was about stress, fatigue, and seeking comfort. I would love to grab a nap at 3pm when I am feeling tired, but I can't—so I go for chocolate. I feel disconnected from my family after a long day and rather than reach out, I scoop myself some ice cream. I feel overwhelmed by the piles of papers on my dining room table, so I have a bite of something sweet to help me cope with the stress.

Here's the thing: food is a really effective and easily accessible way to create a change in how we are feeling. And most of us are conditioned to use food for comfort from a young age. It is easy to understand why so many of us get in the habit of using food as a coping tool.

Personally, I am not against using food as a coping tool. I am against over-using or mindlessly using *any* coping tool. So, I became more mindful and started asking myself what I really need when I feel the urge for dark chocolate. Sometimes I really want something sweet. At other times I can see that I am using sugar to avoid my feelings, so that's when I encourage myself to use a different coping tool. I am also keeping an eye out for any other "moles" that might pop up to fill in the space that sugar once occupied.

One final note: I am here for body positivity, intuitive eating, and taking the focus away from our bodies and what we eat and putting it on our hearts and minds. Please do not allow the experience I describe with sugar to translate into any kind of judgment around your own experiences.

June 22

We Can Name Our Truth and Not Let It Define Us

Hope is being able to see that there is light despite all of the darkness.
~ Desmond Tutu

I am a person who lives with anxiety and depression. I have lived, worked, and loved right alongside anxiety and depression since I was a teenager. The stigma of mental health issues runs deep in our collective psyche, and for years I held shame around my struggles. It took me a long time to name this truth directly because I was afraid that if people knew about my mental health problems they would think I couldn't, or worse, shouldn't, do my work as a therapist. The truth is I have been working as a therapist my entire adult life right alongside these struggles. In some ways, having my own experience with anxiety and depression is an asset because it gives me a deeper understanding of some of the issues my clients face. So today I say plainly, and often, that I am a person who lives with anxiety and depression. This is my truth *and* it is only a piece of my story. Yes, I struggle with anxiety and depression, but there is so much more to who I am. My mental illnesses don't define me. I am more than my struggles, and so are you. It can be healing to name the things we live with, and it is also healthy to remember that they don't define us.

June 23

If You Want to be a Butterfly, First You Have to Become the Goo Inside the Cocoon

During the process of metamorphosis the caterpillar creates a cocoon, called a chrysalis, around itself. Once the chrysalis is complete, the caterpillar dissolves into a soupy goo inside the cocoon which eventually reorganizes itself and emerges as a butterfly. We often have to go through some dark and difficult places to get where we want to be.

The most striking example of this from my own life is when I consciously decided to seek more emotional closeness with my husband. I had been mistreated by so many men that I was afraid to let myself be fully vulnerable with him. After I committed to opening my heart for deeper emotional intimacy in my marriage, I turned into someone I am not. I became insecure, jealous, and fearful. I did not recognize myself. Our relationship went through the roughest patch we had ever experienced. It was one of the darkest times of my life. I had become the goo inside the cocoon. Inside that cocoon I grew and discovered new layers of truth and understanding. I healed old wounds and found the deeper emotional intimacy that I had been craving. It hurt like fucking hell and some days I felt like I would die from the pain of changing. But I didn't. I came out the other side, and my marriage became stronger than ever. I know now that we could not have gotten to where we are today without going through that dark and uncertain time.

Spend some time with your journal today. What's the butterfly that your heart yearns for? Are you willing to become the goo inside the cocoon in order to transform?

June 24

Letting Go is Not My Default

Everything I've ever let go of has claw marks on it. ~ David Foster Wallace

Have you ever met someone who seems to let go of things effortlessly? They easily forgive. They don't ask for apologies; they don't hold on to resentment. I am so jealous of that type of person. Personally, I have a hard time letting things go. I am still carrying around anger about shit from years ago. Maybe it's because my brain likes to replay things over and over and over, well past the point of usefulness. It's partly anxiety, partly a protective thing. If I hold on to every hurtful thing you've ever done to me, then I will be better prepared for the next hurtful thing. (Side note: This is neither rational nor healthy.) Mostly, it just sucks and keeps me stuck in the past.

Letting go is not my default. Releasing does not come naturally for me; I have to work at it. Here are some things that help me:

1. *Meditation.* Sometimes I breathe in "let" and breathe out "go." It's not subtle, but it helps.

2. *Writing.* Get it out of your head and onto the page. Sometimes I light it on fire afterward. Seriously.

3. *Praying.* Ask for help from the *Something More* (God/dess, Source, Universe).

4. *Dancing.* Put on your favorite song and move. Repeat often.

5. *Opening my hips.* Butterfly Pose, Pigeon Pose, hip circles. Daily.

6. *Vocalizing.* Sing, cry, scream—just get it out.

7. *Clearing space.* Releasing physical stuff seems to help with the emotional releasing. Let that shit go.

Is there anything you're holding on to today? Choose one of the techniques from the list above to help you release. If you're like me, you may want to bookmark this page and return to it often.

June 25

Set Down Your Worries

It's going to be all right.
All of the shit will get done.
Or it won't.
Either way it will be okay.

Frantic, anxious energy does not help anything get done.
Quite the opposite.

When you feel the anxiety and fear rising, let that be a reminder to take a break. Step away from what you are doing. Take a few deep breaths. Spend some time in nature. Soak in a salty bath scented with your favorite oils. Light a candle and say a prayer. Put on some music and dance. Go to yoga and cry on your mat. Commit to not compromising your spirit in the name of getting shit done. I know it doesn't make rational sense to take a break when there is so much to do but taking care of yourself will support your work. Set down your worries, even if only for a few moments.

We can trust ourselves. We can trust our process. We can trust life.

What do you need today?
Can you take a pause and give yourself the gift of taking care of your needs?
Can you trust that everything will be okay if you take a break and do something to support your spirit?

June 26

Forgive Yourself

Finish every day and be done with it.... You have done what you could; some blunders and absurdities no doubt crept in; forget them as soon as you can. To-morrow is a new day; you shall begin it well and serenely, and with too high a spirit to be cumbered with your old nonsense.
~ Ralph Waldo Emerson

Forgive yourself,
Let it go,
Let it be.

You did the best you could, and that is all you can ask of yourself, ever.

Beating yourself up,
Holding on to old regrets,
Won't change what has already happened or help anyone,
It just hurts you and keeps you stuck.

Learn from the past and move forward accordingly.

You will mess up again,
You are imperfect,
Because you are human—it's part of the deal.

Forgive yourself and begin again in the spirit of love and kindness.
Repeat as often as needed.

June 27

Advice on Worrying

If a problem is fixable, if a situation is such that you can do something about it,
then there is no need to worry. If it's not fixable, then there is no help in
worrying. There is no benefit in worrying whatsoever. ~ Dalai Lama

I love this advice on worrying from the Dalai Lama. I get stuck inside of
worry all the time. I find that action helps to soothe my worry. If there is
something I can do about the thing I am worried about, I make a plan to
do it. I also have some tools I use when there's nothing I can do about the
thing I am worrying about. I try to replace my worry with prayer. Each
time a worry comes into my mind, I pause and ask for a blessing around
the thing I am worried about. Another technique I use is scheduled worry
time. Rather than allowing worry to take over my day, I set aside a
designated time to worry, such as 7:30pm-8:00pm. If worries pop up
outside of the designated time, I simply let them go. If it feels hard to let
the thoughts go, I jot down a note about the worry so I can reference it
later.

Pause and take stock of how much time and energy you are devoting to
worry. Acknowledge that it is a fruitless practice that often creates more
suffering. Be kind and patient with yourself as you take steps toward
shifting your relationship with worry.

What's on your mind today?
Is there something you can do about it? If so, make a plan to do it.
If not, practice letting go of your worry.

June 28

The Radical Act of Choosing Simplicity Inside of a Complicated World

Many people believe simplicity implies doing without. On the contrary.
True simplicity as a conscious choice illuminates our lives from within.
~ Sarah Ban Breathnach

We live inside of a complex world where we are surrounded by more choices than ever before. I love freedom and possibility, *and* having so many options can also feel overwhelming at times. I think simplicity has become a trend for this very reason. People are distilling their clothing down to capsule wardrobes. There are entire movements around minimalist living. We are clearly craving a reprieve from our complicated world.

You don't have to do anything drastic in order to invite simplicity into your life. Small steps can have a big impact. Some of the ways I invite simplicity into my life are by limiting the number of activities my kids participate in, scheduling unplanned days into my month, eating the same meals over and over, giving gift cards rather than searching for the perfect gift, reading one book at a time (this one is so hard but makes a big difference), having boundaries around social media, engaging in only one task at a time, and spending time in nature.

Today, ask yourself how you can invite simplicity into your life. Take some time to meditate or journal around this question. Trust whatever comes up for you as being exactly what you need to know.

Sometimes the Most Helpful Thing We Can Do is Surrender

We are most deeply asleep at the switch when we fancy
we control any switches at all.
~ Annie Dillard

Sometimes I have rough mental health days. These are the days when there isn't any trigger for my funky mood. Nothing is wrong, per se. I just feel sad and I can't pull myself out of it. On the really hard days, I can't concentrate enough to read, and social media feels like an assault on my nervous system. I often spend the day feeling constantly on the edge of crying or screaming. When this happens I turn to my tried and true strategies: exercising, writing in my journal, baking my favorite cookies, snuggling my people and pets, meditating, and walking by my beloved river. Sometimes things shift and sometimes nothing seems to help. When none of my tools work, I practice surrendering to things as they are. I name where I am, inside of some depression, and work to accept it. I try to relax into it. I reassure myself that it will pass (it always does).

Sometimes we don't know why we feel the way we feel.
Sometimes the tools don't work.
We humans are complicated creatures.

Sometimes the most helpful thing we can do is to simply relax into the truth of the moment; to sit with things as they are without trying to fix or change.

june 30

I Am Here and I Matter

They told me I was too sensitive.

They told me I was weak.

They told me I was the original sin.

They told me I was too loud, too smart for my own good.

They told me I couldn't because I was a girl.

They told me he could do whatever he wanted to do to my body.

They told me I had no recourse.

They told me I had no voice.

They told me to obey.

They told me to stay small.

They told me to stay home.

They told me no one would believe me.

They told me I was dirty.

They told me to be quiet.

They told me I did not have agency over my own body.

They told me I shouldn't because I am a woman.

They told me I was a slut.

They told me boys will be boys.

They told me I was damaged goods.

They told me to shrink so I'd stay safe.

They told me it was all in my mind.

They told me men can't help themselves.

They told me I didn't matter.

They told me I had no purpose beyond serving a man.

They told me that's just the way it is.

And I believed them.

I took all that was said and unsaid as fact.

I did not question it.

I was a woman and therefore, I was less than.

They told me the only way to earn respect, rights, and privileges was to become as much like a man as possible. And I believed them. I thought feminism meant I could be just like a man and therefore earn the respect, rights, and privileges that come along with being a man.

So I worked diligently to prove my rational intelligence, drive, and independence.

I left my 6-day-old baby and went to my college classes.

I earned a 4.0 GPA as single, working mother.

I medicated my menstrual cycle.

I hated my body and punished it accordingly.

I denounced "women's work" and refused to wash dishes or cook meals.

I bought a house to prove I didn't need a man to provide for me.

I earned a Ph.D. so they would take me seriously.

I got a job working for a highly respected man in my field.

I ignored the wise inner whisper and followed orders from the deafening patriarchal voice.

And I felt feminism had sold me a lie. I had worked so hard to embody masculine traits. I was accomplished and successful by all masculine standards. Where was my promised happiness? Why did I feel so empty and unfulfilled?

I decided to give the wise inner whisper a chance. I started to follow her lead. I began to spend time in spaces she craved, to read books she felt drawn toward. I started to question everything I had previously accepted as "the way it is." I began to understand the connection between being born a girl in this society and feeling innately flawed.

My eyes were open. I saw through all the lies I had been fed. I wept for all the ways I had disowned myself, my feminine nature. I let myself come home to the truth, to feel it deep in my bones, that I was equal and I did matter. That I didn't have to perform anymore. I didn't have to try to be like a man. I could be a woman and be enough, more than enough. I understood feminism to mean that I deserve equal respect, rights, and privileges *as I am*—to be honored as a woman in her own right.

I rediscovered my voice.
I reclaimed my body.
I honored my cycles.
I proclaimed my worth.
I am here and I matter.

july 1

Women and Wanting

What messages have you received about women and wanting?

Women are here to serve and, thus, are not allowed to want.
Women should work hard to stay in control.
Women should not want or enjoy sex.
Women should stay small, literally and figuratively.
Women should not be trusted; their desire is powerful, scary, and sinful.

These messages and others are handed down to us through our culture, our media, our schools, our families, and our friends. To say we women have a complex relationship with our wanting is to put it mildly. We are taught from a young age that a "good girl" or "good woman" forgoes her own wants and needs to care for others. This is why women are generally overworked, underpaid, and exhausted. Many women don't even know what they want; they've never allowed themselves to consider such a thing. Other women are aware of what they want but are living their lives based on what they think they "should" be doing.

Grab your journal and try this: I want _____, but _____.

Make a list of what you want and listen to what comes up immediately afterward. Chances are you will hear the "shoulds."

I want to go to yoga tonight, but I should stay home with my family.
I want to eat pizza, but I should have a salad.

I want to learn to paint, but I should focus on getting the house organized.
I want to take a nap, but I should play with my child.
I want more, but I should be happy with what I have.

What shoulds come up for you when you make a list of what you want? Where did you get these ideas? Are they serving you, or do you want to release them?

july 2

Above All, We Are Women in Our Own Right

I am a mother and a wife.
These roles come with a set of expectations.
These ideals are not necessarily mine; they were handed down to me.
They are reinforced for me every day by the world we live in.

A good mother puts her kids first.
A good mother does not work outside the home.
A good mother does work outside the home.
A good mother enjoys being a mother at all times.
A good mother is fulfilled by being a mother; she does not need anything more.

A good wife puts her spouse first.
A good wife has the house clean at all times.
A good wife maintains a thin body.
A good wife does not bother her husband with her needs.
A good wife takes care of the children.

Buying into these expectations and ideals is harmful.
At the end of the day, what is left for us?
The truth is, we are more than our roles.
We are women in our own right.
We deserve to center ourselves inside of our own lives.

My truth is...

Motherhood alone is not enough for me.
I have many dreams that have nothing to do with my children or my marriage.
Sometimes being a mother is overwhelming and I want to run away.
My house is only clean every other week when I pay someone to clean it.
I am disorganized.
My car is always a mess.
I have a lot of needs. A lot.
I prioritize myself, and I am a good mother and wife.

Women are caregivers.
We are the nurturers.
We hold so much.
We are many things to many people.
Above all, we are women in our own right.

Spend some time with your journal today. What are the roles you play? How do they relate to you considering what you want out of life?

July 3

What Fears Are Holding You Back from Dreaming?

You gain strength, courage, and confidence by every experience in which you really stop to look fear in the face. ... You must do the thing you cannot do.
~ Eleanor Roosevelt

I believe that letting ourselves dream is part of self-love and self-care. Nothing is too small or too big when it comes to dreams. Dreaming is an invitation to allow yourself to consider what you want. You might dream of running a 5K, redecorating your bedroom, learning to speak Italian, or starting a business. As you begin to explore your dreams, let go of any comparison or judgment that comes up and allow whatever arises to be just right for you. You can trust yourself.

Sometimes we don't allow ourselves to dream because we are afraid. We might worry that we will lose our friends if we follow our dreams and start to change. We may be afraid that our families will judge us if we say what we really want out loud. Sometimes we think we are too old for dreaming or that we will become destitute if we follow our hearts. What are your fears when it comes to dreaming? I believe that simply naming things diminishes their power.

Grab your journal and list the fears that are holding you back from dreaming. If you feel open to it, you might share your fears with someone close to you. Observe how the fear shifts as you name it, whether only to yourself in your journal or to another person.

july 4

In This Life List

Twenty years from now you will be more disappointed by the things that you didn't do than by the ones you did do. So throw off the bowlines. Sail away from the safe harbor. Catch the trade winds in your sails.
Explore. Dream. Discover.
~ Mark Twain

Everything I have in my life was once simply a dream—my children, my husband, our home, my yoga studio, my community, my career, my dog, that perfect red lipstick, those sexy grey boots, that painting on the wall, these books that surround me. When it comes to dreaming there is no right or wrong, nothing too big or too small. There is only you, the longings of your heart, and bridging the space between the two.

What do you need in order to say yes to dreaming? Are there shoulds or fears lingering in your mind? Take a moment to consciously let them go, or at least set them aside for a bit. My hope is that you open to possibility and allow yourself to want. Let this invitation be a spark that reignites the burning desires inside of you. Let's invite our hopes, wishes, and dreams out to play. I'm asking you to let go of what you think you know and open up to the vulnerable joy of dreaming.

Let's begin to give voice to our dreams. I find it's easier to start with wild dreams that seem to be far off in the future. For today, grab your journal and create an "In This Life List" of hopes, dreams, and wishes that you want to experience during your time on this planet.

july 5

Imaginary Lives

You do not have to be good.
You do not have to walk on your knees
for a hundred miles through the desert, repenting.
You only have to let the soft animal of your body
love what it loves.
~ Mary Oliver

The Artist's Way by Julia Cameron is an amazing guidebook to reclaiming our creativity. It is full of soul-stirring questions, and today we are going to continue giving voice to our dreams with one of my favorite prompts from the book: naming our imaginary lives. Some of mine are a stay-at-home mom who homeschools her kids and grows her own vegetables; a Buddhist nun who lives a life of spiritual devotion; and a writer who lives alone on the coast. We are not necessarily going to pursue our imaginary lives, but they can offer us clues to what we are longing for inside of our life. For example, I might research planting a small vegetable garden, taking a spiritual retreat, or spending some time at the beach as a way to honor my soul's desires.

Carve out some time for yourself to sit with this prompt. Remember that your dreams and longings are sacred. If you could wipe the slate clean and create an imaginary life, what would you do? Who would you be? Today, make a list of five imaginary lives.

july 6

If Money Were No Object

Impossible is just an opinion.
~ Paulo Coelho

When it comes to dreaming about what we want, one of the biggest blocks is money. Money is a very real issue for many people in this world and I do not want to discount that truth. It is difficult to dream about the future when financial difficulties force you to focus on meeting basic needs in the present. However, money can also be entangled with many other things, from our feelings of safety and security to our sense of worth. Most of us have a complicated relationship with money. I am asking you to set all that aside for a few moments for the sake of today's prompt. We may not be able to bring our if-money-were-no-object dreams to fruition now (or ever), but we can look for clues about what we want. And this may help us to take a baby step toward those big dreams. We are practicing opening up to possibility by removing some of the most common blocks to dreaming.

Consider what you would do if money were no object. How would you spend your days? Spend 10-15 minutes journaling your answer. Allow yourself to just write without editing or censoring. Stay curious and have fun!

july 7

Let Go of Perfectionism

Perfectionism is the voice of the oppressor, the enemy of the people.
It will keep you cramped and insane your whole life.
~ Anne Lamott

Perfectionism holds us back from pursuing our dreams. So many of us don't do or try things because we are afraid we will not do them well. One of my mantras is *"you have to be willing to do something poorly before you can do it well."* This mentality has helped me do many things that initially felt scary and out of reach, such as start a business, learn to ask for what I need inside of my relationships, and write this book. The other way perfectionism shows up for many of us is through waiting for perfect conditions before doing something we want to do. Many women are waiting for ideal conditions before they go after their big dreams—things like dating, becoming a parent, switching careers, asking for a divorce, or going back to school—as well as their smaller dreams—things like trying yoga, reaching out to an old friend, cleaning out the closet, or learning to cook. Perfection is a myth. When we buy into it, we put our lives on hold. Let's opt out and start living—right here, right now inside of our messy, imperfect, and very real lives.

Spend some time with your journal today.
What you would do if you didn't have to do it perfectly?
What would you do if you weren't waiting for perfect conditions?

july 8

Visioning

Intuition is a spiritual faculty and does not explain, but simply points the way.
~ Florence Scovel Shinn

Visioning is the process of creating a visual representation of what we want—both the things we are calling forth and the feelings we are craving. I believe it is also a way to connect with our intuition. A popular way to work with visioning is to create a vision board by cutting out images and words from magazines and pasting them onto paper or poster board. I often don't understand the images and words I am drawn to cut out until months or years later. For example, I once felt pulled to create a vision board with many pictures of beautiful fruits and vegetables. It didn't make sense to me at the time, but a few months later I ended up becoming a vegetarian. It feels like my inner self speaks to me through the process of creating a vision.

One of my teachers, Hannah Marcotti, introduced me to two additional ways to work with visioning: vision books and vision cards. A vision book is a blank journal that can hold many pages of collages. Vision cards are just what they sound like—cards with images and words glued onto them. I have used index cards or blank flashcards to create these. Creating a vision card or a page in a vision book takes less time than making a vision board, making it easier to incorporate the practice into your daily or weekly routine. Vision books and cards are fun to make, and I appreciate that they are easily stored.

Our visions, in whatever form we choose to create them, serve as reminders of what we are calling forth. Visioning is one of my favorite self-care activities. It fuels my creativity and feels almost meditative.

For today's activity, you will need a stack of magazines, scissors, glue, and whatever you'd like to paste your vision onto (a piece of paper, blank journal, or cards). Visioning is meant to be fun! Let go of trying to create a beautiful end product and instead focus on relaxing into the process. Stay open to possibility and the magic of discovering the messages and dreams waiting within the magazines. Allow yourself to clip anything that pulls you in, even if (especially if!) it doesn't make sense right now. When you feel ready, glue your words and images down.

july 9

You Can't Have It Both Ways

It took me a long time to learn that it's okay to say no, especially inside of my relationships. For most of my life my default was to say yes to whatever was asked of me by someone I love. I always said yes because I liked to think of myself as a *very nice, super accommodating* person. Part of my identity was that I was exceedingly easygoing, never said no, and just went along with whatever was asked of me. People responded very well to me as a *very nice, super accommodating* person, but what happens when you are a *very nice, super accommodating* person is that you hurt yourself, over and over, in big and small ways. You are not a good protector of your time and energy because you are so concerned about pleasing other people. For years I didn't even know that I was selling myself out like this. I just knew that I liked making people happy and that most of the time I really didn't mind saying yes.

Eventually I had to learn to say no in my relationships because I burnt out and couldn't go on with the over-giving and over-functioning while disregarding my needs. I came to see the hard truth that you can't have it both ways: you can't practice self-care, say no, and have healthy boundaries while also being a *very nice, super accommodating* person. You have to choose. I decided to choose honesty and self-care. I decided to say goodbye to my *very nice, super accommodating* self and live inside of the discomfort of trying a new way. I learned that it is safe for me to say no and that I am allowed to have needs inside of my relationships. I discovered that my relationships could survive hurt and disappointment. And here's an important point—nothing catastrophic happened when I made these changes. I am still loved.

Spend some time with your journal today. Do you struggle with saying no? If so, where and when does this show up in your life? How can you experiment with setting boundaries to protect your time and energy?

July 10

Words as Self-Care

By words we learn thoughts, and by thoughts we learn life.
~ Jean Baptiste Girard

I love words. Words can be an anchor grounding me back to myself, an inspiration that uplifts my spirit, and a touchstone that calms my mind.

Reading and writing are two of my favorite activities. They bring me joy on an everyday basis and offer me solace when I am having a hard day.

Here are some other ways that I use words to support my self-care:

1. *Choosing a word or phrase for the day, month, or year.* This is a beautiful way to stay connected to your intentions.

2. *Repeating a mantra silently or aloud.* You can use an existing mantra or write your own. Saying mantras can help calm fear and worry. This is also a helpful practice for when you are working on changing thoughts and beliefs.

3. *Reciting a favorite poem or prayer.* This practice can shift your day by offering a moment of mindfulness. I love the poetry of Mary Oliver, Nayyirah Waheed, and Rumi. I encourage you to explore and find your own favorites.

4. *Collecting inspiring quotes.* You might want to start a Pinterest board or do it the old-fashioned way and jot down your favorite quotes in a notebook.

How can you use words to support your self-care today?
Choose an idea from above or create your own practice.

july 11

On Being Seen and Heard

Being seen.
Being heard.
Showing up.
Speaking up.

These things bring up so much for us, especially as women. I believe that all women come into this world with an innate fear of showing up and speaking up because throughout history women have literally been killed for everything from simply existing to speaking their truth to power. We carry these wounds in our collective unconscious. We have also been taught from a young age that there are rules about when and how it is acceptable for us to be seen and heard.

Here are some common messages about being a woman:

Don't be too loud, too big, too pretty, too plain, too smart, too strong.
Don't go to the store without makeup on.
Don't go out without a bra on.
Don't wear that.
It's your fault because you wore that.
Why are you dressed like a boy, like a slut, like a prude?
Who do you think you are?
You're fat, you can't wear that.
Why are you so skinny? Eat a burger.
That shirt violates the dress code; you'll distract the boys.

Why did you say that? You're being such a bitch. You're being dramatic.
Are you on your period?
Girls can't do that.
Girls shouldn't do that.

The rules are never-ending, and they are even more complex for women with intersecting marginalized identities such as race and sexuality. The truth is, it is not safe for all women to be seen and heard inside of our current society. Let's de-condition ourselves from the harmful messages we have received and work together toward a world where all women can show up and speak up without fear for their safety.

Today I invite you to name the messages that you have been given about being seen and heard as a woman. Let them bubble up to the surface. We can only rewrite and resist what we can name.

July 12

You Deserve to Be Seen During the Good Times and the Bad

Staying vulnerable is a risk we have to take if we want
to experience connection.
~ Brené Brown

I have this tendency to isolate myself when I'm going through something. Things get hard or confusing and I get quiet, I pull away. Maybe this habit is a remnant of shiny, happy me—an old habit of only showing up when I have good things to share, of not letting others see me be sad, confused, or scared. I am lucky because I have people in my life who won't let me hide when I am struggling. They give me my space and they also say, *"Hey, you don't seem okay. What's going on? I'm here and I love you."* They coax me out of my shell and invite me to be seen inside of my truth. Inside the shell, the isolation, is where depression brews and shame thrives. I start to think, *"I can't tell anyone what's going on in my head. I am all alone."* If I stay there too long, it gets pretty scary. When I come out of the shell, when I turn toward people rather than away during my times of distress, I start to feel less alone. Sometimes I even get the awesome feeling of, *"Hey, it's not just me!"*

Today, I invite you to practice turning toward people rather than away from them when things feel hard. You deserve to be seen, to be witnessed with love and kindness, during the beautiful times, the hard times, and everything in between.

July 13

Your Genius Matters

If you are human, you have a calling: to live your genius.
~ Gay Hendricks

I once went to driving school in order to reduce the amount of a speeding ticket I had gotten. I walked into the same community college classroom where I used to give lectures on Developmental Psychology and spotted the grumpy-faced instructor fiddling with the computer and muttering under his breath. He appeared to be pretty much exactly what I'd expected—a man in his fifties with a gruff demeanor. I grabbed a seat and wondered if there was a way I could read my book or return emails during the next three hours. Then he started addressing the class and his whole demeanor shifted, taking my mindset right along with it. I sat up a little straighter, captivated by his lecture. It was clear he was operating from a place of genuine care and interest. I could see it, but more than that I could *feel* it. I didn't even touch my phone until we took a break 90 minutes later. I was sincerely engrossed. *In traffic school!* He was talking about reaction time, adjusting your side mirrors, and merging—and somehow it was interesting. I could feel there was more to this guy than met the eye.

And then it happened. He told us a story about when he was 19 years old and studying Pre-Law as an exchange student in Germany. He had been driving home after his last final exam and fell asleep behind the wheel. He drove his car head on into a pole and was in a coma for six days. He was temporarily paralyzed from the waist down and lucky to be alive. Eventually he recovered and decided to come home to the U.S. and teach driver safety. He wanted something good to come from his trauma. *He wanted his story to mean something.* This was the magic I was feeling— a beautiful connection between his "why" and his work. He was in his zone of genius. This was how he was able to make driving school feel like Oprah's Lifeclass.

The zone of genius is an idea put forth by Gay Hendricks in his book *The Big Leap.* The zone of genius is the place where our talents and passions intersect; the place where time expands and we're operating in the flow. When we are in our zone of genius we are doing work that we love and it shows. We all have our own zone of genius. My driving school teacher reminded me of the importance of pursuing our passions. He reconfirmed for me that when we follow our hearts and do what lights us up, we brighten the world around us.

Your genius matters. If you haven't found it yet, keep looking. If you aren't living it yet, keep moving toward it in whatever way you can.

july 14

Selfies as Self-Care

Self-portraiture is one of my self-care practices. Taking a picture of myself helps me to pause and bring a moment of mindfulness to my day and invites me to see myself with love and compassion. Snapping a selfie is one of the ways I mark my journey and honor the truth of how I am feeling on any given day. I often share my selfies on social media along with a few words describing my truth in the hope that someone out there might get that amazing, "Hey, it's not just me!" feeling.

I want us to show up and be seen. I want us to tell each other the truth about our lives. I want us to tell the world the truth about what it is like to be a woman inside of this patriarchal society. Selfies are one way that we can begin to do that. I believe that when enough of us begin to show up and tell the truth about our lives, we will eliminate that special kind of loneliness that comes with being a woman in this culture.

Today, I invite you to play with taking some pictures of yourself. Let this be easy—no need to dress up or use fancy equipment. Your phone camera will work just fine. As you take your pictures, release any judgment that arises and see yourself with love and compassion. If you feel called to, share your selfie with a friend or on social media. Let's practice showing up and being seen.

july 15

Managing Medical Appointments

Medical appointments can be triggering. I know women who have been traumatized by doctors, including some who now avoid seeking medical care because of their past experiences. I have had the experience myself of feeling steamrolled by a doctor. It's an awful feeling. Things like being offered treatment options without a full explanation of the risks and benefits and having to make a decision without proper time to research, have left me feeling confused and angry. I've been afraid to speak up and advocate for myself and my children in various medical situations. I've left appointments feeling powerless and stupid. I understand that often the issues at hand may feel like no big deal to the doctor because they encounter them every day. But for the person experiencing the issue, it *is* a big deal. I wish more doctors would remember this.

In an ideal world, doctors—especially white, male doctors—would understand privilege and power and would take this into consideration when working with patients. *But we live in a far from ideal world.* And we have internalized the principles of this world, this patriarchy that we live in. Some ways this has shown up for me with medical appointments: I haven't spoken up for myself because I have been taught to be quiet; I have felt stupid for feeling unsure and uncomfortable because I have been taught that women are over-emotional and dramatic; I have acquiesced to a man in a position of power because I felt small and unimportant. It is important to note that these are my experiences as a white woman. Navigating medical appointments can be exponentially more challenging for women of marginalized identities.

In our culture we have been conditioned to hand our power over to medical professionals. I want us to reclaim our voices and reaffirm our worthiness so that we can work in respectful collaboration with our doctors. I practice empowering myself before medical appointments by pausing to breathe and connect with my power. I remind myself that I deserve to be informed and that I am in control. I give myself permission to advocate for myself or my child. I take the time to mindfully and intentionally reinforce my worth and my right to be heard. Because of the messaging of patriarchy, this is not my default mode of operating. I will continue to consciously practice until I have internalized my right to be heard. Remember that you deserve to be treated with patience and respect by your doctors.

July 16

How to Say the Thing You Think You Can't Say

What do you feel like you can't say?

We don't have to say everything that we think and feel. Honestly, we probably shouldn't. These instructions are for when there is something you know you need to say, something you want to share, but you are holding back because you feel afraid of being judged or rejected. It can feel scary to be honest and vulnerable. But we get to choose. We can hold the truth in and stay "safe," or we can let it out and risk the possibility of pain in service of true connection. Truth-telling is an evolving practice for me. Here is my process for being brave and saying the thing you think you cannot say:

1. *Don't just say something, sit there.* I feel a lot of things very intensely. Rather than react impulsively, I prefer to sit with my feelings so that I can respond mindfully. My favorite ways to be with my feelings are to meditate and journal. These practices help ground me in my truth.

2. *Talk it out with a neutral(ish) person.* I make decisions based on my own inner wisdom, which I access by noticing how things feel in my body. Sometimes part of my process to access my inner wisdom is talking to other people. Working with a therapist is ideal because you have someone truly outside of the situation. If you don't have a therapist, a trusted friend is an amazing resource. When choosing a friend to talk with, be clear about what you are looking for—is it advice or just someone to listen? Choose someone who can hold space for the particular issue at hand. I like to ask, *"Would you be willing to listen without giving advice while I talk this through?"* or *"Would you be willing to tell me what you think and give me some advice?"*

3. *Write down what you want to say.* This will help you get clear. It also activates our logical thinking brain that sometimes goes offline when we are dealing with an emotionally-charged issue. You might start with the prompt *"I can't say"* and see where it goes from there. Often I find it helpful to write a letter to the person. Even if you don't give them the letter, your thoughts will be fresh in your mind when you have the conversation.

4. *Keep yourself safe.* Determine if the person you want to express yourself to is safe. Are they capable of receiving your words and responding appropriately? Or will they twist things or use your vulnerability to manipulate you? We can't always

safely express everything that we might want to directly to the person involved. The good news is you can still heal by expressing yourself in other ways such as therapy, movement, art, and ceremony.

5. *Just say it.* If you determine that the person is safe, choose a time and place to express yourself, being mindful of when the other party is most likely to be open to hearing you. Again, I like to ask for permission before I start talking. You could say something like, "*Hey, I have this thing I'd like to talk with you about. Is now a good time?*" If the person says no, respect that. You can follow up with, "*Thank you letting me know now is not a good time. When would be better for you?*" Personally, I love when people say no to me because it lets me know that they are honoring their boundaries. I feel safer with people who hold their boundaries because I know they will respect mine too. When the other person is ready, go ahead and say the thing you think you cannot say. If it is too hard to talk, send an email or a text or read from the letter you wrote.

6. *Really listen.* Open your heart and receive what the other person is saying in response. Stay present and grounded in your body. Drink a glass of water, take some deep breaths. Be brave and have the conversation.

7. *Notice.* Observe how you feel after expressing yourself. What was the outcome? Were your needs met? Did you learn something new?

8. *Celebrate.* Give yourself credit for being brave! Applaud your strength and courage, no matter the outcome of the conversation. You said the thing you thought you couldn't say, and that is a big deal.

July 17

Unpack the Lies You've Been Told and Reclaim the Truth of Your Worthiness

I know, personally and professionally, that we all walk around every day with a head full of lies. We believe that we are not good enough. We believe that we are alone. We believe that we are ugly, stupid, or damaged. These are lies. We were not born with these ideas. We have picked them up throughout our lives from growing up inside of this patriarchal culture. Believing these lies about ourselves is dangerous. A lie is the first form of violence toward oneself. When we believe the lies we tell ourselves, we engage in further violence toward ourselves. We say hateful things to our reflections in the mirror, we starve ourselves, we disown our truth. Sometimes we literally harm ourselves or even take our own lives. The spectrum of violence toward ourselves exists because we believe the lies we've been told. The truth is, we are each worthy, loveable, and amazing in our own special way. I want us to tell ourselves these truths and more. Because the truth heals. Because telling the truth about our lives is how we get free. Because the antidote to violence is truth. We will not harm what we hold sacred, and we are all sacred.

Spend some time with your journal today. What are the lies that you've been told about yourself? Write them down so that you can let them go. Reclaim the truth of your inherent worthiness and lovability. Commit to practicing non-violence toward yourself in your words, thoughts, and actions.

july 18

When There Are No Words

When there are no words,
I will find my breath,
I will lean into the ache in my gut,
I will let the tears fall.

When there are no words,
I will sit beside you with love and grief in our hearts,
I will feel into our connection even if we are strangers passing
on the street,
I will cry and hope and pray for all of us, even as I know it is not enough.

When there are no words,
I will really feel the sun on my face,
I will fold the laundry with gratitude,
I will be here now, more than ever.
When there are no words,
I will take a break from social media,
I will go outside and notice the bunnies at dusk,
I will remember the good in this world. *There is so very much.*

When there are no words,
I will pray through the tears,
I will cling to the beauty,
I will hold my girls a little tighter.

When there are no words,
I will give myself time and space,
And then I will find a way to speak,
Because I must, *we must*, say something.

When there are no words,
I will not give in to the feelings of helplessness,
I will refuse to be part of the problem by staying silent,
I will begin by speaking their names.

I wrote this in June 2016 after the mass shooting at Pulse nightclub in Orlando, Florida. It's about my experience of feeling stunned by fear, anger, and sadness while also knowing I have a responsibility to take action toward creating positive change. It's a feeling I have frequently in our world today. May we overcome hate and violence, and may our words, thoughts, and actions move the world closer to love and justice.

july 19

Wantings and Prayers

Change me Divine Beloved into One who is wildly open to the New. Grant me the willingness to experiment and play. Free me from rigid patterns that no longer serve. Let me feel adventurous and spontaneous, knowing that the more I open to life, the more it opens to me.
~ Tosha Silver

I want all the peonies.
I want long, lazy days at the beach.
I want to live my life as my prayer for the world.
I want to feel safe.

I want to chase my dreams, even when it feels like someone else has already done what I dream of doing.

I want to spend an entire day reading.
I want an epic marriage.
I want a house on the water with an amazing porch.
I want to be seen, *really seen.*
I want to tell the stories I hold in my soul.
I want to eat veggies straight from the garden.
I want words inked across my forearm covering the scars of the past.
I want freedom, joy, and beauty.
I want more time to do nothing.

I pray to be free inside of my wantings.

I pray for ease, for space.
I pray to feel like I belong.
I pray to be the mom they deserve.
I pray to understand that I am enough, even on my worst days.

I pray to hold on to, to live inside of, the moments of soul-stirring awe at this life that is beautiful and hard all at once.

I pray to be vulnerable inside of love.
I pray to use my voice, even if my words come out timidly.
I pray to stop comparing myself.
I pray to forgive myself as easily and gracefully as I forgive others.
I pray to be brave enough to change.

I pray to embody what it truly means when I whisper *Om Shanti Shanti Shanti.*

Spend some time with your journal today.
What's calling you?
Make a list of current wantings and prayers.

july 20

Let Go of Expecting People to Read Your Mind

Many of the problems we have in our relationships come from assuming that other people know, or should know, what we want or need. The truth is people cannot read each other's minds, and even your partner or closest friends may not know what you want or need in any given situation. The healthiest way to get our needs met is to directly ask for what we want and need. I can hear you now, "*I shouldn't have to ask for what I need, he should know.*" Or another common response, "*It doesn't mean anything when she does what I want if I have to tell her what to do.*" If you want happiness and peace inside of your relationships you need to let go of these ideas and practice communicating what you want. As the saying goes, uncommunicated expectations are premeditated resentments. The people who care about you truly want to meet your needs, they just may not know how to best do that. Let go of expecting people to read your mind. Communicate your needs directly and notice how this shifts things inside of your relationships.

july 21

Make a Wishlist for the Month

You are allowed to want what you want. You do not have to apologize for, justify, rationalize, or defend your desires. So often we fear being selfish, silly, or impractical when that is exactly what we need more of—self-care, play, frivolity. Life can be so damn serious, and it's hard to dream inside of that seriousness. I love the imaginary lives exercise (see July 5 if you missed it) because it can feel so challenging to allow ourselves to want within our reality.

Today I invite you to revisit your imaginary lives. Mine were a stay-at-home mom, Buddhist nun, and writer living alone on the coast.

Look to your imaginary lives for clues about what you are craving. For me, that is joy and ease in my parenting, dedicated spiritual practice, and solitary time devoted to writing.

Finally, create a wishlist of ten things you would like to feel, experience, or create over the next month—ways to feed those desires within your life here, now. My wishes might include having dance parties in the kitchen with my daughter, increasing my daily meditation time, taking a workshop at the local spiritual institute, and spending an afternoon alone writing at a coffee shop.

Hold your wishes close at heart as the month unfolds and be open to magic. Things may not show up exactly the way you envisioned; they might be even more amazing than you could have imagined! Consider creating a wishlist each month as a way to stay connected with your desires. You can do this anytime, but the New Moon is an especially powerful time for naming our dreams.

July 22

Ask for a Sign

I believe in magic and synchronicity.
I believe in a divine love connecting us all.
I believe a benevolent source has my back.

And sometimes I lose my faith and trust in Spirit. Sometimes I feel like
nothing makes sense and I have no idea what I am doing. Sometimes I feel
anxious and alone on my path. This is when I ask for a sign, something to
let me know that I am being held and guided.

Feathers have long been a symbol of faith, trust, and magic for me. I often
find them right when I need to be reminded that I am not alone. I have a
friend whose messages come to her from license plates and another who
finds signs in songs she hears on the radio. You can receive a sign in any
way that resonates for you.

*Today, I invite you to ask for a sign from The Universe/God/Source (whatever
you call the Something More).*

Sometimes the Path of Evolving is Hard and Lonely

The spiritual journey is individual, highly personal.
It can't be organized or regulated.
It isn't true that everyone should follow one path.
Listen to your own truth.
~ Ram Dass

Sometimes the path of evolving is hard and lonely. So, why do we do it? I think we do it because we can't *not* do it. The path chooses us as much as we choose it.

Personally, the more inner work I do, the more I learn I have *more* inner work to do. Sometimes I get frustrated with this truth and I just want to turn back, to return to life before I was on this path of spiritual work and self-discovery. There are many times when the path feels hard and I just don't want to do the work. Sometimes I turn my back on my path completely. I stop my practices and fill in the space by mindlessly eating and watching television or scrolling through social media. I can never go on this way for too long though; my soul always pulls me back toward my path. I find it helpful to simply accept that sometimes the path of evolving will be hard and lonely. This way, when I find myself inside of those feelings I don't make it into a bigger deal than it is. Instead, I am able to see the challenges as an expected part of the process of evolving, to practice self-compassion, and to keep moving forward.

Spend some time with your journal today. Where are you on your path of evolving? How are things feeling today? If all is well, spend a few moments in gratitude. If things feel hard or lonely, spend a few moments practicing self-compassion.

July 24

Practice Staying with Yourself

Being human is hard. There are moments of feeling ungrounded in our bodies, unkind in our minds, and unsure in our hearts. It is understandable that we would want to run away from these experiences rather than turn toward them. I invite you to practicing staying with yourself. This means simply being with your truth in the moment without trying to fix anything. Stay and be where you are, even the uncomfortable places. Instead of rushing to try to change things, allow yourself to practice communing with whatever is happening within you.

Don't confuse not running away from your feelings with not taking care of them. Just because you are practicing acceptance and surrender does not mean that you shouldn't engage in the practices that help shift things for you. We can get stuck in our feelings if we abandon self-care in the name of staying with ourselves. I believe staying with yourself and being in your feelings means practicing self-care right alongside the feelings, not to try to change what you are feeling, but to commune with it. Writing it out, crying in Child's Pose, or calling a friend for support are different than avoiding your feelings by shoving them down, overworking, or using substances to numb out.

There is a difference between pain and suffering. Being where you are, even when it is painful, and practicing acceptance doesn't mean you have to suffer. We can learn to walk this middle path of allowing and honoring, of releasing resistance to our pain, while also doing the practices to take care of our pain. Often, once you accept and honor your feelings, they shift without any fighting or forcing. Remember that your feelings deserve love and kindness. Practice staying with yourself during the uncomfortable times.

July 25

Declare Your Intentions

I believe that The Universe listens when we declare our intentions and that from the moment we say what we want aloud things start shifting in the unseen. Begin today by making a declaration to yourself. This could be a dream you have, a role you want to step into, or a feeling you want to embody. Claim your intention in the present tense. For example, *"I am going back to school; I am an artist; or I am enough."* Repeat your intention often. Say it in the mirror, include it in your meditation practice, or write it in your journal. Trust that these practices will inspire some magic on your behalf. Share your intention with others and the magic amplifies exponentially. People will offer to help you, resources will land in your lap, and synchronicities will become your new normal. When we are aligned with our higher self, the place where our wild, *divine* dreams come from, The Universe can't help but conspire on our behalf.

What do you want to call into your life? Declare it today.

july 26

Awareness + Understanding + Choice = Change

Sometimes creating change in our lives feels overwhelming. How do we go about releasing unhelpful thoughts and behaviors so that we can build new habits and ways of being? I find it helpful to break the process of change into three steps.

The first step toward creating change is *awareness*. We can build awareness of our patterns through methods of self-inquiry such as meditation and journal writing. This helps us identify what we would like to change.

After awareness, the next step is *understanding*. Why do we do the things we do? This requires a willingness to look at our own inner workings through self-study. Time spent in introspection, reading relevant books, and therapy can contribute to understanding.

The final step in creating change is *choice*. Will we repeat our patterns or try a new way? If we struggle with choosing a new way to think or be, it can be helpful to revisit the step of understanding to learn more about what is going on underneath the surface.

Spend some time with your journal today. Think of something you would like to change (this could be a thought or behavior) and consider where you are with regard to awareness, understanding, and choice. Let go of any judgment that arises and allow yourself to simply notice. Let what you discover be information that can support your journey of change.

july 27

It's Not Just You

I don't share to teach or convince others, I share to make those who feel the same as me feel less alone. ~ Unknown

We are not alone in our struggles. This truth comforts me. Today I want you to know that it's not just you. Whatever you are feeling or going through, there is someone out there who can relate. Someone who would feel comforted to know they are not alone in feeling guilty, angry, happy, jealous, sad, or scared. There is so much performing and pretending in our current world, much of it driven by social media. This is why I share what I am going through in life as openly as I do online and in my writing—because I hope someone might see themselves reflected and feel the amazing relief that comes with realizing *it's not just me.*

It is important to note that I don't publicly share everything in my life. I believe we can be authentic and still keep some of our stories private. To me, having boundaries around what we share and with whom we share it is part of self-care. I also check in with myself about my intentions before I share. I do my own work around processing before I share things so that I can offer my experience without the expectation of anything in return.

You don't have to share your truth widely in order to make connections. It isn't necessarily healthy or wise to post our experiences for public consumption. The truth is, it is just as powerful to talk about what you are feeling or going through with one person in your life. Who can be your safe place for sharing? How can you show up in your whole truth today in service of connection?

july 28

Let Go of the Idea of Achieving Balance in Your Life

I try to avoid focusing on bringing balance into my life because it feels like yet another ideal put on women. I like to think instead about mindfully responding to my life and intentionally choosing where I focus my time and energy, with permission to change as often as needed (sometimes hourly!). Some things in my life—such as family time, self-care, and work schedules—are non-negotiable. But aside from those structures, I shift my open time and space as needed. Some days, weeks, or months I am more focused on one area or another. If I have a big project at work, I will spend more time working than relaxing with my family. On the other hand, in the summer I typically plan to work less so I can have more time to be with my family. There are also times when I am more outwardly focused and other times I dedicate myself to turning inward. For example, I try to schedule my work and social events during the first three weeks of my menstrual cycle and leave the last week for more alone time.

There is no right or wrong when it comes to how we devote our time and energy. There is only what feels right for you, doing the best you can to honor that, and the permission to change at any moment. Accepting the cycles, honoring the ebb and flow, and releasing any ideas about needing to be consistent invites peace and flexibility into our lives. Let go of trying to achieve the elusive ideal of balance and instead honor whatever is true and needed for you day to day, or even moment to moment.

july 29

Change Comes in Many Forms

Change comes in many forms. Sometimes we have a hand in creating change, and other times things change whether we want them to or not. Sometimes things burn down and we start over from scratch, and other times the shifts happen more slowly and gently. We can't predict what will come our way in life; we can only learn to flow more easily with the inevitable changes that life will bring. I have had the experience of my whole world being turned upside down in a moment, and I have had the experience of craving change and feeling like things were progressing at a snail's pace. I have suffered both from resisting change and yearning for it. There is peace to be found inside of surrendering to change, in whatever form it may come.

Spend some time with your journal today. What is your relationship to change? What changes are occurring in your life right now? What pace of change are you currently experiencing? How you can release resistance and find ease within the changing nature of life?

July 30

The More You Have, The More You Can Give

Sometimes joy and abundance can feel uncomfortable. We worry that we are being selfish or that somehow our success takes away from others. The truth is we all deserve a life full of soul-nourishing belongings, relationships, and experiences. People who are worried about being selfish are not in danger of being selfish. Your joy and abundance does not take away from others. When that belief pops up, call it what it is—the old voice of scarcity and fear. Your joy supports other people's joy, and your abundance supports other people's abundance. The more you have, the more you can give. This is true for everything from emotional energy to money. Open up to receive, knowing it will allow you to give generously in return.

Spend some time with your journal today. What is your relationship to joy and abundance? Are there any areas where you are blocking yourself from receiving due to feeling undeserving or fear of being selfish? How have you shared your joy and abundance in the past? How would you like to be able to give in the future?

july 31

Some Thoughts on Life Outside the Comfort Zone

I once had a yoga teacher who I adored *and* found very intimidating. She was kind but stern, and her classes were intense. She had a gift for taking her students outside the comfort zone and helping us see that we could show up in a bigger, bolder way. She taught me that I was capable of going deeper and further in my yoga practice than I had imagined. During the time period in my life when I took her classes, she was exactly what I needed—someone to push me to the next level, a place I had not been willing to take myself. These days I practice a more gentle form of yoga, but I practice taking myself out of my comfort zone in other ways.

Contrary to today's typical personal development advice, I don't believe we need to be constantly pushing ourselves outside of our comfort zone. I think there are times in our lives when staying in the comfort zone is healthy and represents good self-care. I also think it is important to consider context. It is probably not wise to push out of the comfort zone in all areas of our lives simultaneously. We need some steady ground to stand on as we challenge our limits.

I like to conceptualize the comfort zone as ranging from 0 (feeling bored or in a rut) to 10 (pushing our limits as much as we can). Think about the different areas of your life, such as work, relationships, health, and finances. Where would you put yourself on the scale of 0-10? Where do you want to be? If there is an area of life where you'd like to come out of your comfort zone a bit, make a plan about how you can pursue that goal. Remember not to hand your life over to some platitude about living outside the comfort zone. You get to choose. Discern what feels right for you and proceed accordingly.

august 1

What Would You Do If You Didn't Have to Prove Your Worthiness?

We don't have to do all of it alone. We were never meant to.
~ Brené Brown

Most women I know, personally and professionally, struggle with some version of feeling not good enough. We feel like we have to work to earn love and respect. We think we have to prove our worthiness through our accomplishments or by acting in certain ways.

Why do we do this?
Because our society constantly feeds us images of the "perfect" woman.

And we compare our imperfect reality to this perfect, nonexistent woman and decide that we don't measure up. So, we run around trying to prove our worth by over-working, over-committing, and over-spending until we end up exhausted, anxious, and overwhelmed.

Personally, nearly all of my choices until I was 30 years old were motivated by trying to prove to the world that I was a good mother, wife, daughter, friend, *woman.*

These days I am pretty well grounded in living my life based on my inner authority, but sometimes I still need to check myself because it is easy to fall into my old ways of performing and people-pleasing.

What would you do if you didn't have to prove your worthiness?

How would you move your body?
What would you wear?
What would you eat?
What would you create?
What would you say yes to?
What would you say no to?
What would you buy or not buy?
How would you spend your time?
Who would you spend it with?
What would you say or write?

Take some time with these questions; really feel your way into them. Let yourself imagine a life where you don't have to hustle for your worth. Give yourself permission to do what feels supportive and sustainable, even if it is not necessarily what will please others.

august 2

Healing Through Writing

Let me fall if I must fall. The one I will become will catch me.
~ Baal Shem Tov

Writing is how I mark time. I write (mostly) every day in my journal, and I usually write a weekly love letter to share with my community of online readers. Something about putting into words what I've been experiencing brings me a sense of completion and closure.

I've always known this, but it took me some time to be able to articulate it. Now I know that I need to name what is going on for me before I can heal it. I need to take the time to deconstruct what I'm feeling, to understand why something is bothering me, and to acknowledge what it is bringing up for me. I need to be able to put it into words. This is why my brain sometimes goes around and around about distressing things. It is trying to find the words to explain my feelings; it is working to describe what often feels indescribable. This is why I write. To translate that which feels inexplicable into a language that lets me name my truth—to give voice to the pain, the joy, and everything in between. The act of writing allows me to release, move forward, and step out of the story.

Today, I invite you to spend some time writing. This can be for your eyes only or you can share with others if you feel called to do so. What's on your mind today? Is there something asking for attention or needing healing? Set a timer and free write for ten minutes. Check in with your mind, emotions, and body after you write. Depending on how you feel after this practice, consider adding writing to your regular coping toolbox.

august 3

When Your Brain Can't Bring Peace

My brain can't bring peace. It can't bring life. For that, I had to let go and hover over the reef, traveling into the black—a nothing, a tiny nothing paddling and kicking across the expanse of blue, taking deep breaths and heading for the shore, all I know of safety, buoyed by ancient waters pulled forever by a cratered moon. ~ Janelle Hanchett

At one point in my life when I was struggling hard with depression, I had this old story I would replay in my mind pretty much every day. It was a story of deep hurt, and it quickly turned into a story of my unworthiness, which quickly turned into a story of *I'm not safe*, which flowed into a story of *OMG this is horrible and I can't handle it*.

The facts were one thing, and my feelings were quite another.

No matter what I did I could not let go of this story. Sometimes I could catch myself and pause the story at one point or another with varying degrees of success. But I could not let go of this story. Not through therapy, not through journaling, not through talking, not through fighting, not through writing it down and lighting it on fire, not through praying and begging for help.

Not through thinking about it.
My brain couldn't bring peace.

I couldn't think or reason my way out of the pain; what ailed me couldn't be solved by my mind. In fact, I couldn't trust my mind when it came to this story. It was lying to me, playing tricks on me by twisting things up and around and around. Not being able to rely on my mind was very difficult for me to accept. I am analytical. I have a tendency to be over-attached to my mind and over-identified with my intellect. But when I was stuck in this negative thought cycle, I couldn't think my way out of it. Instead I needed to tap into my soul, the *Something More* within me— the place within that is beyond thoughts and stories. That is where unshakeable peace lives.

So I made up my mind (ha!) that I was going to try an experiment. When the story popped up, instead of thinking more or journaling or trying to flip to a positive affirmation, I decided I was going to breathe. Specifically, I would notice my breath flowing in and out, my belly rising and falling. I invited my breath to help me let go, to lead me back home to my Self—the me that is beyond thoughts, emotions, or my physical body. My core, my spirit, my essence. Because that place within me is peace, is love, is pure, is true—and it is always available for me to tap into, at any time.

As soon as I decided on this plan, I began laughing hysterically at myself. I knew I was not going to be able to follow through. It sounded like an amazing plan, but I know myself and my attachment to my mind, and it just wasn't going to happen that way. So I did this instead: I gave myself ten minutes to try to use my mind to bring me peace. During that time I would write, think, or talk, and then afterward I would breathe and work on letting go and connecting with my soul. Eventually, I did let this old story go. I'm not sure how. It was probably some combination of time passing, therapy, and divine intervention. We can never know exactly what will bring us relief, so why not tap into all of our resources—mental, physical, and spiritual.

Everything Is Not Your Fault

One day I was backing out of the driveway at my office.

During the day, the street is packed with cars parked up and down both sides, making it difficult to see. Although I looked before I backed out, there was a car coming. The driver swerved around me. I raised my hand in a friendly wave and mouthed, "I'm sorry!"

She gave me the finger.

As I pulled away there was a car coming in the other direction, and the driver gave me a dirty look and shook her head at me. I immediately felt the muscles in my back tense up and my eyes filled with tears. *Wow, I am such an asshole*, began the familiar chorus in my head. *Wait*, I caught myself before I went too far down that path. *I made a mistake.* I waved and apologized. *I am not an asshole; I'm just a person who made a mistake.*

This is a tiny, inconsequential example of how I tend to assume that everything is my fault.

I'm not sure why. Maybe it's because it lets me feel like I have control. If it's my fault then I can somehow be in charge of creating change. In the past, this pattern of assuming I am always to blame has kept me tolerant of toxic situations. I thought that if I was just more kind, more patient, more hardworking, more more more....

If I was just good enough, then things would be better.

I think a lot of empathic, sensitive, spiritually-minded beings do this. We are so good at personal responsibility that we take on everything, even things that are not ours. It can be a dangerous habit. This mode of assuming I am at fault has kept me quiet, thinking that I didn't have a right to have any needs. It has kept me passive, believing that I didn't deserve to assert myself.

Let's shift this pattern.
I am not always wrong— and neither are you.
I am not always right—and neither are you.

Let's take responsibility for our behavior (wave and say sorry), and let's hold people accountable for theirs (even if you're pissed, it's not okay to give someone the finger).

august 5

Hold Your Intentions Close to Your Heart and Release Expectations

The distinction between intention and expectation is important.
Intentions are about how we want to show up and what we want to feel.
Expectations are about how we think things or people should be.

Intentions are an important part of my spiritual practice. I set an intention every time I practice yoga. I set intentions for each of the courses I teach. I set an intention before I enter into a social gathering. I set an intention whenever I work with a healer, such as during massage, acupuncture, and energy healing. Declaring an intention helps me to focus my awareness and direct my energy toward what I want to experience. Intentions also help me live my life with mindfulness. On the other hand, when I get caught up in expectations I often experience stress, anxiety, and anger.

Let's use a social gathering as an example. If I go into an event with expectation—say, that my child will behave a certain way or people will react to me in a certain way—then I will likely end up frustrated because I can't control other people's behaviors or reactions. But if I go into an event with the intention of love and connection, then I have the ability to shape my experience because how I feel is not attached to anyone else's behavior. I can always invite myself to return to love and connection, no matter what else is going on around me. This is the power of intention.

Today, I invite you to set an intention. This could be for your day in general or for a specific part of your day like a meeting, picking up your kids, or eating your meals. Consider how you want to feel and put it into words. Let your intention be a guidepost that you connect with throughout the day. Observe how this shifts your experience of today.

august 6

Just Be

Everything that's created comes out of silence. Your thoughts emerge from the nothingness of silence. Your words come out of this void. Your very essence emerged from emptiness. All creativity requires some stillness.
~ Wayne Dyer

I am a doer. A go, go, go kind of person who really loves to get shit done. I hated Savasana, the final resting pose at the end of yoga class, for the first five years of my practice. (You want me to just lie here and do nothing?!) The truth is, I still hate it sometimes. Just being, resting in the white space, is a challenge for me. And I know it is essential.

Essential to a life well-lived.
Essential for getting quiet enough to hear my own voice.
Essential to my creativity.
Essential for refilling my internal well.

So I make myself practice doing nothing.

Today, I invite you to find 15 minutes to just be. Let this be a spiritual practice. Take a comfortable seat on the floor or in a chair. Set a timer for 15 minutes. Close your eyes, if that feels supportive today. Just be—with your breath, your mind, your self. Witness whatever arises without pushing it away. Invite yourself back to the present moment over and over again. Notice how you feel when the 15 minutes are over and consider adding this practice to your daily or weekly routine.

august 7

Be Patient with Your Process

Patience is also a form of action.
~ Auguste Rodin

Show up for yourself every day.
Take time to tune in and connect with your truth.
Trust your own timing.
There is no *one* place you need to be, no *one* thing you need to do.
There are many ways to arrive.
You don't need to figure everything out today.
All will be revealed in divine timing.
Be patient with your process.

august 8

Don't Wait to Share What's Inside of You

Our job in this life is not to shape ourselves into some ideal we imagine we ought to be, but to find out who we already are and become it.
~ Steven Pressfield

I believe that we each have gifts inside of us—art longing to be created, ideas waiting to be articulated. Often we don't share what is inside of us because it is not fully formed or we feel it needs to be more polished before we put it out in the world.

What gems are you holding inside of you, thinking that they are not ready to be shared with the world?

It's okay to share thoughts and ideas that are still forming in your mind.
It's okay to write or say or do something imperfect.
It's okay to be in process and to let people see that.

Waiting until something is "complete" or "ready" is a form of perfectionism and one way we fall into never sharing what is inside of us.

Today, I invite you to take a risk. Share the beauty and inspiration that is within you, even if your creations or ideas are newly formed or still in process. It will be a gift to yourself and to whomever you share it with.

august 9

There Is No Arriving

[G]ive yourself permission to allow this moment to be exactly as it is,
and allow yourself to be exactly as you are.
~ Jon Kabat-Zinn

One morning I was walking my puppy by the river near my house and pondering something that had been bothering me. There, among the quiet of the trees and water, with the company of only my dog and the birds, I found relief from what I had been struggling with for so many days. I felt a sense of peace, as if I were wrapped in a blanket of comfort there among the trees. It was a beautiful moment.

And then it began to rain. Hard. I stood where I was and looked out at the fog over the water. I took in the lushness of the trees surrounding me, and I just let it rain. I did not fight the rain. I did not think, "Shit, I don't have an umbrella." I just surrendered to the rain, stood in the moment, and soaked up the blissful feeling of peace.
And a moment later, I started to attach to it.

Oh, this is magical. I don't want to lose this feeling. I don't want to go back to the confusion and the sadness and the fear that I was feeling.

But I did.
Not right in that moment, maybe not even that day, but eventually.

Of course I did.

Because I am human.

Because we are all constantly in flux.

Because there is no arriving, no completion to this path of learning and growing and healing.

Accepting this truth gives us the freedom to surrender to where we are in the moment, to let that be enough, while we also move toward where we want to be. Wherever you are landing today, allow it to be a step on your path even as you release any attachment to arriving somewhere in particular.

august 10

Save Your I'm Sorry's

It takes years as a woman to unlearn what you have been taught to be sorry for.
~ Amy Poehler

Women tend to over-apologize.

We say "I'm sorry" for everything from our lunch order (*"I'm sorry, can I have the dressing on the side?"*) to expressing our beliefs (*"I'm sorry, I disagree with you."*). In some cases we practically apologize for our existence. Saying "I'm sorry" implies that we have done something wrong. I believe there is an impact on our sense of self when we repeatedly apologize for things that do not warrant an apology, such as our preferences, needs, or opinions. "I'm sorry" means I am full of sorrow. Let's save the phrase for when we truly mean it, when we've done something that makes us feel sad and regretful.

Today, notice how often you say, "I'm sorry."
Do you mean it in the true sense of the phrase? Or is it just a habit?

august 11

Being Honest About Our Needs

People who are "nice" hold truth inside until they reach a breaking point and then they become dangerously inappropriate; I know because I used to be such a person. ~ Deborah Adele

The truth—in all senses of the word—is important to me. I feel uncomfortable if I tell even the tiniest of lies and work hard to be impeccable with my word.

One place where I struggle with being honest is when it comes to voicing what I need. I will still shove the truth down in order to do what I think will please others or what I think a "good" mom/wife/friend/therapist would do. But I am not doing anyone any favors when I do that because I muck up the energy of the interaction with my dishonesty. Even if I am doing what I think is kind, I am tainting it with the ickiness that is a lie.

Think about all the tiny ways we say yes when we mean no.
These are small violences against ourselves and others.

When I am intentional about being honest about my needs I do things such as the following:

Take a nap when I am tired.
Say no to social engagements.
Ask for a back massage when I am aching.
Take a bath when I am craving some alone time.
Sometimes in order to prioritize my needs I might not be able to give 100% at work or home. Chores may be left for the next day (or the next person!), emails and voicemails may sit unanswered, and I might not have quality one-on-one time with my kids or my husband or my friends.

And yet, the world keeps spinning.

And I find that after I have given myself the gift of meeting my needs, I can approach my tasks and my people with kindness, presence, and an open heart.

Today, practice being honest about what you need. Observe how doing so impacts your mind, mood, and energy, as well as your interactions with others. You will likely discover that being honest about what you need is good for you and everyone around you.

august 12

Would You Be Willing?

Communication is of paramount importance in creating healthy relationships. We are not formally taught how to communicate effectively, and many of us did not have healthy role models when it comes to how to talk to one another. This seems to be especially true when it comes to asking for things. We say things to our partners like, *"Why can't you ever..."* or we scold our children, *"How many times do I have to ask you to...."* This type of phrasing puts the other person on the defensive. Next time you have a request, try beginning with, *"Would you be willing to...."* Notice how this simple shift impacts your interactions.

august 13

Relationships Are Made Up of Agreements

Relationships are made up of agreements. We agree on certain parameters for how we will treat one another, spend time together, and more. If you live with someone, there are agreements about how you will manage your living space and share household responsibilities. If you co-parent with someone, there are agreements about how you will raise the child. It may feel odd to think of our relationships as being made up of agreements because many of us have not explicitly discussed the agreements inside of our relationships. Often we assume we are in agreement with others. The truth is, outside of abusive behavior, there are no right or wrong agreements inside of relationships; there is only what feels okay for both people. Agreements can also change over time as we shift as individuals or the relationship itself evolves.

One of the keys to successful relationships is explicitly defining agreements. Don't assume that the other person knows what you expect from them. Take the time to get clear on what you want from your relationships and communicate it directly. Be prepared to negotiate your expectations or to receive "no" as an answer when you ask for what you want. Continuing to expect something different than what a person has told you they are capable of or willing to do creates resentment. If you cannot come to an agreement with the other person, you can choose to shift your expectations or to leave the relationship.

Is there an agreement you need to discuss with someone in your life?
Take the time to address it today.

august 14

The Connection Between Empaths and Narcissists

When someone shows you who they are, believe them the first time.
~ Maya Angelou

Empaths are people who can sense and feel other people's feelings. They often feel drawn toward helping people. Narcissists are controlling and manipulative. People who develop narcissistic traits are typically deeply wounded from experiencing trauma. Empathic, sensitive women are often drawn toward narcissistic people because they have a strong desire to heal others, and narcissists need a great deal of healing. Empaths also have the gift of seeing the best possible version of people, which can cloud their ability to see the reality of the person before them. Because empaths love to help others, they sometimes stay in unhealthy relationships and continue believing things will change if they just try harder or give the narcissist more time.

The truth is, a relationship between an empath and a narcissist cannot be healthy. Due to the nature of these personality types, the empath will give to an unhealthy degree, and the narcissist will continue to take well past that point.

It's not your job to heal or save anyone except yourself.
It's okay to walk away from people.
You deserve healthy, nourishing relationships.

august 15

Hobbies Can Just Be Hobbies

If you've come to life to truly experience life, there's enough room
for many interests, curiosities, activities that spark enthusiasm,
and quiet nights doing none of it.
~ Mari Andrew

In the world of personal development there is a lot of talk about pursuing your passion and earning a living doing something you love. The truth is, it can be freeing to just allow a hobby to be a hobby. It relieves the pressure that comes with trying to earn money through our creative practices. Besides, we don't need to monetize everything in life. The idea that we should is capitalist bullshit. We can do things simply for the enjoyment and fulfillment they bring to our lives.

What can you do just for fun today?

august 16

You Can Take Back Your Yes

Have you ever agreed to something in the moment and then felt a sense of dread when you thought about it later? Personally, when someone asks me to do something my default response is yes. I often say it without thinking things through. So I have had to learn the art of taking back my yes. I usually say something simple like, *"Things have changed and this will no longer work for me,"* or *"I've had some time to think more about it and I can't be there/do that."*

You can take back your "yes." Women generally think this is a radical idea. It can be a bit uncomfortable in the beginning, but once you have some practice, it feels refreshing to be honest and to honor what you need. You can change your mind. Your "yes" can be revoked at any time for any reason you choose, whether it pertains to completing a task, going to a social event, or anything else you might have agreed to that no longer works for you.

Spend some time with your journal today. Do you tend to say yes without thinking things through? Is there anything that you've recently agreed to that you'd like to change your mind about? Practice pausing before you agree to things to give yourself time to consider what you really want and know that if you agree to something and change your mind, you can take back your yes.

august 17

Speaking Up About Our Needs Is a Gift to Others

Sometimes we think that we are being kind or helpful when we don't speak up about what we need in order to keep the peace or make others comfortable. This is how I operated for most of my life, and at times, I revert back to this behavior because I want to please people, even if it means sacrificing my own needs. Like many women, I want to be perceived as nice and likeable. But denying our needs is not healthy and creates resentment over time.

I am honestly thrilled when someone tells me no or otherwise asserts their needs inside of our relationship because it feels like a permission slip for me to do the same. I feel like I can trust them to tell me the truth, and that makes me feel like I can trust them with my truth in return. Speaking up about our needs is a gift to ourselves and those around us. Imagine if we all practiced being honest about our needs. We would probably disappoint each other once in a while, but we would survive. And we would be able to trust that when someone says "yes" it is wholeheartedly true and not given out of obligation or fear.

How can you speak up about your needs today?
Can you give yourself permission to be honest, even if it might disappoint others?

august 18

We Don't Have to Tolerate Discomfort Just Because We Can

If your compassion does not include yourself, it is incomplete.
~ Jack Kornfield

I spent a fair amount of my life powering through difficult situations. I can tolerate a lot of stress and discomfort, and sometimes this translates into me not taking care of my needs because things aren't *"that bad."* The truth is we don't have to tolerate discomfort just because we can. In fact, just because you *can* do something doesn't mean you *should.*

I believe all pain deserves attention and that we deserve more than simply getting by; we deserve to thrive. We don't need to keep living with discomfort just because we can survive inside of it. We don't have to push through and wait for things to get to a breaking point before we make a change. We are allowed to take steps toward healing and feeling the way we want to feel right here, right now.

Spend some time with your journal today. Is there a physical or emotional situation where you have been tolerating discomfort? How would you like to feel? What steps can you take to make the situation feel better? How can you thrive rather than just survive?

august 19

Take a Social Media Break

Social media has many benefits. It's a great way to connect with people, it provides a plethora of information and inspiration, and it can be a positive influence on our lives. However, there are also many downsides: it puts us into comparison mode, encourages us to mindlessly scroll for hours, and disconnects us from our bodies. Creating boundaries around our use of technology is an important piece of self-care. Social media breaks can provide us with a much-needed respite and help us connect more deeply with ourselves.

Today's invitation is to take a social media break. There are many ways to do this. You could start small by setting a no social media window, such as 8pm-8am, or go bigger and take social media apps off your phone, for one day per week or one weekend a month. Choose what feels doable for you and pay attention to how you feel during your social media break. This is a powerful practice for resetting your mind and body. If you'd like to further explore your relationship with your phone, I recommend the book How to Break Up with Your Phone *by Catherine Price.*

august 20

Spend Time Alone

In solitude we give passionate attention to our lives,
to our memories, to the details around us.
~ Virginia Woolf

How often do you spend time alone?
How does it feel to be alone with your thoughts and feelings?

People have differing needs for alone time. For me, time alone is the most important piece of my self-care. As an introvert, my mood and energy are directly correlated with the amount of time I spend alone. When I go too long without alone time, I often become irritable and anxious, and sometimes I even have physical symptoms, like pain in my body or trouble sleeping. I think it is important to spend time by yourself whether it feels essential or not. There is so much wisdom to be gleaned from simply *being* with ourselves. I understand this idea can feel uncomfortable. Many people purposely avoid spending time alone because there are thoughts and feelings that they don't want to face. Know that running from yourself doesn't work in the long run. The day will come when you find yourself emotionally or physically unwell; our minds and bodies only allow us to run from ourselves for so long. The truth is that healing comes from facing ourselves and acknowledging our inner truth.

If spending time alone feels uncomfortable, it's okay to start small. Can you sit in the quiet with yourself for five minutes? Or take a 20-minute walk without your phone? Carve out some alone time to just be with yourself today.

august 21

When There is So Much To Do

When there is so much to do, take time for self-care, especially when you feel like you don't have time. Relaxing creates time, I swear.

Take a nap.
Slow down.
Spend time in nature.
Soak in a salty bath.

When there is so much to do, create space to do the most important stuff. Let the rest go.

Take things off your calendar and to-do list.
Delegate.
Cancel.
Let it go undone.

When there is so much to do, practice self-compassion.

Give yourself a break.
Talk to yourself kindly, like you would to a friend.
Give yourself permission to not do everything well.
It's okay if the laundry goes unfolded or you half-ass your way through a work meeting.

When there is so much to do, stay present.

I know you can check out and plow through. Don't.
Be in your body.
Be in the moment.
Stay, feel, breathe.

When there is so much to do, take action.

Make a list.
Do the hardest, most necessary thing first.
Get it done, one step at a time.
You've got this.

august 22

What Do You Love About Being You?

We must fall in love with ourselves. I don't like myself. I'm crazy about myself.
~ Mae West

Most of us spend a lot of time pondering our faults and picking ourselves apart.

Let's do the opposite. Let's honor ourselves. Let's claim our gifts.

Grab your journal and make a list of 25 things you appreciate about yourself. Include everything from the small stuff like the color of your eyes to the bigger things like your compassionate heart. What do you love about being you?

The Special Kind of Loneliness of Being a Woman

Sometimes it feels like there is a special kind of loneliness when it comes to being a woman.

Women are caregivers.
We are the nurturers.
We hold so much.

And systemically there is very little support set up for us. We are faced with issues such as no paid maternity leave, the wage gap, and gender roles that expect us to do the majority of housework and child care even if we work outside the home. We also grapple with constant exposure to impossible ideals for our bodies, our homes, our sensuality, our mothering, our emotions, and our careers. The message is that we are supposed to be perfect women and we are supposed to do it all on our own. Perhaps worse, because we have internalized these ideals, we struggle to share our truth for fear of judgment, which further isolates us.

The antidote to the special kind of loneliness that comes with being a woman in our culture is connection through truth-telling. When we share the truth about our lives we let other women know that they are not alone in their struggles. Women telling their real-life stories to one another also helps to dismantle the impossible ideals that are portrayed by the media.

Let's opt out of pretending we're fine when we're not.

Let's opt out of trying to meet impossible ideals and judging ourselves when we can't.

Let's opt out of trying to be perfect women with perfect bodies, homes, and families.

Instead, let's tell each other the truth about what it's like to be a woman inside of this culture. Let's connect with one another, love and support each other, and come together to change the systems that create the special kind of loneliness of being a woman.

august 24

Release Tension from the Body

Sometimes I wake up in the morning with my hands balled into fists. I notice that people often walk around with their shoulders tensed up to their ears. I know many women who struggle with tightness in the jaw. We hold stress in our bodies in so many ways. Often, we are unaware that we are clenching our fists, jaws, or stomachs as we go about our day.

The way we carry and position our bodies influences our thoughts, feelings, and behaviors. Tensing our muscles sends messages to the brain that we are in danger and should be on high alert, which in turn increases our anxiety response. Creating calm and open feelings in our bodies sends message to the brain that we can relax.

Pause right now and drop your awareness into your body. Where do you feel tightness or tension? Breathe into the area and invite some release. Try clenching and unclenching your hands a few times and notice the impact. Notice as tension leaves the body and relaxation takes its place. You could also try progressive muscle relaxation, which involves tensing and releasing various parts of the body. It is an excellent tool for managing tension in the body, as well as anxiety in general. You can search online for a guided version if you'd like to further explore this practice.

august 25

Practice Using Your Voice

Freedom lies across the field of the difficult conversation.
And the more difficult the conversation, the greater the freedom.
~ Shonda Rhimes

Speaking up can be particularly challenging for women. We are socialized to be quiet and agreeable from a young age. If speaking up feels challenging for you, know that you are not alone. Find small ways to begin using your voice. Speak up about what you really want for dinner or which movie you'd like to see and work your way up to speaking your truth about the bigger things over time.

Today, find one small way to practice using your voice.

august 26

We Don't Need Huge Expanses of Time to Create
the Change We Crave

One of my biggest blocks when it comes to creating change and working toward my goals is thinking I need big chunks of time. Sometimes it is a matter of *wishing* I had big chunks of time. The truth is we don't need huge expanses of time to create the change we crave. Furthermore, spending a few minutes every day on a project or goal is often more effective than devoting a big chunk of time to it once in a while.

What have you been avoiding because you feel like you don't have enough time? This could be anything: cleaning out your closet, starting a business, learning to knit, or beginning a meditation practice. Devote 5-15 minutes to it today and notice how you feel afterward. Can you find 5-15 minutes every day this week? What about this month? Small steps taken consistently add up to big change.

We Are All Divine Love Embodied

We are all divine love embodied.
We suffer when we forget this truth.
We harm ourselves and others when we disconnect from our inherent, divine nature.

When I stay connected to the truth that we are all divine love embodied, everything else is easier. I am kind, patient, and compassionate with myself and others.

Because when I connect with the truth that we are all divine love embodied, I don't doubt my worth and there isn't any space for negative beliefs about myself.

Because when I connect with the truth that we are all divine love embodied, I speak my truth with love and kindness and advocate for those in need of protection.

Because when I connect with the truth that we are all divine love embodied, I can forgive myself and others for our very human mistakes.

The truth is I am divine love embodied and so are you.

The truth is we are all already enough, perfect and whole just as we are in this very moment.

The suffering we experience within and without is a forgetting of this sacred truth.

Every violence and oppression stems from the forgetting of this truth.

I believe it is our duty as humans to do whatever it takes for us to remember the truth that we are divine love embodied. This is our work, perhaps our most important work, because when we are connected with the divinity within ourselves and one another, we create peace and love. We will not harm what we hold sacred, and the truth is we are all sacred.

Ask yourself what connects you to the place of divine love inside you, the truth of your being, and then find a way to do it today. Try to connect with this place within yourself every day. I believe remembering the truth of our inherent divinity will help us release the spectrum of internal violence that spans from negative self-talk to suicide and the spectrum of external violence that spans from talking over each other to murder. Connecting with the divine love within you each day helps shift this world a little closer to love.

august 28

Cooking or Baking as Self-Care

Spending time in the kitchen can be therapeutic. I find chopping vegetables for soup to be meditative. Baking chocolate chip cookies brings me comfort. I know some people who love to make bread from scratch and others who even create their own recipes! Those things are beyond my skill level, but I still enjoy spending an afternoon in the kitchen. Cooking or baking settles my nerves; it feels grounding to use my hands to create something, as though I am coming home to some ancient place within myself.

Spend some time in the kitchen today. Prepare something from scratch and allow it to be an act of self-care. Invite your mind to take a backseat and let the work of your hands bring your awareness into your body.

august 29

Moon Rituals

I work with the Moon as a mirror. ~ Ezzie Spencer

Connecting with the cycles of the moon is a beautiful way to bring ritual into our lives. There are eight phases of the moon cycle, but a simple place to begin is by noting the New and Full Moon. The New Moon (or Dark Moon) is about new beginnings. It's a beautiful time to make wishes or set your intentions for the upcoming month. The energy of the New Moon encourages going inward. We can work with it by spending time alone in contemplation through journal writing or meditation. The Full Moon is an energetic time and encourages action. It's an ideal time for releasing what no longer serves you. We can work with this energy by getting clear on what we want to let go of and releasing through ceremony, such as writing down what we want to release and burning the list.

Spend some time with your journal today. Do you feel connected with the moon? How would you like to honor her changing energies each month? A beautiful practice to start with is simply to go outside and look for the moon each night. Perhaps you'd like to dive in deeper and look up the New and Full Moons each month and record them in your calendar. A simple New Moon ritual is listing your intentions for the month. A simple Full Moon ritual is to write down what you would like to release. Consider adding these rituals into your monthly schedule. You can practice them by yourself or with a group.

august 30

Tune into Yourself Before Consuming Outside Information

With social media, books, news, videos, television, and the internet, our world today is full of an unprecedented amount of data. A study in 2011 found that we take in five times more information every day than we did in 1986, and it seems probable that that number is only increasing over time. While it is amazing to have so much information at our fingertips, there is a downside to it. Namely, it is difficult to have room for any of your own thoughts or ideas when you are constantly taking in other people's writing, pictures, and videos. I am not suggesting that we completely stop taking in information, but rather that we prioritize checking in with ourselves over consuming outside information. Many people wake up and scroll on their phones. They start their day by filling their heads with other people's thoughts, making it hard to hear their own inner voice. Today's invitation is to practice tuning into yourself before consuming outside information.

How can you prioritize connecting with your inner self?

This might mean starting your day with meditation or journal writing or setting a boundary around when you consume outside information, such as not checking your phone or computer before 9am or after 9pm.

You Are a Person, Not a Project, and Also, It's Okay to Want to Change

[T]he curious paradox is that when I accept myself just as I am, then I change.
~ Carl Rogers

I am naturally driven toward personal growth. I have a deep desire to learn more and be a better human. I love this about myself *and* I recognize that I can be way too hard on myself. I have to remind myself that I am a person, not a project.

This dance between self-acceptance and the desire to change fascinates me. I have learned to discern between when to accept myself as I am and when to accept myself as I am and work on changing (because I believe we should approach change from a place of self-love and self-acceptance). The answer is simple, but not necessarily easy: I ask myself if the desire to change is coming from outer authority or inner authority.

There are two ways to check in on this:

1. I ask myself what messages I have in my mind about what is bothering me and where they are coming from.

2. I check in with my body because I know that is where my wisdom lies.

Here are two examples to illustrate:

The year I turned 40 I gained some weight. I continued to squeeze myself into pants that were just a little too tight for a year. I tolerated an entire year of discomfort because I kept thinking that my body would change back to what it was before. As I gained weight, I had thoughts, almost daily, about how I could and should change my body: *You should do a cleanse. You should do a juice fast. Try keto. Intermittent fasting. Blah, blah, blah.* There is no shortage of disordered eating advice in this world. Thankfully, I recognized all those thoughts for what they were—the product of living inside of a patriarchal culture that worships the thin-ideal. *No thanks, I'll pass on that plate of bullshit.*

So when those thoughts came up, I acknowledged them as unhealthy and sent them on their way. I reaffirmed to myself that I would not restrict or punish myself in any way to try to lose weight. But somehow I kept thinking that my body would revert back to its previous size. I wasn't accepting that it had changed. That the body I was in—right then and there—was my new normal.

Then one day I went and bought new pants in a bigger size. It was not a momentous occasion. I just quietly decided not to keep stuffing myself into clothes that didn't fit. I felt amazing in my new pants—sexy, confident, beautiful, comfortable. Accepting the new version of my body felt so good.

The same week I bought my new pants, I attended a social event. I was talking with a group of women, most of whom I did not know. I was nervous. I wanted to fit in, to be accepted. I was trying to be funny. I was trying to contribute to the conversation. *I was trying too hard.* I was not being the best version of myself. It felt a lot like high school. I ended up saying some things that I did not feel good about. I actually felt kind of gross after it was over. I did not like who I let myself become in order to fit in. I beat myself up pretty good for the rest of the night and even the next morning.

The following day I wrote in my journal about what had happened. I meditated on it. I accepted that I am an imperfect human. I decided to give myself the same advice I give others and view my feelings of guilt as data. I let the ickiness simply be information that I had engaged in some behavior that was not aligned with my highest self. I decided to forgive myself and make a promise to myself that I would be more mindful next time I was in a social situation.

In the example of my too-tight pants, the messaging about my body was clearly from an external source, social and cultural messaging, and I primarily experienced it as thoughts in my mind. In the example about the social situation, the messaging was internal and largely came from my body sensations. Outer authority vs. inner authority.

In general, outer authority is all types of fucked up—especially for women. We cannot trust the messaging we exist inside of because it is inherently designed to undermine our self-love and self-trust. Patriarchy is real and that shitty messaging infects everything in our world. It takes daily effort to unlearn and de-condition ourselves—to reclaim our self-love and self-trust and to connect to our inner authority. Inner authority is honest, kind, and wise. We all have the wisdom of inner authority—it just might be buried underneath layers of social expectations, trauma, and fear.

I invite you to take a few minutes today to check in with your own mind and heart. Are you being guided by outer authority or inner authority? How does it feel? Accept whatever truths arise for you, and if you decide to work toward change, let it come from acceptance and love. Your inner authority will not lead you astray. You can trust yourself.

september 1

Pick One Thing

This month I am going to invite you into some action around your dreams. We will begin by picking one thing to focus on. *This is the part I resist.* There are so many beautiful dreams swirling around in my head and I want to bring them all to life. And I believe I can—just not all at once. Picking one thing to focus on allows us to concentrate our time and energy, and it helps bring our dreams to fruition more quickly.

A dream can be anything you want to experience.

Getting a new tattoo,
Becoming a yoga teacher,
Going on a vacation or retreat,
Redecorating your bedroom,
Decluttering your closet,
Starting a business,
Starting a meditation practice,
Hosting a dinner party,
Knitting a scarf,
Presenting at a conference,
Spending more time with your family,
Making new friends,
Starting a women's circle,
Starting a blog,
Going to an event,
Nothing is too big or too small.

Today, choose the one dream that you will focus on this month. Leave behind any ideas about right or wrong and let your intuition guide you. An exercise that I find helpful is to write each of your dreams on an index card or slip of paper. Create a circle of dreams on the ground and literally step inside of it. Face each dream in turn and tune into your body, noticing how the dream feels. Choose the dream that lights up your body the most.

september 2

Make a List of Action Steps

In every dream brought to life there are tens, maybe hundreds, of tiny action steps. It can feel overwhelming to think about achieving our big goals and dreams. Making a list of small steps helps our big goals and dreams feel more manageable. It also encourages us to take action by breaking the big goal or dream into doable tasks.

For example, here are some action steps for the dream of having a beautiful, clutter-free home:

- create an inspiration board on Pinterest;
- buy new plants;
- flip through magazines for ideas;
- schedule a day off for uninterrupted de-cluttering;
- walk through the house and make a list of to-do's for each room;
- go through a closet and fill a box to donate;
- make a wish list of decorative items.

For today, make a list of action steps toward your one dream that you chose yesterday. Try to break the big goal or dream into micro-movements that feel doable inside of your life. After you make your list, choose one thing to do this week in service of your dream.

september 3

Share Your Dream

There is magic inside of speaking our dreams out loud.
There is power inside of being seen in our wanting.

Amazing things have happened every single time I have taken the step of sharing my dreams with another person. I had a class full of students before I even completed my yoga certification. I found a space to rent for a yoga studio that cost less than my monthly book budget. I found the building that would become my wellness center less than two miles from my house. Saying what I want out loud has led me to connect with incredible resources, amazing people, and powerful healers that all ended up supporting my dreams in their own way. Speaking your dream out loud tells the Universe you are serious. Magic will follow.

One note: when a dream is in its infancy we must choose wisely who we share it with. New dreams are vulnerable and deserve gentle protection. When sharing, choose someone who can hold your dream without projecting their own stuff onto it; someone who can share your vision, lift you up, and celebrate your bravery.

Today, I invite you to share your dream, your one thing, with someone who can support you.

september 4

Find the Feeling Inside Your Dream

Underneath every dream we have is a yearning for a feeling. If you dream of quitting your job, you might be yearning to feel free, happy, or empowered. If you dream of running a half marathon, you might be yearning to feel strong, confident, or vibrant. If you dream of having a beautiful, clutter free home (this is one of my dreams), you might be yearning to feel peaceful, serene, or surrounded by order and beauty.

The beautiful thing about identifying the feelings inside our dreams is that we can find ways to have those feelings right now, within the life we already have.

For example, here some ways I can feel peaceful, serene, and surrounded by order and beauty right now:

1. Buy fresh flowers for the dining room table.
2. Make my bed.
3. Buy a new houseplant.
4. Clear one small area, like a shelf or counter top.
5. Play music at home.
6. Light candles.
7. Create an altar.

Spend some time with your journal today. What are the feelings inside your dream? After you identify them, list at least five ways you can create those feelings inside of your current life.

september 5

Practice Gratitude

Gratitude unlocks the fullness of life. It turns what we have into enough, and more. It turns denial into acceptance, chaos to order, confusion to clarity.
~ Melody Beattie

One of the most powerful things we can do while working toward our dreams is to be thankful for what we already have, to practice gratitude. And gratitude truly is a practice. Our brain has a built-in negativity bias that steers us toward focusing on what is or could go wrong. This is great for keeping us alive and not so great for keeping us happy. Happiness and contentment need to be consciously cultivated.

Today, make a Master Gratitude List of at least 50 things, big or small, that you are thankful for. This will help shift your mind into noticing the goodness inside of your life.

A few examples from my own list: my family and friends, sunshine, dark chocolate with sea salt, Muir Woods, yoga, work that I love, the internet, possibility, fresh fruit, trees, my breath, books, clothes that feel amazing, peonies, puppies, and the ocean.

After you make your Master Gratitude List, go back to the one dream you are working with for this month and make a gratitude list around it. This will help you see the ways your dream is already manifesting in your life.

Continuing with the example of my dream of a beautiful, clutter-free home, here is my gratitude list: our beautiful house in a neighborhood I love, living so close to the Niagara gorge, the grey wall in my bedroom, our bedspread and throw pillows on our bed, the patio in our backyard, the bookshelves in our living room, the big bathtub in our attic, the carpet in our hallways, and the fireplace in our living room.

september 6

Create Structure to Support Your Dream

Our dreams deserve our time and attention. Creating an action plan is a beautiful way to support ourselves as we move toward our goals. Devoting your energy toward your dream in a structured way helps bring your dream to fruition. I like to turn this time spent working toward a dream into a sacred ritual. The creative muse loves predictability—you show up for her regularly and she will show up for you. And all dreams are creative, no matter their nature. We are creating something that doesn't yet exist— whether it is a feeling, a thing, or a relationship.

Plan and schedule the action you will take toward your dream and infuse it with joy. If you want to host an elaborate dinner party, create a special Pinterest board and spend ten minutes every day looking for inspiration. Buy yourself a special candle that you only burn while planning your dinner party. If you want to start a meditation practice, commit to setting your alarm 15 minutes earlier three days a week. Set up a beautiful meditation corner with cushions and incense. If you want to write a book, block out an hour every Sunday to write. Buy yourself a special tea or seltzer that you drink only while writing.

Today, I invite you to create some structure around taking action toward the one dream you chose to work with this month. What will you do and when will you do it? How can you infuse the sacred into this time devoted to your dream?

september 7

Times I've Been...

As we move toward our dreams, it is natural to experience periods of fear and doubt. You may be trying to do something you've never done before. You might feel overwhelmed by the bigness of your dream. You may worry that you are unequipped for the task at hand. These worries are to be expected; they are part of the process of moving toward your dream. One of my favorite tools for navigating these moments of fear and doubt is to remind myself of positive and successful experiences I've had in the past.

What do you need to be reminded of right now? Grab your journal and make a list. Use one of the ideas here or create your own. Keep your list nearby for whenever you need a confidence boost. You've got this!

Times I've...

- *been brave*
- *taken a chance & it worked out*
- *manifested what I wanted*
- *learned something new*
- *persevered and done hard things*
- *made wise decisions*
- *shown strength, determination, or tenacity*

Boundaries

Boundaries are the distance at which I can love you and me simultaneously.
~ Prentis Hemphill

Boundaries are limits we set with ourselves and other people. They help us to protect our time and energy. Most of us have to learn to set boundaries because we have been socialized to ignore our own needs in order to please others. There is a lot of complexity inside of boundary work. If you'd like to explore more deeply, I highly recommend Randi Buckley's work.

A simple place to begin is to discern how you want to feel inside your life. This tends to shift over time, but a key feeling that I want to have inside my life is spaciousness. Once you've identified how you want to feel, you can use it as a guidepost when deciding what you are and aren't willing to do. How you want to feel can inform your boundaries. For example, I am unwilling to attend more than one social function in a day or answer work messages between the hours of 9pm and 8am because those things feel like the opposite of spaciousness to me. Some general boundaries I have that support a feeling of spaciousness inside my life are not taking responsibility for other people's feelings and honoring my capacity when it comes to holding space for my friends and family (even if that means I sometimes have to say no when they reach out for support).

Spend some time with your journal today. How do you want to feel inside your life? What boundaries can support you in feeling that way?

september 9

Sacred Adornment

Know, first, who you are, and then adorn yourself accordingly.
~ Epictetus

I believe adorning ourselves can be a practice in deeper self-understanding, self-acceptance, and self-love. Part of my personal path of awakening included falling back in love with getting dressed. I decided to own my truth, on the inside and on the outside. My beloved earrings and bracelets, flowing clothes, and bright red lips became an expression of who I am and what I love. Now when I get dressed and choose my jewelry and makeup it feels like a gentle affirmation to myself, "*Hey, I see you. I love you just the way you are. Go ahead and show the world.*"

Today, adorn yourself with something that feels true and good. Heavy eyeliner or a bare face, a braid or a mane of messy hair, yoga pants or dress pants, your favorite dress or nothing at all. Whatever your soul desires. Let yourself be seen inside your beautiful truth.

september 10

You Doing Your Inner Work Helps Change the World

We can never obtain peace in the outer world until we make peace with ourselves. ~ Dalai Lama

There is a lot of pain, suffering, and injustice in our world. It can feel overwhelming to think about how we as individuals can impact change. It can feel silly to focus on taking care of ourselves and doing our inner work when there are so many others suffering. I disagree with the notion that we should forgo self-care in service of working toward a more loving and just world. We can't show up to help others if we are depleted. I also believe that we are all connected and that one individual's healing positively impacts the collective experience.

I have learned that one of the most powerful things I can do for all the people I love, which on my best days includes all beings everywhere, is to practice self-care and do my inner work to heal and find peace within myself. Self-care and self-love are anything but trivial; I truly believe these practices will change the world. Doing your inner work does contribute to a more loving and just world. However, this is a space where awareness is vital. If you are a person with privilege, especially white privilege, practicing self-care and doing your inner work is not enough when it comes to creating a better world. Those of us with privilege need to put it to work and use our resources to help create change.

Practice self-care and do your inner work while also devoting time and energy toward dismantling the systems that create injustice in our world.

Protect and Cleanse Your Energy

Other people can impact our energy. This is true of both strangers and people we know. If you are highly sensitive or empathic you likely pick up on other people's energy wherever you go. This is one of the reasons I feel drained when I leave a place with a lot of people in it, such as the mall.

There are techniques we can use to both protect and cleanse our energy. To protect your energy and prevent yourself from picking up other people's, visualize yourself in bubble and imagine that nothing can permeate it. Sometimes I imagine my bubble as encrusted in crystals for an extra layer of protection. Another visual that helps me is imagining I am putting on a cloak when I am going into a situation where I don't want to pick up other people's energy. I allow everything to stick to the cloak and then I imagine taking it off when I am out of the situation and leaving everyone else's energy behind. My favorite way to cleanse my energy is to take a salty bath. I do this at least once a week. Other ways to cleanse your energy include spending time in nature, visualization and meditation around cutting energetic cords that connect you to others, smudging yourself or your space, and working with an energy healer.

Spend a few quiet minutes with yourself today. How is your energy? Do you feel like you pick up other people's energy? What strategies will you use from today's essay to help you protect and cleanse your energy?

september 12

Responding vs. Reacting

Between stimulus and response there is a space. In that space is our power to choose our response. In our response lies our growth and our freedom.
~ Viktor E. Frankl

Responding is a mindful choice. Reacting is knee-jerk behavior; it feels like there is no choice. We spend a lot of time reacting—being triggered without even realizing it, falling into default patterns. We don't pause, we (re)act mindlessly.

A mantra I use to help with this is, "Don't just do something, sit there." Pausing before reacting gives us the opportunity to take a few deep breaths and intentionally decide how we want to respond; it allows us the space to act in line with our values and priorities. Instead of sending the text or posting the status, write it in your journal and decide *if* and *how* you want to say what you want to say. Instead of lashing out in anger, take time to process your emotions so that you can express them in a healthy manner. Instead of automatically agreeing to a task or social event, say you need to think on it and give yourself space to determine what you really want.

Spend some time with your journal today. What is one of your default reactions? How can you invite more intention and mindfulness around it?

You Are Not an All-You-Can-Eat Buffet

You are not an all-you-can-eat buffet.

You do not exist for others to take whatever and however much they please,
They don't get to keep coming back for more,
Walking in and out of your life as they see fit.

You are not an all-you-can-eat buffet.

There are no magical servers behind the scenes, refilling you with what others crave.

When you serve up the physical, emotional, and energetic fuel from your center, you need time and space to replenish that goodness.

You are not an all-you-can-eat buffet.

You decide what is served,
You decide who you will nourish,
You decide when you are welcoming visitors into your heart space.

You are not an all-you-can-eat buffet.

The truth is, all-you-can-eat buffets are not good for anyone.

People may think they love the constant access and plethora of choices, but it is not healthy for anyone involved.

Boundaries are nourishing for the giver and the receiver.

You are not an all-you-can-eat buffet.
This is your invitation to stop acting like you are.

september 14

On Staying Committed During Challenging Times

Storms make trees take deeper roots.
~ Dolly Parton

I have been practicing yoga for almost half my life now. My yoga practice has had its ups and downs over the years. For me, practicing yoga usually involves all kinds of feelings—the joy of feeling alive and in my body, the frustration of a wandering mind, the peace of breath work, the irritation of discomfort in my body, and more—but the majority of the time I feel calm and centered after practicing no matter what I have experienced while on the mat.

However, there have been periods of time when things were different, when I felt just as distracted, cranky, or anxious when I got off the mat as when I got on. When this happens I don't blame myself or the teacher or even yoga itself for this stagnancy. Instead, I remind myself that the things we love just don't do it for us sometimes. We lose the positivity, the turn-on, the appeal for one reason or another. There could be a dozen different reasons why my yoga practice feels dull and lifeless at times. I probably will never know exactly why, and it doesn't really matter. *What matters is what I do with it.* The important thing is that I keep showing up because I am committed to my yoga practice as a vehicle for self-knowledge. I am in it for the long haul, and that means staying during the *blah* parts.

Everything that we love will disappoint us or lose its luster at some point. There have been times when my marriage, my kids, or my work didn't feel uplifting or inspiring. Times when it feels like I am giving so much and not getting anything in return. But I stay. I keep showing up. Because I understand that anything I am involved with long-term will have its ups and downs, that this is part of being committed to someone or something. And I am committed to my marriage, to my kids, to my work, and to my yoga practice. So I don't walk away. I have faith that things will shift.

It is easy to be committed to our people and our practices when things feel great and we are basking in the benefits of the relationship. The test of our commitment is what we do when things are challenging. Can you keep showing up for the people and practices you are committed to when things feel hard or boring?

Let Your Love for the World Be a Verb

The word "love" is most often defined as a noun, yet all the more astute theorists of love acknowledge that we would all love better if we used it as a verb.
~ bell hooks

In many spiritual communities there is a lot of talk about sending light and love. Emphasis is placed on intentions, visions, and the energy we put out into the world. I agree with and support these notions, *and* I also know that they are often used as a spiritual bypass—a way to avoid doing the hard work that needs to be done to bring down oppressive systems and structures.

Personally, I want to embody love, not only through my intentions, but also through my actions. I used to believe that lighting a candle or saying a prayer was enough work on my part when it came to healing the world. The truth is that due to my various privileges and resources, I have a lot of power inside of our current society. And I believe that with this power comes responsibility to take action toward creating a more loving and just world. I want to do more and do better. I want to put my love into action. So, I continue to meditate, pray, send love, and light candles, but now I also make phone calls, send emails, organize free yoga, donate money, read books, share information, and do whatever else I can to contribute to a more loving and just world.

How can you let your love for the world be a verb today?

From Frozen to Fierce

You never know how strong you are until
being strong is the only choice you have.
~ Bob Marley

I was shocked and saddened when Donald Trump won the United States presidential election. I was one of the many people whose bubble of white, liberal privilege burst that day. I couldn't find words and words are how I make sense of the world. I knew I couldn't stay silent, but I felt so defeated.

I felt like patriarchy won.
I felt like racism won.
I felt like white supremacy won.
I felt like homophobia won.
I felt like xenophobia won.
I felt like the abuser won, and when you are a survivor that feels extremely personal.

I felt numb and disconnected. I was struggling to engage socially. I felt scared to speak up and say how I felt. It took me a few days to realize I had been triggered into a traumatic response, that I had frozen. Many people think that when you encounter danger you go into fight or flight mode. They leave out the third possible response: freeze. Essentially, when we freeze, our nervous system registers that we are unlikely to survive if we try to fight back or run away, so we shut down.

So when a man who had bragged about sexually assaulting women was elected president of my country, I froze. Just like I froze when a man came into my bedroom and I lay still like nothing was happening. Just like I froze when my friend ran his hand a little too far up my leg and I said nothing. Just like I froze when I was a waitress and a random man literally grabbed my pussy as I delivered his beer and I just smiled and walked away, assuring a concerned customer that I was fine.

When you have experienced trauma, the freeze response is likely to be triggered even if it is unnecessary. My personal safety was not imminently in danger on November 9, 2015, but Donald Trump being elected to the highest office in this nation triggered my past traumas and left me feeling powerless.

Freezing was adaptive for me when I was a child. The truth is I am no longer small and helpless. I am a grown woman and I have resources—money, education, influence, *my voice*. So I decided not to stand by frozen in fear. Instead, I became fierce. I learned to be a warrior for love and justice. I educated myself. I started speaking up and out. I committed to amplifying the voices of marginalized people. I learned to fight for what I believe in with my wallet, my words, and my actions. I became the fierce warrior that I could not be when I was a little girl.

september 17

Lessons from Burnout

I had been actively working on self-care for years when I found myself inside of burnout. I thought I had self-care pretty well figured out, not to mention I had a business teaching women about it! My self-care plan included drinking lots of water, eating foods that feel good in my body, getting plenty of sleep and exercise, regularly scheduling alone time, writing in my journal, limiting social media and news, getting massages and pedicures, seeing an acupuncturist and a therapist, giving myself permission to say no, and working hard at self-compassion and self-forgiveness. There was one glitch though. I was still focused on serving others first. I allowed myself care only after taking care of others. No matter how exhausted or drained I felt, I would only rest once I had tended to everyone else.

It took experiencing burnout for me to shift this pattern. Burnout forced me to give myself space to heal; I had no choice but to prioritize my own well-being. I am grateful that I recognized I was in crisis and took measures to care for myself, but at the time I felt sad and a bit embarrassed that I had allowed myself to get to this level of distress. And, at the same time, I trust that I had to go through what I did in order to get to where I am now. My work after burnout was to understand what wasn't working so that I could make changes and create boundaries to prevent it from happening again.

Burnout taught me that I cannot push through when I need to rest, that I cannot push down what begs to be expressed, and that I cannot sacrifice my self-care to take care of others. It invited me to actively create a more sustainable version of my life by putting my needs at the top of the list. I was changed by the experience of burnout, and, as difficult as it was to navigate that period in my life, I am grateful for the lessons I learned.

september 18

Go into Your (Metaphorical) Cave

When I was in burnout I dreamed I was walking in my neighborhood and came upon a dying bison. She was weak and struggling to stand. As she fell down and got back up again, clearly fighting to survive, her eyes met mine. I woke up startled and struggling to breathe. I researched and learned that bison represent sacred power, survival, and walking in tune with the Great Mother. They are a symbol of the will to survive and the fortitude to overcome. I believe the bison came to me in my dream to remind me of how close I was teetering on the edge of survival. Not necessarily physically (though I was unwell often during this time period), but spiritually and emotionally. My inner strength was struggling to stand. The divine feminine within me was fighting to survive, falling and getting back up again, but clearly exhausted. This dream felt like a clear message to me: time to course correct.

Also, during this time period one sentence appeared in my journal writing repeatedly, *"I wish I could go into a cave for a while."*

Secluded.
Alone.
In the dark.
Nothing to do.
That is what I was craving.

Alone in the dark with nothing to do might sound depressing, but for a highly sensitive, empathic person like myself, it is rejuvenating. I adore people, and I am blessed to be surrounded by amazing family, friends, and clients. And still the truth is I only fill up emotionally and energetically when I am alone. I didn't really go into a cave after I had the dream about the bison, but I created as many changes in my life as I could to mimic the seclusion and quiet of being in a cave. I took as much off my plate as possible. I took a three-month sabbatical from work, limited my social calendar, and spent my days alone reading, writing, and being in nature. I emerged from my time in the cave as a different woman—a woman more fully grounded in herself, more connected with her intuition, and resolute in her commitment to care for herself.

How can you spend some time in your metaphorical cave? This could be as simple as a few minutes every day meditating or writing in your journal, or as elaborate as planning a solo retreat. Spend a few minutes today dreaming up ways to replenish your soul and commit to an action step toward what you are craving.

Connected to Spirit, Grounded in Soul

At one point along my path I realized I had this image in my mind of an idealized spiritual person who is disciplined, focused, and only puts time and energy into things that lift the world up, things like meditation and activism work. I began to believe that I shouldn't devote my attention to things like creating a beautiful home or revamping my wardrobe because they weren't spiritual pursuits. I observed that my spirituality had started to feel a whole lot like some kind of perfectionism. Specifically, some kind of masculine perfectionism that was instructing me to transcend the mundane and live immersed in the higher world. It felt like the feminine was missing from my spiritual path.

The masculine teaches that the fruits of our spiritual practice are something to work toward and achieve. The feminine says the divine is right here, right now. The masculine says *be consistent with your practices.* The feminine says *embody your life and everything becomes part of the practice.* The masculine says *show up and be steady.* The feminine says *you are a woman and you flow.* I realized I had been giving my spiritual life over to masculine ideals.

Some teachers differentiate between spirit and soul. Spirit is the masculine, "up there" divine energy, and soul is the feminine, "down here" divine knowing. Spirit is the ethereal stuff of heaven. Soul is the mundane stuff of earth. Traditionally, spirit has been prized over soul. The feminine has been wiped from most religions and even many spiritual traditions. When all of this clicked in my head and heart, I grieved once again for the ways I had denied my femininity. It hurt to realize that even in this most important and personal place of connecting with the divine, I had abandoned her.

I believe there is room inside our spiritual practices for both masculine and feminine energies. They each contribute in their own way to the path. I decided that I would aim to live my life connected to spirit and grounded in my soul.

Praying to spirit, listening to my soul.

Consistently showing up for my practices, being open to whatever arises, and releasing the expectation of consistency in myself.

Having faith and trust in something more outside myself, receiving guidance from within, and trusting my intuition.

The stillness and calm that are always available, allowing myself to feel everything.

Structure, nature.
Rooted, flowing.
Divine masculine, divine feminine.
Consistency, change.
Out there, in here.
Learning, knowing.
Spirit, soul.

Write Your Future Self a Letter

The privilege of a lifetime is being who you are.
~ Joseph Campbell

Today I am sharing one of my favorite practices. Writing a letter to your future self is a simple action that creates powerful results. By writing ourselves a letter describing what our future looks and feels like, we set ourselves on the path of turning our hopes and dreams into reality. I have experienced this many times myself and with the women I work with at retreats and workshops. I don't know exactly how it works. I just know that it does.

The faith-trust-pixie-dust part of me believes that getting clear on what we want and how we want to feel pulls it toward us, calling it into reality. The empirical-research-science part of me thinks that getting clear on what we want and how we want to feel makes us more likely to act in line with those goals, thus bringing them into reality. Magic or science? *I choose both.*

I usually forget what I write in my letter almost as soon as I seal it in the envelope. But I do remember the feelings I had as I wrote it. Sometimes I feel calmer and clearer just by writing the letter. This practice also reminds me that whatever is happening in my life at the moment is temporary and that things will change over time. When I am going through something hard it can be easy to forget that the hard thing won't last forever.

Today, I invite you to write your future self a letter. Take some time to get grounded into your most wise self (a few conscious deep breaths usually help me connect with her), and let the words flow. From yourself to yourself, a story of what's to come. Then seal your letter up, write a future date on the envelope (I usually work with 3-12 months), and stick it in your journal for safekeeping. Let magic and science get to work on your behalf.

september 21

Finding Ease in the Transitions

Breathing deeply, I softly invite my yoga students, who are seated with hands covering eyes, to open their eyes into the warmth and the darkness of their palms. In that moment, I feel the gentleness of the transition from final relaxation—the slow, mindful shift from yoga practice into daily life.

My transitions in life don't usually go as peacefully as my transitions in yoga. Often they are more choppy and sloppy than slow and mindful. One of the greatest gifts of my yoga practice is learning to bring the lessons of yoga off the mat and into my life.

If I was there with you today, I would take you gently by the hand and we'd find a spot to sit. The comfiest couch or even a blanket under the sun. I'd tell you you're amazing and help you remember that you're loved; I'd remind you that you deserve to gently ease into this season. I'd ask you what that would look like for you. We would probably make a list because that is how I roll. Together we would remember that it doesn't have to be hard and hurried, that we can invite in ease and calm.

Spend some time with your journal today. What would feel gentle, slow, and mindful as you prepare to transition into the upcoming season? Can you leave some blank space in your schedule for naps, walks, or whatever else you happen to need on any given day?

september 22

Make a Seasonal Bucket List

To the attentive eye, each moment of the year has its own beauty, and in the same fields, it beholds, every hour, a picture which was never seen before, and which shall never be seen again.
~ Ralph Waldo Emerson

One of the ways I like to honor the changing seasons is to make a bucket list of things I'd like to experience for winter, spring, summer, and fall. I list seasonal foods to enjoy, places to visit, and activities to do. I create the list with my husband and daughters, and we post it on our fridge as a reminder of the fun things we want to do. This practice helps me pause and notice the change in seasons, and it encourages my family to prioritize how we want to spend our free time.

Make a seasonal bucket list. You can make your list for the year all at once or pause at the start of each season to write it down. Consider inviting your family and friends to join you in this practice.

How to Do the Thing You Think You Cannot Do

We can do hard things, even things we never thought we could do.

Here is some advice on how to do the thing you think you cannot do:

First, make a list of all the times you've done things you never thought you could do. Remind yourself that you are a brave badass. Because you are.

Second, take exquisite care of your body. You might think drinking wine, eating ice cream, and watching Netflix will make it easier to do the hard thing, but trust me, I speak from experience when I say, those things won't help you in the long run. Drink water, eat your veggies, go outside, sweat, stretch, get enough sleep.

Next, enlist the power of your mind. There are (at least) three parts here.

(1) *What is the story you are telling yourself about this hard thing? Is it true? Can you know for sure? Is it helpful? Write a new story.* It is important to literally write it down. Read it in the morning and before you go to bed. This helps to reprogram your mind around the hard thing.

(2) *Watch how you talk about the hard thing to other people.* Words are powerful. Speak the new story out loud, over and over.

(3) *Consciously choose your thoughts about yourself, others, and the world in relation to the hard thing.* Create a mantra or affirmation to support you

before and during the hard thing. Write it on a sticky note or program it into your phone as a reminder and repeat it often.

Then, call on the power of Spirit. Pray. Meditate. Visualize. Ask for a blessing. Get quiet and listen intently to what comes through. Imagine yourself doing the hard thing and everything going swimmingly.

Finally, just do the hard thing. We often build things up in our minds, which can keep us stuck. Dig deep, find the courage, and just do it. I promise that you will feel better on the other side of doing the hard thing.

september 24

Therapy Is Not Just for When You Are in Crisis

I have been in and out of therapy since I was 18 years old. Although it was a crisis that originally brought me to therapy, since that time I have returned for a variety of reasons. Sometimes I've gone because my struggles and patterns were glaringly illuminated and I wanted to heal them. Other times I've gone simply because I wanted the specific kind of support therapy offers.

I wish more people understood that you don't have to be in crisis to seek the help of a therapist. Structured time and space for reflecting on your thoughts and feelings with a qualified professional is powerful at any stage of your life. Therapy is the tool that has most changed my life, and I highly recommend it. If you've hesitated to reach out to a therapist, ask yourself why. In our current culture there is a lot of stigma around seeking help for our mental and emotional health. Sometimes we have internalized that stigma, which interferes with us reaching out for support. Set aside any judgments you may have around therapy and consider if it might be helpful for you.

september 25

Dreaming vs. Doing

If you contemplate air without breathing, you will die.
~ Unknown

I love to dream. I make lists of all the things I want to create and vision pages about how I want to feel. I thrive inside of thinking, pondering, and imagining. Sometimes I hang out in the dreaming stage too long. The truth is we have to take action in order to make our dreams a reality. All dreaming and no doing doesn't get us very far.

What are you doing to move toward what you want? I think small, daily actions are the most powerful tool for making our dreams a reality. Today, make a list of at least ten steps toward the life you've been dreaming of. Commit to doing something on the list this week.

Reframing Triggers

Life has created certain challenges for you. But the purpose hasn't been to imprison you. The purpose has been to set you free, to provide you with lessons, experiences, circumstances that would trigger growth and healing. Life has been provoking, promoting, urging you to grow, stretch, learn, heal. Life has been trying to break you out of your prison.
~ Melody Beattie

I used to spend a lot of time and energy trying to avoid triggering people. I worked to craft comfortable environments and experiences for my family, friends, and clients. At a certain point, I started to wonder if I was being helpful or harmful. I considered that trying not to trigger people may just be another form of attempting to control their experiences. I started to understand triggers not as something terrible to be avoided at all costs, but as part of the path of growth and evolution. I began practicing trusting people to manage their own emotions and have their own journey so that I could release the urge to try to create some ideal environment where no one would be bothered.

An example of how I did this comes from teaching yoga. When I first started teaching yoga I would freak out if there were any outside noises during class. I'd hear noise from the apartment above the studio and my heart would start racing. *There are people here trying to relax!* Now that I've released trying to control everything so people will be comfortable, when I hear noise from the apartment above us or a fire truck comes racing by with sirens blasting, I pause and tell the class how thankful I am for the distractions because it helps us practice returning to our breath and bodies no matter what is going on around us. The outside noises help us translate the mindfulness we are curating on the mat out into our daily lives, where there are always plenty of distractions from the present moment. The trigger is part of our growth.

Spend some time with your journal today. Do you try to control other people's experiences? Can you reframe triggers as part of the path of growth and evolution? Can you trust the people around you enough to allow them to have their own journey?

september 27

Your Needs Matter

I once set down my mat in yoga class, and then someone came and put their mat touching mine. I shifted over a bit. Class started, and I realized there was a ripple in the flooring under my right hand that was uncomfortable and distracting. For the first few minutes of class I told myself to just deal with it, that it wasn't such a big deal. *How many times a day do we say this to ourselves?* My mind was convinced that if I got up and moved my mat it would distract the teacher and the other students. My default response was to suffer through and not bother anyone else. It took a solid five minutes before I convinced myself to just get up and move. *Before I remembered that I deserve to take care of myself, that my needs matter too.*

This is a simple, almost silly, example, but it illustrates the work it takes to flip our default setting from, *"Shhhh, don't bother anyone with your needs"* to, *"My needs matter and I deserve to take care of them."* Like how it took me nearly a year of regular appointments to ring the bell and ask the acupuncturist to turn the heat up when I was cold. Like how when I have to pee twenty minutes after I just used the bathroom and I hesitate to get up and go again. Like how I struggle to accept that I need so much time to sleep, take baths, and eat chocolate during my premenstrual week. Taking care of these simple needs is powerful because these minor, daily actions help me to create a new default. They shift my mindset and affirm my worthiness so that when it comes to the big stuff—boundaries, following my dreams, and asking for help—I have a beautiful reservoir to tap into that reminds me I deserve to take care of my needs.

Spend some time with your journal today. Do you know that your needs matter? List some times that you took care of your needs, big or small, and some times that you didn't. Notice how you feel as you look over the two lists. Look for ways to meet your needs today, whether it is something simple like moving your yoga mat or something more complex like asserting yourself with a co-worker. Remember that every action adds to the reservoir and helps create a new default of knowing your needs matter.

september 28

What You Say and Do Matters

I remember a particularly difficult week when my oldest daughter, Megan, was a teenager. I had worked six consecutive days in the office, wasn't feeling well, and was preparing to go out of town for a retreat. My youngest daughter, Lainey, was sick, and Megan was feeling really stressed about her SATs. I was trying to help her understand that even though the test feels so important, it doesn't actually mean that much in the grand scheme of life. I felt like I was failing everyone that week, especially Megan. I had tried not to pass on my perfectionism to her, and yet somehow it felt like I had as she was crying in frustration and screaming awful things at me. I did my best to just keep breathing and give her space while also loving her and letting her know I was there for her.

That week I did my usual self-care practices right alongside all my work and home stuff. I got a massage, went to acupuncture, took my herbs, showed up at yoga class, drank my tea, and wrote in my journal. I worried that none of it mattered, that even though I was trying so hard to model self-care and self-love, the only thing that Megan noticed was the weeks when I worked six consecutive days.

And then she posted on social media that I'm her best friend; that she saw a heart within a broken wall and it reminded her of me; that I taught her to see love in everything; and that she knew it would be okay even though it was a hard week. I realized that what I say and do *does* matter, that she was paying attention to the whole picture.

I know sometimes it feels like you are talking to a wall,
I know some days it seems like no one recognizes your effort or example.

They are listening and noticing, I promise.
What you say and do matters, I swear.

Please don't give up.

Just Show Up

Writing is like breathing, it's possible to learn to do it well,
but the point is to do it no matter what.
~ Julia Cameron

Sometimes we prevent ourselves from pursuing our dreams by putting conditions around what we want. When I am feeling this type of resistance, I use this mantra: *just show up*. It helps me let go of expectations and simply *put my ass where my heart wants to be,* as author Steven Pressfield says.

If you want to run, lace up your sneakers.
If you want to meditate, sit on your cushion.
If you want to practice yoga, unroll your mat.
If you want to write, come to the page.
If you want to paint, go to the canvas.

You don't need to be a certain way.
It doesn't have to be a perfect day.
The house doesn't have to be clean.
Your to-do list doesn't have to be empty.

Just show up for yourself and your dreams.
Come as you are and let go of any ideas about the outcome.
This is the practice. This is how we bring our dreams to life.

september 30

Put a Container Around Your Work

Before technological advances like email and smartphones, you went to work and then came home. The boundaries between work and home were more concrete. In our modern world, it is easy to work during our time at home. Some employers even *expect* that we will be available by phone or email during off-work hours. It is easy to allow work to invade your personal time. This lack of a container around work time is not sustainable or healthy. This applies to people who don't work outside the home as well. It's easy to spend all of our time doing chores. Part of self-care is having a container around work time.

If you work outside the home, set a boundary around when you are willing to spend time on work projects and answer work-related phone calls, text messages, and emails. For example, you might say that you won't do anything work-related after 7pm on weekdays or that Sundays are a completely work-free day. If you don't work outside the home, set a boundary around when you will stop doing household and parenting-related tasks. For example, you might decide that you won't do any chores past 8pm or that your kids have to amuse themselves until 7am (if that is an age-appropriate expectation). There may be times when you make exceptions to your boundaries, such as if you are working on a project with a tight deadline or one of your kids is sick. This is okay; we just want to make sure it's not our normal operating mode to be always working.

Spend some time with your journal today. What boundaries do you have in place for your work inside and outside of the home? How can you put a container around your work time?

Plan a Vacation

Oh, the Places You'll Go!
~ Dr. Seuss

Plan a vacation and take some time to get away from daily life, even if it's only for a night.

For renewed inspiration.
For relaxation, deeper than the kind we can get on our days off at home.
For new places and novel experiences.
For reignited creativity.
For self-love and self-care.
For restoration.
For a fresh perspective.
For fun and for play.
For creating memories.
For remembering you are more than just the sum of your work.
For just not thinking about anything for a bit.
For coming home reinvigorated and full of beautiful ideas.

october 2

Fear and Resistance Are Part of The Process

Sometimes we feel afraid when we get what we want. Honestly, this *usually* happens to me. I hope and pray for something, I work hard to make it come to fruition, and then I freak out when it does. My body will be buzzing with the pulse of, *"Yes, this is it!"* and *"Oh my god, it's all happening!"* and then it starts. The voice of fear and resistance, *"What the hell am I doing? Who do I think I am? I can't do this."* Often my body and brain try to pull me back into a space that feels safer by sabotaging my progress, *"Who cares that it makes me feel sick and tired, I want some chocolate cake! Shopping, I should go shopping. I'll just take a nap and ignore the work that needs to be done today."* I've learned to recognize this response in myself and to simply call it what it is: fear. I am afraid that I don't deserve to be happy and successful and that whatever I'm experiencing is too good to be true. I worry that I can't pull it off or that my buzzing-with-happiness, magical self will make other people uncomfortable.

On my best days, I am able to not eat the cake or go shopping or freak out or quit. Sometimes it takes me a few days of those behaviors to recognize what is happening. Ultimately, I have learned that fear and resistance are simply part of my process of change and growth. As I evolve there is a part of me who is afraid. She wants to keep me small or dull me down so that I will be safe. She is a frightened little girl. I don't try to push this part of myself away. I reassure her that it is safe for me to be happy and successful. I witness her with gentle compassion and send love to her, but I do not let her run the show. Instead, I move alongside the fear and resistance as I keep taking steps toward my dreams.

october 3

What Are You Doing With Your Life?

I thought I had to surrender my questions, doubts, and intuitions of darkness in order to believe again. Increasingly, I learned that the great spirits of religious traditions do not solve all questions but live in the questions, and return to them again and again, not as a circle returns, but as an ascending spiral comes to the same place, each time at a higher level.
~ Rabbi David Wolpe

Life is complicated, and it's easy to feel confused on the path of personal and spiritual growth. There aren't any answers. There isn't even a destination. There is only the process and learning to flow with it.

Spend some time with your journal today and check in with yourself:

What are you doing with your life?
Is ego or spirit leading the way?
Are you living with intention or just going through the motions?
Are you devoting your time and energy to your priorities?
Do you feel present and connected inside of your life?

Approach Your Fears

Do the thing. Don't die. Repeat.
~ Rebekah Borucki

Some of our fears are logical and help us stay safe. However, we also have irrational fears that don't serve us, such as being afraid to try new things, speak up, or take a risk. These fears grow stronger when we avoid the things we are afraid of. I think it is important for us to have the experience of approaching our fears so we see that we can cope with challenging situations. Also, many times we will learn that the thing we were afraid of wasn't actually that scary after all. If we regularly practice approaching our fears, we will eventually feel less afraid. We may even become comfortable with things that used to terrify us. I have had this experience with resting in Savasana and public speaking, both of which I now enjoy, even though they used to give me severe anxiety.

Spend some time with your journal today. What fears are not serving you? Is there an area in your life where you are afraid to speak up or pursue what you want? Is there an activity or hobby you would like to try but you've been nervous about getting started? What are you imagining it would be like to approach your fears? Are you willing to be brave and experiment with taking a step toward the fear? What possibility lies beyond your fears?

october 5

Just Because You Start Something Does Not Mean You Have to Finish It

Time is a precious resource, and part of self-care is being mindful of what we give our attention and energy to. Just because you start something does not mean you have to finish it. You are allowed to change your mind at any time. Practice honoring your preferences with the little things (like setting down a half-read book that you're not enjoying or turning off a movie that you don't like) so that you can honor your needs with the bigger things (like excusing yourself from a party or ending a date early).

october 6

Now is the Right Time for Joy

Don't wait for everything to be perfect before you decide to enjoy your life.
~ Joyce Meyer

So often in life we wait for ideal conditions before pursuing our joy. I didn't do one of my favorite self-care rituals, taking a bath, for years because I wished I had a deeper tub. As you might've guessed, soaking in my good enough tub felt amazing once I got over myself and just started taking baths. We postpone joy because we are waiting for ideal conditions with small things (like meeting up with friends or having sex), as well as bigger things (like starting a family or taking a trip).

Let's release the idea of a right time for joy.
Listen to the longings of your heart; don't ask them to wait.
Now is the right time.

october 7

Begin Again

Tell me your secrets and ask me your questions. Oh, let's go back to the start.
~ Coldplay

I was having a particularly hard night. Sadness weighed heavy on my heart, and I was disappointed in myself for the disconnected and irritable way I'd been showing up inside my life. I'd just spent time with a friend in an attempt to stop isolating myself, and I was still feeling lonely. Driving home, I caught a glimpse of a sliver of moon illuminated against the navy sky and it brought me hope. On the radio, Chris Martin was singing about going back to the start. I gazed into my rearview mirror and saw a couple kissing at a red light. I remembered love is the only way. I gently invited myself to begin again.

We will have many hard days inside of this thing called life. We will mess up and act in ways we're not proud of. We will hurt people and be hurt by people. Our hearts will ache. We can't go back and change the past, but the beautiful thing about life is that we can always choose to begin again.

I Define My Pace

Nature does not hurry, yet everything is accomplished. -Lao Tzu

This is a poem about choosing to slow down inside of a fast-paced world. Today, I want you to know that you don't have to run along with everyone else, you can define your own pace.

Glorification of busy,
Guilt when it feels too comfortable,
Choosing to embrace ease,
I define my pace.

Limbs moving,
Music pumping,
Sinking into Child's Pose,
I define my pace.

Sickness lingering,
Fear of disappointing,
Staying in bed,
I define my pace.

Mind racing,
To-do list growing,
Making soup and sipping tea,
I define my pace.

Declarations made,
Imagining eyes watching,
Taking one step at a time,
I define my pace.

Technology failing,
Tears falling,
Taking a break,
I define my pace.

Time flying,
Brain rushing,
Body slowing,
I define my pace.

october 9

The Sweet Spot Between Stagnating and Striving

I have been a seeker and still I am, but I stopped asking the books and the stars.
I started listening to the teaching of my Soul.
~ Rumi

When it comes to personal growth and change, I have a habit of going from one extreme to the other. I find myself either hanging out in the comfort zone for too long or overdoing it and pushing into overwhelm. I have been on a lifelong journey to find the sweet spot between stagnating and striving. For me, this in-between place is a combination of the inspiration, creation, and excitement that feels like it's missing when I'm stagnating, along with the rest, ease, and breath that feels like it's missing when I'm striving.

I've found a few things that help me stay in the sweet spot. Closing my eyes, taking a few deep breaths, and connecting with my inner self guides me toward my next steps. Spending time with my journal helps me with clarity, perspective, and focus. Slowing down supports me in maintaining my breath so that I can move toward my goals in a mindful way. Staying connected with my priorities helps me ensure that I don't trade how I want to feel for what I want to create. I also find it helpful to remind myself that I can do everything I want to do, just not all at once.

The space does exist where you can feel the way you want to feel while working toward your goals. Spend some time with your journal today. Do you tend toward stagnating or striving? What can help you stay in the sweet spot between the two?

october 10

Over and Over and Over

In my world there are some sure signs that shit has gone awry. I start keeping score in my relationship with my husband, tallying up how many hours we've each spent handling childcare and household tasks. I crave sugar and eat foods that leave me feeling nauseous and tired. I fall asleep in front of the TV instead of snuggled in my bed. I ignore my friends and spend too many hours working. I hear myself saying yes when I mean no.

In yoga, ahimsa (nonviolence) is the highest ideal. Negative and judgmental thoughts, overindulgence, eating foods that don't nourish me, engaging in draining behaviors, overworking, not protecting my boundaries—these are tiny acts of violence against myself. Like anyone, I fall into these old habits sometimes due to stress. Part of my personal path is learning to act, think, and speak in integrity with my highest self no matter what is going on around me and within me. I want to live from my center even amidst the storms of daily life. When I find myself falling into old destructive habits, I simply invite myself to start over.

I begin with forgiveness. *I forgive myself for choosing out of alignment with my highest self, for these tiny acts of violence against myself.*

I release the past, whether it was a moment or a month. *With a deep breath I blow my past self a kiss and let go of any lingering self-judgment.*

I choose self-love and self-care. *I choose actions and thoughts that support myself. I schedule time for a walk in the woods, a yoga class, or a salty bath to help me recalibrate. I whisper kind words to myself as I gaze into the mirror.*

I begin again, as many times as I need to—sometimes ten times or more before noon.

Forgive, breathe, release, self-love and self-care.
Over and over and over.
Forgive, breathe, release, self-love and self-care.
There is nothing to achieve.

Instead, I practice.
Slip up.
Start again.
All from a place of nonviolence, love, and compassion.

Change Comes in Many Forms

In 2008, I took a look at my life, saw a series of neatly checked off boxes—house, husband, healthy child, "good" job, retirement account, health insurance—and thought, *"Why am I not happy?"* A year later, I had reinvented my life. It was a period of dramatic change. It was intense, exciting, and scary all at once. Ultimately, I quit my job in order to pursue my dream of opening a wellness center.

Five years later I started to have the same feelings of discontent. This time around I had created my own boxes—another child, successful private practice as a therapist, yoga studio, wellness center—but the feeling was the same. I was grateful, but I had fallen out of love with my life. Reinvention had pulled me out of my funk all those years ago, so I thought that was what I needed again. I filled my vision books with words about reinvention and change, and I waited for the reinvention to arrive. It never came. The truth is, I didn't need a reinvention. It wasn't 2008. I wasn't living my life by someone else's standards. I wasn't disconnected from my truth. Looking for my next thing didn't bring me happiness. It brought me confusion, anger at my confusion, fear, and sadness. The word "reinvention" stared up at me, implying I needed to become something new, and it started to really piss me off.

Slowly I began to realize that everything I wanted was right in front of me and my heart was simply calling for some subtle adjustments. I had thought that feeling stuck and sad meant I didn't like my life. But you can be inside of a life you love and feel sad and stuck sometimes. I realized I was not interested in creating a dramatically different version of my life, and I threw all of my reinvention clippings in the garbage. The changes that occurred at that time in my life were quiet and mostly internal. They were powerful in a gentle way. There was no drama, no earth-shattering moment. Sometimes that is how change happens.

october 12

Let Your Life Be Your Prayer for the World

I aim to live my life as my prayer for the world. My deepest prayer for the world is "May there be peace, love, and justice for all." Here are some of the actions I take in support of that prayer:

Educating myself on social justice topics.
Speaking to my children with kindness.
Donating money to causes I care about.
Lifting up the voices of marginalized people.
Meditating on peace.
Honoring my limits.
Lighting a candle and saying a prayer.
Volunteering my time.
Going to therapy and learning to break unhealthy patterns.
Making altars.
Counting my blessings.
Looking people in the eye.
Helping people in need.

Let your life be your prayer for the world. What is your prayer for the world? How can you live your life in alignment with your values?

An Untamed Woman

You were once wild here—don't let them tame you! ~ Isadora Duncan

An Untamed Woman is connected to her truth and lives from her center.

An Untamed Woman embraces all the beautiful, messy parts of herself.

An Untamed Woman understands there are gifts to be mined from the shadow parts of her soul.

An Untamed Woman flows with and honors nature's cycles.

An Untamed Woman understands there is a time for growth and a time for rest.

An Untamed Woman knows who she is and does not apologize for it.

An Untamed Woman loves her belly and honors it as her power center.

An Untamed Woman dances with her edges while holding her boundaries.

An Untamed Woman is guided by desire, open to possibility.

An Untamed Woman is brave, badass, wild, and powerful.

Spend some time with your journal today.
What would it mean for you to untame yourself?

october 14

Single-task

Warning: this might be your least favorite essay in this book.

We love to think that we are amazing multitaskers. The truth is there is no such thing as multitasking. Our brains cannot do more than one thing at a time. When we think we are multitasking we are actually doing what is called task-switching, which is just what it sounds like: switching from one task to another. Research shows that task-switching is bad for our brains. It makes us less efficient, and there is some evidence that it may actually change the structure of our brains. One recent study found that high multitaskers had less brain density in the anterior cingulate cortex, a region responsible for empathy as well as cognitive and emotional control.

Today, I invite you to single-task.
Do one thing at a time.

When you are eating, eat. Don't scroll on your phone or watch TV or write emails. Just eat. When you are talking to your kid or your partner or your friend, stop everything else and really be present with the person in front of you. When you're walking the dog, just walk the dog. When you're washing the dishes, just wash the dishes. When you're cooking dinner, just cook dinner. You get the idea. Do one thing at a time and give it your full attention. Give it a try today. It may be uncomfortable at first; I know it was for me. With practice you will come to enjoy single-tasking. And your brain will thank you!

october 15

You Are Allowed to Choose Yourself

You are allowed to choose yourself.
You are allowed to do what is best for you.
You are allowed to prioritize your needs.
You are allowed to pick what feels right to you.

Where did you learn otherwise?
Who benefits from your believing that what you need and want isn't a priority?

Women are conditioned to put themselves last, to choose the needs and wants of others above their own. Women provide the bulk of unpaid labor in our society and do the majority of caregiving and household tasks, even when they work outside of the home. Women also put in tons of emotional labor and take on most of the mental load in our culture. Emotional labor, as defined by author Gemma Hartley, is "the unpaid, invisible work we do to keep those around us comfortable and happy." The mental load is the planning, scheduling, negotiating, and problem-solving work required to manage daily life. Considering all the physical energy, emotional labor, and mental work we put into our careers and relationships, it is understandable that we often make decisions based on what we think will keep the peace or make others happy. The truth is you are allowed to choose yourself, and if other people are disappointed or hurt by that, you don't have to manage their feelings. You are only responsible for your own emotional wellbeing.

You are allowed to choose yourself. Start today. Find a small way to honor what you want and need.

Knowing vs. Embodying

One of the biggest things I have learned on my own journey is that it is one thing to know something and another to embody that knowing. I spent years relating to self-care from a place of cognitive understanding—thinking, writing, reading, and teaching. I understood and believed in the practices of self-care but had not integrated them into my body. A good example of this disconnect is the story I told on January 12 about going to yoga because it was scheduled in my calendar even though I was exhausted and really needed to rest.

For me, *knowing* is our knowledge and beliefs about something; *embodying* is about moving that knowledge down into the body. One is about the head and the other is about the heart. One feels prescriptive and the other feels intuitive. I believe knowing and embodying are both integral pieces of our self-care practice. I know from my own experience, and that of the women I work with, that we sometimes stop at the point of knowledge and don't fully integrate our beliefs into our bodies. A few ways to move from knowing into embodying are checking in with your body throughout the day, noticing how she feels when you are making a decision, and practicing letting your body, rather than your mind, guide your choices.

Spend some time with your journal today. Are you approaching your self-care practice from a place of knowing, embodying, or both? Are there any shifts you'd like to make to move your practice more into your body?

Self-Care at Work

It is important to carry our self-care practices into our work environment. Most of us spend a good portion of our day working. How we integrate self-care into our work hours will vary based on several factors, such as our profession, our environment, and how much freedom and flexibility we have. Here are a few general ideas that you can use as a framework to build your own plan for self-care at work.

1. *Honor your boundaries and set limits.* It is vital that we have boundaries around the time we spend working. In our current world, it is rare for work to end when we clock out. Most people attend to work-related tasks, emails, or text messages during their "off-hours." Create limits around the hours you work at home or when you will answer work-related calls or messages. This is important to do if you work for yourself as well. As an entrepreneur, it is easy to always be working. Consider designating work hours for yourself. Think about limits within your job as well. For example, as a therapist, I have learned my personal limits around how many clients I can see in a row without a break (three) and how many clients it feels good to work with in a day (six is my max).

2. *Take time for self-care every day.* Set aside a few minutes for self-care before you begin your work for the day. Spend the time doing whatever feels nourishing for you. For me, this is my morning journal writing time. In the past I have exercised before

work, spent time reading an inspirational book, or meditated. I know other people who enjoy a contemplative cup of coffee or a walk outside. Make this self-care time non-negotiable in order to reinforce to yourself that your well-being is a priority.

3. *Listen to your body.* Learn to tune into your body and what it needs. Many of us live from the neck up, especially at work. Part of self-care is listening to your body and honoring its needs as they arise. This includes everything from pausing to eat when you are hungry to taking a bathroom break as needed. In some occupations, such as teaching, it is particularly challenging to honor your body in this way. Do the best you can within the reality of your job, even if it means you have to wait until after work to take care of your need for a nap or a walk.

4. *Be aware of your beliefs.* What do you tell yourself about self-care and work? When I had a job working for someone else, I believed that my needs were not important. I thought that taking care of myself and setting boundaries meant I wasn't as good as my colleagues. I was able to shift my mindset while still working in this position, and when I started practicing self-care at work, I found that not only was I was happier, but I also accomplished just as much in a shorter amount of time. By taking good care of myself, setting limits, and taking breaks, I became more efficient at my job.

5. *Honor your strengths and preferences.* Do the things that you are good at and enjoy and let go of the rest. I know—it's a beautiful idea but challenging to implement fully. Do what you can within your particular situation. For me, this looks like delegating tasks,

hiring help for certain aspects of my businesses, and referring out non-ideal clients.

6. *Take time off.* Americans are notorious for not using our vacation days. Schedule time off regularly. Personally, I have a non-negotiable lunch break every day and I don't work during that time. I also take Fridays off from work every week, and I schedule time off every quarter, even if I don't travel. How can you build some time off into your week, month, or year?

Spend some time with your journal today. Create a self-care plan for work. Include simple, small things like one minute of breathing a few times a day, as well as more involved plans like a summer vacation. Self-care is good for you and good for your work.

october 18

Look for the Opportunity to be Kind

The single act of kindness throws out a root in all directions,
and the roots spring up and make fresh trees...
~ Frederick William Faber

Look for the opportunity to be kind today.

Who can you help?
How can you spread some love in the world?

A few ideas: buy coffee for the person behind you in the drive-thru line, smile and make eye contact with a stranger, give out five compliments, bake something and bring it to a neighbor, send a friend a text message telling her why you love her, surprise someone with flowers, bring in your neighbor's garbage can, offer to watch a family member's kids, leave a sticky note with a positive thought on the mirror in a public bathroom, or pause and tell the manager about a positive experience you've had in a store or restaurant.

october 19

Schedule It In

I use a planner, The Planner Pad, that has space for six different to-do lists each week. I love it because it allows me to divide up my tasks for home and my four businesses. I use the other column for my self-care. When I make my weekly to-do lists on Sundays, I start with a self-care list. I schedule self-care into my week the same way I schedule my other priorities. This helps me keep my self-care activities at the top of my mind and encourages me to follow through on my promises to myself. Today's invitation is to schedule in your self-care the same way you would a doctor's appointment. Maybe even charge yourself a cancelation fee if you don't show up? I'm joking, but it's not a bad idea.

Spend some time with your calendar. What are the most important pieces of your self-care? Journal writing, reading, salty baths, exercise, time in nature, meditation, seeing friends? Schedule at least one self-care activity into your calendar for the week. Consider doing this every week.

Keeping Track is Whack

I created the mantra "keeping track is whack" for myself because I have a habit of keeping track in my relationships. I'll add up how many hours my husband spent taking care of our daughter and compare it to how many hours I spent doing the same. I'll remind myself that I texted my friend first the last three weeks or that I have asked someone to make plans more times than they've asked me. I feel a pit in my stomach just typing out those behaviors. They are not in line with who I want to be in this world. Keeping track feels petty and immature to me. It doesn't lead to anything useful; usually I just stew in my own self-righteous anger. The truth is, a lot of factors impact who handles child care tasks, texts the other person first, or asks to make plans. When I keep track in my relationships, what I am really doing is looking for evidence to support the story that I do more than the other person and therefore I am not valued in the relationship. The keeping track is really about me wanting to feel loved and appreciated, which is a very human need that I can have met in other healthy ways.

Keeping track builds resentment and creates icky energy inside our relationships. If you have a tendency to keep track like I do, feel free to borrow my mantra. Also, explore the story behind keeping track and what need it might be pointing toward. Find healthy ways to get your needs met so that you can release behaviors that don't feel aligned with who you want to be in the world.

october 21

What Are You Waiting For?

I'll take up yoga when the kids start school.
I'll call for the appointment once things settle down.
I'll speak up after the holidays.

So often in life we put off the things that are important to us, whether it is exploring an interest, taking care of our health, or advocating for our needs. We find excuses and wait to take action. In some ways it's understandable. Life is busy and we all have so much on our plates. The truth is there will always be something pulling our attention away from what we want and need. It is simply the nature of life. We get to choose—keep waiting or decide to pursue our wants and needs now, right alongside the busy-ness of daily life.

Spend some time with your journal today. What have you been putting off because you are waiting for ideal circumstances? How can you take action today?

october 22

One Foot in Front of the Other

As a highly sensitive person who also has a proclivity toward anxiety, my nervous system sometimes falls into disarray. I might wake up in the middle of the night inside of anxiety, with my heart racing and my mind spinning. On the really hard days, I can feel my body buzzing with anxiety and my mind moves so quickly that it is hard to think straight. When this happens (and I am able to notice that it's happening), I pause and repeat one of my favorite mantras—"just do the next right thing." That might mean taking a shower, eating a meal, going to work, meditating, or unloading the dishwasher. Whatever the next right thing is, I do it by putting one foot in front of the other.

If my mind is really all over the place and I can't rein it in, I'll schedule my day out 30 minutes at a time. When I am in that kind of headspace, it helps me to break things down to the smallest possible (achievable) steps. Also, every time I feel overwhelmed (which can be every hour), I stop and drink a glass of water or take a few deep breaths. I try to repeat encouraging words to myself too: *It'll be okay. This is temporary. Tonight, today will be over and I'll unwind in the bathtub or in bed watching TV.*

It is rare now for me to feel this way, but anxiety and overwhelm used to be my everyday experience. If you're still there, my heart is with you and I want you to know that one foot in front of the other is a beautiful place to begin. If that doesn't make sense to you, try drinking a glass of water, taking three deep breaths, and making a list. Just like everything in life, anxiety is temporary, and small steps can help you create a shift in your experience.

october 23

Just Like Physical Health, Mental Health Takes Work

Keep going.
That's all you have to do, ever.
You really don't have to be amazing,
or fierce or beautiful or successful or good.
Just keep going, please.
Slowly is fine.
Crawling is fine.
No feeling is final.
Except hope.
~ Glennon Doyle

I believe that we have to actively work toward feeling the way we want to feel and that just like physical health, mental health takes work. Personally, I need practices to support my mood—tools for managing stress, anxiety, and depression.

Today, I am sharing a few things from my toolbox in the hopes that you find something useful.

1. *Old story, new story:* This is one of my go-to tools. First, you write out your old story, the tale you are currently telling yourself about the situation. And then you write a new story. You don't lie to yourself and say everything is great when it isn't. Instead, you write a more positive take on the situation that is still reality based. Once I write the new story I read it at least once a day to

help rewire my mind around the stressful thing. For example: *Old story: Ugh, I have so much to do this week. I will never get it done. I hate this. Why does this always happen to me? New story: I have a lot on my plate this week. I will approach my tasks with intention and focus. I will ask for help. I will be okay if I can't get everything done. I will practice taking care of myself inside of the busy-ness.*

2. *Facts vs. feelings:* Sensitive, empathic people often turn feelings into facts. To use this tool create two columns—in one list your feelings, in the other list the facts. This helps us get out of our emotional brain and back into our thinking brain. For example: *Feelings: I am invisible. No one cares about me. Facts: There are many people who care about me, but they aren't mind readers. If I need support I need to reach out.*

3. *1% better:* This is a behavioral strategy I use when I am in a funk. You simply ask yourself how you can make the task or the moment 1% better. For example: *Putting on my slippers while making breakfast in the morning so my feet will feel warm and cozy, lighting a candle when I get to my office to remind me that it is a sacred space, and playing uplifting music are tiny steps that add up to a shift in my mood.*

4. *Movement:* I cannot overstate the importance of movement for relieving stress and uplifting your mood. The impact is even greater if you can do your movement outside. For example: *Walk in your neighborhood, do some yoga in your chair, dance to your favorite song, shake it out, ride your bike, swim laps, or chase your kids around the park.*

5. *Mindfulness*: Three words: This shit works. Mindfulness means paying attention, on purpose, in the present moment, without judgment. So often our minds are replaying the past or worrying about the future. Mindfulness invites us to be here now. For example: *Meditate or breathe consciously (simple diaphragmatic breathing is an amazing tool). Use an app for meditation (I like Calm, Headspace, and Insight Timer) or search online for free videos. Pause and pay attention to the moment. Let go of judgment. Be where you are. Breathe.*

6. *Connect*: Do not stay in the darkness alone! I know you want to. I know you think you will bother other people or be a downer. It's just not true. You matter. You deserve love, attention, and kindness. Your people care about you and want to be there for you. Seek connection. For example: *Text a friend. Set up a coffee date. Make the phone call to reach out. Go to therapy. Find a group to gather with, online or in person. If it's the middle of the night and you don't want to wake your people, connect with your higher power or go outside and pray to the stars and the moon. Remind yourself that you are not alone.*

I hope these tools help in some small way to bring peace and joy into your heart today.

october 24

When You Can't Get Exactly What You Need

This is a moment of suffering. Suffering is part of life. May I be kind to myself in this moment. May I give myself the compassion I need.
~ Kristin Neff

When I find myself on the brink of overwhelm, I pause and ask myself what I need. Often the answer is an entire day to myself. Spending time alone is how I refill my inner well. However, taking an entire day to myself is usually not feasible. So I ask myself, *"What can I get that is close to that?"* This allows me room to get creative and brainstorm how I can meet my need for alone time within the realities of my life. I might do something like send my dog to daycare, go to a yoga class in the evening, take a long bath, or find some time to go out by myself to a bookstore or coffee shop. We may not be able to give ourselves exactly what we need, but we can get creative and find some close approximations, some small steps that can create powerful changes.

What do you need today? Can you get it for yourself right now? If not, what are some actions that you can take today that will move you closer to what you need?

october 25

The Middle Part Just Isn't as Sexy

When I was in the midst of writing this book I woke up at 2am one night, disoriented by a dream about an old lover. I hadn't thought of this man in ages, and it confused me even more when I calculated the years since we had been together—20. How is it possible that I am old enough to have a lover from 20 years ago? I had trouble falling back to sleep. My mind wouldn't let go of this dream. It had nothing to do with the old lover and everything to do with the symbolism of the dream, which boiled down to a question of whether or not I still wanted to be with this man if things weren't going to be easy, if they weren't going to be exactly as I had imagined at first sight.

But here's the thing: the dream wasn't really about a man at all, it was about this book.

I am so good at starting things. I love generating ideas, dreaming, and envisioning the end result. It's all the stuff in between starting and finishing that gets in the way. The middle part just isn't as sexy, right? I think this is true of so many things—they start off exciting and new and then become... not so exciting and new. It's easy to lose interest or move on to another new idea. How can we stay the course when something is important to us? How do we navigate the ups and downs of a long-term project without giving up?

Here are my ideas (and the techniques I used while writing this book):

1. Take daily action toward the goal, even if it is for five minutes.

2. Know the *why* behind your goal and remind yourself of it often.

3. Stay connected with the big vision. I think it helps to have a clear picture of where you are going and how you will feel when you get there.

4. Set small goals, track your progress, and celebrate your accomplishments.

5. Seek support and accountability.

Sometimes the middle part is hard, but if we want to achieve our goals, we need to stay the course. Are you in the middle of a goal or project? How can you use the five steps listed above to support your progress?

october 26

Living in Alignment

The opposite of love is not hate; it's indifference. ~ Wilhelm Stekel

My mission in this life is to help women reclaim self-love and self-trust. I work with women in service of my mission through therapy, yoga, writing, and teaching. I have aimed to consciously incorporate social justice into my work from the start. I chose to purchase and rehabilitate a building in the inner city so that services like therapy and yoga could be more accessible to people from socioeconomically and racially diverse backgrounds. I have consistently worked with therapy clients pro bono and on a sliding scale. I have offered free community yoga classes at the studio. I have volunteered my time teaching yoga for groups at the local city mission, schools, domestic violence shelter, and breast cancer support groups. I have offered scholarships for the yoga studio and my online Badass Self-Care® classes.

Nearly a decade into being an entrepreneur, I began to feel a disconnect between my mission and some parts of my work. I realized that what was bothering me was that a certain level of privilege was necessary in order to participate in yoga. Yoga is a beautiful, transformative practice that should be accessible to all. We are all worthy and deserving of its gifts of presence, connection, and peace. Yoga is not thin, white women doing headstands on the beach. Yoga is not even about physical postures of the body; it is so much more. In 2018, I decided I no longer wanted to participate in a version of yoga that required privilege to enter the room. I converted my yoga studio to 100% pay-what-you-can.

Privilege is complex and includes many layers. I know that moving to pay-what-you-can only addressed economic privilege. I understand that this shift in my business model was a small thing in the grand scheme of our capitalist society. But it was something that I could do. It is something that more closely aligned my values, my mission, and my work. It was a step in the right direction. I am a privileged white woman, and I am determined to use my resources in service of creating a more loving and just world. Your identity may be different or it may not. Either way, today I invite you to consider how you can use any privilege you have for good— whatever that may look like in your corner of the world.

Coherence in the Closet

One day I hadn't done laundry and couldn't find anything to wear to work. There was a black dress with white polka dots stuck in the back of my closet. I hadn't worn it in years, but it still fit, so I put it on and started getting ready for work. I noticed my body felt super uncomfortable, like I wanted to crawl out of my skin. I sometimes have that type of physical reaction to certain materials or textures, but this wasn't that experience. The dress was soft and comfortable. I realized it was because the dress was from a different time in my life when I was a different version of myself. I felt out of place inside it. I physically couldn't show up in the world inside that polka dot dress because it didn't match my insides. Now I try to create coherence in my closet by having clothing and accessories that reflect who I am in my heart, even as it shifts over time.

Spend some time with your journal today. Do you feel like your outsides match your insides? Are your clothes and accessories reflective of who you are in your heart? If not, how can you take a step toward creating coherence in your closet?

october 28

You Can Honor Your Capacity and Work Toward the World You Want to Live in

For me, forgiveness and compassion are always linked: how do we hold people accountable for wrongdoing and yet at the same time remain in touch with their humanity enough to believe in their capacity to be transformed?
~ bell hooks

One of my intentions in this life is to open up and feel it all. I spent decades disconnected from my emotions and my body in an effort to keep myself safe because I believed I could not handle everything going on from the neck down. This is a common response after trauma. Often the emotions and body sensations are so overwhelming that our survival instinct kicks in and we disconnect. When we experience ongoing trauma, this disconnection can become a habit, and what began as an adaptive response can become a coping mechanism that interferes with our ability to fully inhabit our lives long after the danger has ceased.

At one point I took my intention to open up and feel it all to the extreme of feeling what was happening to other people—my friends and family, my clients, even strangers across the world—as if it were happening to me. When I did that I thought I was being a compassionate, empathetic person, but really I was being codependent and setting myself up for physical and emotional burnout. Sometimes I still slip back into this over-corrected form of feeling my feelings. I can be like a sponge soaking up all the feelings around me and making them my own.

This sometimes happens to me around the news and social justice efforts. I go so far into feeling my own feelings, and everyone else's, that I become overwhelmed. I don't want to look away because I want to be informed and show support for the movements that I am passionate about. And I also know I need to take a break because I start to slide down into a not great place of feeling helpless, enraged, and so fucking sad. It's a conflict between my need for self-care and my desire to be of service. This comes up for me quite often. Is it okay for me to take a break from education and activism? People of color don't get a break from racism. Millions of people are affected by and don't get a break from transphobia, homophobia, fat phobia, and ableism. It is their daily lived experience.

I don't want to be a fragile white woman who retreats to her bathtub every time things get a bit uncomfortable. And I don't want to live inside of burnout. I don't have hard and fast answers here. Here is what I believe today: our capacity varies and we need to honor that. Capacity varies from person to person, as well as within a person. We are each having our own unique experience, and it is important to honor our truth, whatever it may be in the moment.

It's okay if you can't watch the news.
It's okay if you can't, or don't want to, speak up.
It's okay if you need a break.

Your service to this world may be writing in your journal.
Your service to this world may be being kind to your children.
Your service to this world may be writing to your elected officials.
Your service to this world may be taking care of you and only you.
Your service to this world may be having a conversation with your kids.
Your service to this world may be sharing an article on social media.
Your service to this world may be meditating.

Your service to this world may be reading a book and educating yourself.
Your service to this world may be registering voters.
Your service to this world may be marching or protesting.
Your service to this world may be making art.
Your service to this world may be healing your own wounds.
Your service to this world may be donating money.

I do want to ask each of us—especially the white, heterosexual, cis-gendered women— to take the time to connect within and ask if we are doing what we can do to create a more loving and just world for everyone, not just the people who look like us. Again, what you have the capacity to do may vary from day to day or year to year. My prayer is that you do something—whether it be internal, inside of your family, inside of your community, or inside of our larger culture. All steps toward love and justice matter.

october 29

Where Are You Already Feeling It?

Did you know our brains have a built-in negativity bias? We are literally wired to notice what is wrong. Our brains developed in this way because it is adaptive to scan for danger; it helps us stay alive. The thing is, we don't really need to be doing this all the time. We no longer roam around in nature, hunting and gathering. We have homes and cars and grocery stores. But we have the same brains from all those years ago when we needed to stay vigilant to stay alive.

The good news is that we can rewire our brains. We can learn to focus on the positive, on what is working and feeling good. I am not suggesting we ignore problems or negativity. I am *definitely* not of the "good vibes only" camp. I *am* a nerd for neuroscience though, and I'm intrigued by the impact focusing on the good can have on the brain.

So today I invite you to pause and notice where you already have peace, happiness, and joy. Right here, right now. Where do you already have the feelings that you crave?

Here is my list:

Feeling the sunshine streaming in through the window
Walking by the river and being among the trees
Waking up snuggled in bed with my husband, daughter, and puppy
Coming home and seeing mums and pumpkins on my front step
Writing in my journal
Soaking in a salty bath with essential oils
Reading
Practicing Yoga
Looking at pictures of my family
Meditating on my breath
Making plans with my friends
Looking up at the night sky

Maybe Healing Individuals Is How We Heal the Collective

When you pray, move your feet. ~ African proverb

The more I deepened my exploration of social justice, the more strongly I felt pulled toward working at a systems level. This is partly because the systems we currently live inside (e.g., sexism, racism, homophobia, transphobia, ableism) are so damaging and partly because I can't un-see how systems impact individuals' struggles. In our culture, we tend to attribute everything to the individual. If someone is doing well, it's because that person worked hard. If someone is struggling, it's because they didn't try hard enough or something is wrong with them.

This just isn't true.
It's narrow-minded and it's dangerous.

Systems have a major impact on us as individuals and cannot be ignored when it comes to working toward healing, love, and justice. I spent months wracking my brain trying to figure out how I could affect change at a systems level. Should I go back to school and completely shift my career field? Should I run for a political office? (*I definitely do not have the constitution for that!*) Then one night in the bathtub (naturally!) something clicked for me... systems are made up of individual people! Even if we aim to change a system, that change will likely come at the individual level. I think this is true even when we are thinking about changing policies and institutions. Who makes the change? People. We still need to work at the person-to-person level.

Change is about creating a critical mass (of individual people). Working toward change at the person-to-person level can feel slow. Sometimes it feels overwhelming, and often it feels like it's not enough. The truth is this just might be the way to heal the collective, person by person. After much contemplation, I decided to continue doing my healing work at the individual level through my practice as a psychologist. *And* I aim to work at a collective level whenever possible. For me, working at the collective level means professional endeavors such as writing, teaching, and facilitating groups, and personal actions like voting, sharing on social media, and donating money to organizations doing the important work of trying to change the world for the better. These are the things that I can currently do with my resources and skill set. What you can do may be different. That's okay—we need all of us!

If you want to help heal the collective, start with one person—yourself!

If you have more to give, touch the life of another person or a group of people.

Parenting your child can help heal the collective.
Speaking up can help heal the collective.
Writing can help heal the collective.
Friendship can help heal the collective.
Going to therapy can help heal the collective.
Loving your partner can help heal the collective.
Meditating can help heal the collective.

Just do something to help tilt the world a bit more toward love and justice. Each individual action *does* matter.

I Became Real

You become. It takes a long time. That's why it doesn't often happen to people who break easily, or have sharp edges, or who have to be carefully kept. Generally, by the time you are Real, most of your hair has been loved off, and your eyes drop out and you get loose in the joints and very shabby. But these things don't matter at all, because once you are Real you can't be ugly, except to people who don't understand.
~ from The Velveteen Rabbit *by Margery Williams*

I was going to hustle and prove my worth, but instead I got a cold and spent the day in bed.

I was going to make a Pinterest-inspired tablescape, but instead I had a dance party in the kitchen filled with dirty dishes.

I was going to do one more thing, but instead I took a long hot shower, flossed my teeth, and gave myself a foot massage.

I was going to look the part, but instead I fell in love with ink on my skin and beads on my arms and purple stain on my lips.

I was going to be a good girl, but instead I opened my mouth up wide and spoke the truth.

I was going to stay small and try to fit in, but instead I let out my loudest laugh and threw my head back in joy.

I was going to be a rising star, but instead I quit to follow my wild dreams.

I was going to choose, but instead I created space for all of it.

I was going to spend my whole life trying to fit into neat little boxes, but instead I became real.

Does Your Calendar Reflect Your Priorities?

Things which matter most must never be
at the mercy of things which matter least.
~ Johann Wolfgang von Goethe

Part of self-care is knowing what is most important to us and honoring those priorities through our actions.

Take a moment now and consider your top three priorities. There are no right or wrong answers. Your priorities might include family, health, self-care, work, creativity, spirituality, or anything else that is important to you.

After you've written down your top three priorities, take a look at your calendar or planner for the past month and note how much time you've devoted to your priorities. For example, if you listed family as a priority, how many hours each week are you spending on family activities? Or if you listed health as a priority, how often did you move your body or take the time to prepare healthy meals? If you notice a disconnect between your priorities and how you spend your time, think of a few steps you could take to bring things into alignment.

november 2

What Are You No Longer Willing To Do?

What you eliminate is as powerful in shaping your life as what you incorporate.
~ Chani Nicholas

Today, I invite you to consider what you might stop doing in order to more fully honor your values and priorities.

This could be general:

I will no longer say yes when I want to say no.
I will no longer spend time with people who belittle my dreams.
I will no longer hold back my feelings in close relationships.

This could be specific:

I will no longer check email after 9pm.
I will no longer eat in my car.
I will no longer work on Saturdays.

Spend some time with your journal today.
What are you no longer willing to do?

Honoring Our Feminine Nature

Changing Women. We begin again like the Moon.
~ Terry Tempest Williams

We are not the same women today that we were last year, last month, or even last week. It is our feminine nature to change, flow, and be inconsistent. However, we live in a masculine culture. Masculine energy is linear, directive, and consistent, and in our society we are generally expected to show up and be the same each day. This expectation disconnects us from our feminine nature and can lead to emotional and physical suffering, such as anxiety, depression, and issues with our sacred reproductive organs.

We all have feminine and masculine energy inside of us. One is not better than the other; they are simply different. Many of us have internalized patriarchy, and we deny, resist, or even despise our feminine characteristics such as sensitivity, receptivity, and inconsistency. We are taught from a young age that being female/feminine is weak, less than, something to be avoided, compensated for, and hidden. This message is so ubiquitous it can be difficult to notice. It is within everything from scolding boys to not be "girly" to someone asking if you're "on the rag." We can learn to recognize and de-condition ourselves from these damaging messages.

Personally, I lived (unconsciously) from a place of denying my feminine aspects until I was in my mid-thirties. My masculine energy has served me well in so many ways. It put my ass on a hard wooden chair at community college six days after my first daughter was born. *(I get teary-eyed every time I think of that young woman so afraid of not succeeding that she went against every instinct in her body and left her newborn baby.)* My masculine energy kept me up until 4am waiting tables to pay the rent and woke me back up at 8am for class. It helped me complete a dissertation, buy a home, get a job, and build a business. My masculine energy makes lists and gets shit done.

Now that I am connected with and honor my feminine energy, I cannot imagine living without her amazing guidance. My feminine energy makes things beautiful, juicy, and fulfilling. She invites me to slow down, to surrender, and to open up to receive. She brings me messages of truth that make my whole body tingle with recognition. She keeps me safe even when my masculine energy tells me I'm being irrational. She makes my life feel deeper and more connected, more alive. My feminine energy helps me raise my children with unbridled love, serve my clients with compassion, and deeply know my connection with the divine.

We all have masculine and feminine energy in us, and both of these energies are helpful and important. Culturally, we have been taught to ignore and deny our feminine energy. Reclaiming this part of ourselves is vital in our journey toward self-love and self-trust.

Spend some time with your journal today. What are the messages you have received about femininity? When are you inside of your feminine energy? How can you honor your femininity? What does your feminine, intuitive self want you to know?

november 4

Understanding Our Menstrual or Moon Cycles

Understanding our menstrual or moon cycles helps us design our lives in a way that honors our cyclical nature. Because I am a menstruating woman, I live and work by my menstrual cycle. If you do not menstruate, I encourage you to use the moon cycle as a guide.

In brief, there are four parts to our menstrual cycle, and they correspond to four parts of the moon cycle. Don't worry if your menstrual cycle does not match up with the moon cycle. Follow whichever cycle feels right for you or blend the two in some way.

Menstruation/New (Dark) Moon:
- feminine energy
- a beautiful time for going inward & setting intentions
- many will feel more tired
- incubate and dream for the new cycle ahead
- intuition is heightened
- rest, hibernate
- turn inward by journal writing, meditating, visioning

Pre-Ovulation/Waxing Moon:
- masculine energy
- energy is increasing
- an ideal time for taking some action on your intentions & goals
- strategize, brainstorm, network
- start new projects

Ovulation/Full Moon:
- masculine energy
- peak time of the month in terms of energy and mood
- an ideal time for socializing & dating, as well as working on projects
- put yourself out there—speak, host an event

Pre-Menstruation/Waning Moon:
- feminine energy
- may feel more tired & increasingly sensitive
- as my friend Michele Lisenbury Christensen says, a new layer of truth shall be revealed during this time—anything you've been holding in will rise to the surface
- an ideal time to slow down—take naps, go to bed early
- prepare to let go of whatever didn't work this month, anything you would like to release
- if you can, take time off from work or decrease expectations at work
- skip social commitments and take more time for self-care
- bring your awareness inward through meditation and journal writing

It is important to remember that we are each unique individuals. There is no right or wrong experience of your menstrual or moon cycle. The intention is simply to learn more about yourself so that you can use the information to support your self-care. You may not resonate with the above descriptions. For example, some women feel more tired and cranky during ovulation. Let go of judgments and tune in to notice what is true for you. Let's honor our feminine, cyclical nature in whatever way feels most authentic.

If you are a menstruating woman, tracking your cycle is a beautiful practice for learning more about yourself and how you respond to various phases. Day 1 is the day you begin your bleed. If you are not currently menstruating, track according to the moon cycle with Day 1 being the New Moon. You can track using a journal or by creating a chart. There are also many period tracking apps available. I like to note my mood and energy levels each day. Jot down anything that feels relevant for you. One month of tracking will give you some insight into how you respond to various parts of your cycle. The longer you track, the more you will learn about yourself and your cycles! For a deeper dive, Lisa Lister has two great books on honoring our menstrual cycle: *Code Red* and *Love Your Lady Landscape*.

november 5

I Want to Be Honored

I want to be honored.

The realization came slowly and then all at once, tears streaming down my face. I have been merely tolerating myself in so many ways.

Justifying my choices.
Apologizing for my needs.
Not taking myself and my work seriously.
Making self-deprecating comments as some mixed-up way of protecting myself from pain.

Continuing to believe that I am less than in so many ways.

I do not want to be tolerated, especially by myself.
Acceptance, love, respect—even these are no longer enough for me. I want my body, my work, my beliefs, my practices to be honored, celebrated, and revered.

I cry, releasing and blessing each of my self-inflicted wounds as they float into consciousness.

I send love to my past selves and breathe forgiveness down into my bones. I will no longer justify, belittle, or minimize myself.
I will honor myself.

november 6

Explore the Untold Stories

Until the lion learns how to write, every story will glorify the hunter.
~ African Proverb

One of the consequences of patriarchy is that women's stories have been purposefully and systematically removed from (or altered by) our social institutions of religion, education, and government. Consider the witch hunts. "Witch" used to mean wise woman or healer. Before patriarchy, women were revered for their bodies and their gifts. The truth is, worshipping women and the feminine is not conducive to a capitalist society that focuses on competition and productivity. So the wise women, the witches, were systematically hunted down and eliminated. This is just one example from hundreds of years of oppressing women's voices.

Not learning about women and not seeing our stories in popular culture has a deep impact on us. We are missing role models. We are deprived of the validation that comes from seeing someone like us on the screen or the page. This void is exponentially more pronounced for women of color, the LGBTQ+ community, and people with other marginalized identities.

Today, I invite you to begin to learn about the untold or lesser-known stories of women. There are many ways you can dive into this prompt. You could ask your mother, grandmother, or aunt to tell you about her life. You could watch a movie or television show that centers women's voices, such as Hidden Figures, Pose, *or* The Handmaid's Tale. *You could go to the library and check out a book on goddesses or feminine archetypes. Some of my favorites are* Awakening

Shakti *by Sally Kempton*, Goddesses in Everywoman *by Jean Shinoda Bolen, and* Witch *by Lisa Lister.*

november 7

Protect Your Resources

Modern society is set up in a way that often depletes women, individually and collectively. Women do the bulk of emotional labor and other unpaid labor such as caregiving and child care. We deserve to protect our inner and outer resources. We are each responsible for knowing what boundaries we need in order to thrive. We are allowed to be discerning about who and what we give our time and energy to.

Spend some time with your journal today and think about your resources—inner and outer. Consider your emotional, energetic, physical, mental, financial, and spiritual resources.

What is the quality of each?
Where do you feel depleted?
Where do you feel abundant?
How do you allow yourself to receive?
Where do you deliberately give?
Where are you leaking resources?

What places need some adjusting in your life? It might be a relationship, a habit, or even an environment. How can you begin to protect your resources?

I Hope They Say

There is so much I want to give to my daughters. Things I want to tell them and teach them, beliefs about themselves and lessons about the world. I don't know how to say it all so I try to show them instead. I wonder how they see me, how they will remember me when I am gone.

I believe that people do the best they can with what they have. And I believe, I *know*, that sometimes it isn't enough. I believe that I do the best I can and I know that sometimes it might not be enough, especially when it comes to parenting my daughters. I want the absolute best for them and I am not my absolute best all the time. I try my hardest to do all the things that I know make me the best version of myself, but sometimes I still fuck up. I am working hard to heal and unlearn and be better for them. I hope they see that. I hope that is part of how they remember me.

I hope that when I am gone they say,

"Our mom told us she loved us ten times a day. We used to tease her that she couldn't leave a room without saying 'I love you.'

"She felt everything intensely, including her love for us. To be loved by her was a magical thing—she made you feel so seen, so important. As many things as she had going on, she always made time for us. She answered the phone when we called her in the middle of the night crying. She left a sink full of dirty dishes to have a dance party with us in the kitchen. Every silly thing we said as kids she treated as serious business. She always made us feel important and special.

"She was smart and intense and beautiful and I can see now that she suffered in her own struggles. She worked throughout her life to heal, to be the best version of herself. She wanted to give that to us. Our mother was as brave as she was kind. She went through a lot in this life but she never let that define her. She owned her truth without being consumed by her story."

It might seem morbid, but I think about how I want to be remembered because it helps me become who I want to be. In the end, I hope that they will say that I loved them fiercely, that I did the best I could, and that it was enough.

november 9

How to Love Yourself When You've Been a Real Asshole

Despite all of my inner work, I have moments of being a real asshole.

I have this idea of who I am—a kind, loving, and patient person. And I am that person a lot of the time but I can also be mean, irritable, and downright awful sometimes. When these moments of being a real asshole strike and I show up as the worst version of myself, it throws me into shame and self-loathing. At this point on my path, I am able to recognize that I have a choice when I land in this place. I can stay in it and get pulled down low, or I can choose another way. Here is how I choose another way:

The first thing I do is use my favorite technique for shifting my self-talk. I imagine what I would say if one of my friends or clients recounted the same situation to me. *Because I would never talk to another person the way I talk to myself in those moments.* So I imagine my friend or client sitting before me and tearfully explaining what a real asshole she's been and how she isn't sure she can ever forgive herself. I imagine her asking me, *"How do I come back from this?!"* I know I'd reply to her kindly and gently (as opposed to the disgust and anger I sometimes pile on myself). This helps me to start saying to myself what I would say to her. *"I love you no matter what. We all mess up. You are doing the best that you can. There is no point berating yourself because you can't go back. What you need right now is kindness and compassion toward yourself. These mean thoughts just keep you stuck."*

Next, I talk with someone who can safely catch my emotions about what I've done. If I don't share the truth with a safe, kind person it starts to grow a layer of shame over it—a bigger layer of shame than is already there. Usually I call my husband crying and telling him that I am the worst person in the world. He assures me that I am not and finds a way to make me laugh. After sharing with him, I feel a little lighter, as if the weight on my shoulders is starting to lift.

Then I go on and do something kind for myself even though it feels like I don't deserve it after my shitty behavior. This helps me shift my perspective and stop the inner dialogue about how awful and undeserving I am. Doing something kind for myself when I least felt like I deserve it is a beautiful way of loving myself and reinforcing my inherent worth.

Finally, I decide to forgive myself and begin again. That is how it happens. You simply make up your mind to do it. Every time a mean thought comes back up, I let it be a reminder to send myself love and forgiveness. I commit to taking exquisite care of myself so that I can be the person I want to be. I promise myself that I will try harder to breathe or walk away next time I am in a triggering situation so I don't act like an asshole. I affirm to myself that I am always doing my best, even in my worst moments, and that that is enough. *That I am enough.* I promise to love myself even when I have been a real asshole because love is actually exactly what people who are acting like assholes need.

november 10

Be Your Whole Self

Most of my adult life, I rebuked household chores. My husband did the grocery shopping and cooking, as well as most of the daily tasks like dishes and laundry. We hired someone to clean our house. Then my husband's schedule changed and it didn't make sense for him to continue to carry the brunt of the household chores. I started doing the dishes and folding the laundry more often. I began to cook and even grocery shop here and there. I learned that I enjoy taking care of my family in this way. I find peace and fulfillment inside the routines of daily living. The truth is my husband probably still does the majority of these tasks, but I contribute more now than I have in the past.

I hadn't ever let myself consider that I might enjoy household chores because I was so hyper-focused on not being forced to do them simply because I am a woman. I had cut off parts of who I am (or might be) out of fear and internalized misogyny. When I started doing more household chores I found joy inside of them, not because I was playing a role or trying to be a "good" woman, but because I had discovered a part of myself that enjoyed caring for her family in this way.

I understand the immense privilege of even having options when it comes to household chores. This essay might fill you with anger or just feel totally unrelatable. I wrote it because it is my experience, my truth. You have your own truth and I honor that. One thing we all have in common is that we live inside of patriarchy. And patriarchal culture devalues household chores; it demeans anything inherently connected with the feminine. I bought into this patriarchal nonsense for so long and it led me to deny parts of myself. I am telling you this story because I don't want any of us cutting off any parts of ourselves. I want us to own our whole selves. I want us to live our whole truth. Whatever that might look like for each of us.

november 11

Accept All the Parts of Yourself

What parts of yourself do you struggle to accept?

Your mind? Your body?
Your belly? Your breasts?
Your dreams? Your fears?
Your femininity? Your masculinity?
Your shadow? Your light?

We are complex, often contradictory beings.

How can you begin to welcome in all the parts of yourself with love and acceptance?

november 12

Take a Self-Portrait as an Act of Self-Care

It's about turning the camera on ourselves and yes, knowing that inner critic is probably going to rise up. But we don't stop there. We cultivate our own voice, choosing to not listen to our inner critic when it tries to make us stop and put away the camera in shame. We take another photo. We reclaim that voice and our personal power back. It's a conscious choice to choose self-compassion over self-critique again and again until our critic isn't our go-to response.
~ Vivienne McMaster

Some days it feels really hard to look into my own eyes. Yet, I crave being seen. One of my self-care practices on those days is to take a self-portrait. I turn the camera on myself because I know it holds the power to create a shift. I may look away or even close my eyes, but simply taking the picture and seeing myself shifts my energy. I am able to step closer to self-love, self-trust, and self-forgiveness.

Today, I invite you to play with taking a photo of yourself. No need for special equipment, a camera phone works beautifully. If it feels more comfortable, close or avert your eyes as you take the picture. Notice how pausing to capture an image of yourself creates a shift in your day, your mood, your pace, your breath.

My Children Are My Greatest Spiritual Teachers

My children are my greatest spiritual teachers. Through my relationship with them I become aware of unfinished business within myself.

They illuminate where I am stuck.
They challenge all the fantasies I have about who I think I am.
They keep me humble.
They invite me to love unconditionally.
They show me how to forgive.
They remind me to forget everything I think I know.
They challenge me to meet them where they are, as they are and without expectations.

Through them I learn to surrender my resistance to life as it is.

A story to illustrate:

I am driving to pick up my daughter. As I make my way through the streets of Niagara Falls, I practice my favorite informal meditation. It's simple: as I drive I send lovebeams and positive thoughts out to people I pass on the street. So I'm driving along thinking about what an enlightened person I seem to be today, spreading love all around the city. I start to think I've got it all figured out. I even begin to write a social media update in my head so I can share my amazing lovebeams-while-driving idea with all my friends. Surely they will like and comment away on my status, reinforcing my awesomeness. I pull up to my daughter's friend's house, get out my phone, and see a text from her asking me to pick her up an hour and a half later.

Suddenly I am fuming.

All my enlightened lovebeam shit has flown out the window in less than a second.

I respond, "I'm here right now. And I might kill you."

She replies, "I didn't ask you to pick me up."

I read back over my text messages where she most certainly *seemed* to ask me to pick her up. I screen shot our messages and I'm about to send them to her along with a text emphasizing what a jerk she is. Then I decide no, I will post the messages on Facebook where surely all of my friends will side with me and affirm her rudeness. Yes. And I will tag her, *of course.*

Somehow I remember to take a deep breath.

The breath creates a pause.

In the pause I remember Miss She-Who-Beams-Love-To-Strangers. *You know, the person I thought I was two minutes ago.* I send a text to my daughter that we had a miscommunication and I will see her later. I start driving home and resume beaming love. I even beam some to my daughter.

My children are my greatest spiritual teachers. As I raise them, I raise myself. May I remember this truth, and may I be grateful for the journey.

november 14

Set Boundaries to Support Your Priorities

Go back to the three priorities you identified on November 1. Now that you have clarified what is most important to you, it's time to consider what boundaries can support you living in alignment with your priorities. For example, if you've decided that family is a priority, then you might set a boundary of not taking any phone calls during family dinners. Or if health is a priority, you might define a boundary of no longer going to work when you are sick.

Spend some time with your journal today.
Write down five to ten boundaries that can support your priorities.

Connect with Your Wild Woman Self

There was a time in my life that I did not wash my hair every day. That might not sound unusual to you, but it was a big shift for me. Once I started skipping a day here and there, I became intrigued and decided to see how long I could go without washing my hair (turns out it's five days).

During this time, I deepened my relationship with my hair by noticing how it changed as the days went on and trying different hairstyles (lots of braids and buns). The not-washing also invited me to love my hair in all its variations, helping me to love myself in all my variations. From clean and fresh on day one to dirty and wild on day five. The simple act of not washing my hair (or non-act, really) brought me closer to my wild woman self in ways I could not have predicted.

For me, my wild woman self is the self who is in tune with her cycles, her longings, and her core self. The self who remembers she comes from nature. The self who is connected to the Earth and the trees and her own instincts. My experiment with not washing my hair has long since ended, but I have stayed connected with my wild woman self through other methods, including spending time in nature, embodiment practices, and creative outlets.

Spend some time with your journal today. How can you connect with your wild woman self? If you're looking for a resource to explore this idea more deeply, I highly recommend the book Women Who Run With Wolves *by Clarissa Pinkola Estés.*

Embracing Our Cycles

I love when the Full Moon arrives. Each month as she grows fuller I become more energized and creative. My joy expands and I am able to see so much possibility before me. I fall deeply in love with my life. As the moon wanes I lose some vibrancy and hope, almost as if her waning light takes some of mine with it. I struggle to embrace this cycle. I want to be the lit-up, expansive version of myself all month long. I think many of us strive to show up as an idealized, consistent version of ourselves. We want to be our smartest, most organized, kindest, sexiest, most patient self every day. This is a form of perfectionism grounded in patriarchal conditioning. The truth is we have cycles, just as the luminous moon does. She doesn't judge her changes or try to fight her waxing and waning. She just hangs out in the sky knowing that her light is always there, even if we can't always see it.

I am learning to embrace my cycles. Knowing that there is a time for creativity and a time for rest, a season for growth and a season for destruction. Releasing the idea that one aspect is better than the other. Welcoming all the cycles of life and understanding that each is a necessary part of the whole.

november 17

Are You Trying to Shrink Your Emotional Expression?

There is a particular moment from an anniversary party at the yoga studio years ago that stands out in my mind. It was toward the very end of the celebration, and a group of us circled up together for a toast. I looked around at the beautiful space that I had built and gazed into the eyes of the gorgeous humans that make up our community, and I was overwhelmed with emotion. I was moved to tears, tears that I held back.

I feel things a lot. The intensity of my emotions used to scare me, but now I see it as one of my superpowers. Sometimes I hold back from fully expressing myself because I worry about being too much for people. I worry that I will make people uncomfortable with my big feelings, which is why I held back my tears during that toast. Yet I know that when another person opens up and allows me to witness them in their full expression, I feel blessed to be trusted with their truth. It doesn't shut me down but cracks me open. Naked vulnerability feeds my sensitive soul.

Spend some time with your journal today. Are you trying to shrink your emotional expression? If so, where did you learn you needed to do that? What would it feel like to express your feelings more fully?

november 18

Some Thoughts on Owning Our Stories

Owning our story can be hard but not nearly as difficult as
spending our lives running from it.
~ Brené Brown

To me, owning our stories refers to the process of acknowledging, naming, and integrating the truth of our lives. I have been on a journey of owning my story in one form or another since I was 18 years old. Deciding what, when, and how to share is an ongoing, ever-evolving practice for me. I have noticed there is a lot of talking about owning our stories in the personal development world. This can feel like a beautiful invitation or an unwanted pressure. Sometimes it can feel like we are doing it wrong if we aren't sharing every honest detail of our lives with everyone we know.

The truth is, owning our stories is a process—a very personal process.

The truth is, there is no right or wrong when it comes to owning our stories.

The truth is, we get to decide what to share with people, as well as when to share it.

The truth is, the owning can be internal or external, quiet or loud, bit by bit or all at once.

The truth is, some things can be kept tucked inside the pockets of our hearts and that doesn't mean that we aren't owning them.

Fear, Anger, and Other Beautiful Things

This being human is a guest house.
Every morning a new arrival.
A joy, a depression, a meanness,
some momentary awareness comes
as an unexpected visitor.
Welcome and entertain them all!
~ Rumi

Sometimes it feels like the world is yelling at me to feel good, all the time.

How to be fearless!
Find happiness now!
Transform your suffering!

I adore personal development and self-help, *and* I need to call bullshit on this line of thinking.

Fear, anger, jealousy, sadness—these are part of the human experience. And I want to experience being human as fully as possible.

How beautiful that our intelligent bodies communicate danger to us. How beautiful that our feelings tell us when a boundary has been violated. How beautiful that an emotion can be a compass toward our desires. How beautiful that we can love so much as to feel heart-wrenching sorrow.

The message that so-called negative emotions are a problem to be fixed as quickly as possible robs us of so much. When we deny or rush through our feelings we miss out on valuable information. When we do not claim our fear, our anger, our jealousy, and our sadness, we deny parts of ourselves. We shrink our experience and create a layer of shame around our truth.

Our feelings deserve space to be witnessed and held without judgment.

Give your fear love.
Allow your anger voice.
Let your jealousy teach you what you really want in life.
Invite your sadness to illuminate the stories lying just beneath it.

I am not suggesting you act on your every feeling.
I am not suggesting you wallow or stay stuck.

I am suggesting you allow yourself to feel how you feel, to embrace the whole range of emotions that move through you, to spend some time with the stuff you'd rather skip over. I am suggesting unconditional self-acceptance, which in and of itself is hugely transformative. Let's release judgment and comparing of our feelings. Instead, let's get curious. Stay open. Breathe. Meditate. Journal. Share with safe people. Dance it out. Stop holding shit in. Cry when we feel like crying. Stop pretending like everything is okay when it's not. Let go of the belief that we are the only one with our particular struggle. Let us begin practicing unconditional self-love of our whole beautiful, messy selves by honoring all of our beautiful, messy feelings as guides, as gifts. Because they are.

november 20

Create a Self-Care Basket

It can be challenging to find time for our self-care practices, especially as we head into the holiday season. A strategy that I use to encourage myself to pause for a few minutes of self-care every day is to create a self-care basket. I gather up my favorite self-care tools and put them together in a beautiful basket. It helps to have a basket of supplies at the ready so that I don't have to spend time looking for what I need to relax. Plus, having everything in one place makes it more likely that I'll sit and unwind. The basket also serves as a visual reminder to take a few minutes for myself each day. I like to place it next to a comfy chair in my living room.

Create a self-care basket. You might include a book, your journal, art supplies, magazines, and anything else that supports your self-care practices. Place the basket where you will see it so that it can serve as a reminder to take some time for yourself every day.

Keep Caring for Yourself and
Keep Fighting for Love and Justice

Now is not the time for us to give up or get stuck in despair.
Now is the time for us to practice what I call Badass Self-Care®.

It's called Badass Self-Care® because women taking care of themselves
inside of this patriarchal culture is an act of defiance. When we say, "I
matter and I deserve to take beautiful care of myself," we are breaking
down the social constructs we have been conditioned to follow; we are
changing society. This is exponentially truer for women of marginalized
identities (such as women of color and LGBTQ+ women). Caring for
yourself is part of how we change the culture of misogyny, racism,
transphobia, and homophobia.

We need you to care for yourself now more than ever.

Even amongst the death and destruction and all the horribleness that is
our current reality. *Especially now.*

Because your suffering does not cure the suffering of others. Only your
health—your healing—can help heal others.

Because you cannot give from an empty well, and you cannot fight while
running on fumes. You must replenish.

And we must do the work of breaking down these systems of white supremacy and patriarchy that have created the havoc we are now living inside.

Not one or the other—both. Self-Care and Action.

Do what fills your well so that you have the energy to fight for the world you want to live in. Go outside and look at the sky, the stars, the moon, the trees, the rivers, and oceans. Be with your people. Have real talks with them about what is going on. Cry. Hold each other. Take action together—write letters, make calls. Educate yourself, be informed, *and* know when to take a break from the media. Watching and re-watching news coverage is traumatizing. Share what you learn with others, on social media and in person.

Keep caring for yourself and keep fighting for love and justice.
We need you now more than ever.

The Art of Doing Nothing

Taking a bath is one of my most beloved self-care rituals. I like to use a generous amount of Epsom salt, essential oils, and really hot water so the bath stays warm for at least an hour. While I soak in the bath I check social media, read a book, or watch television. At one point, I noticed that my bath wasn't feeling as relaxing. I got curious about this and realized that I had turned my bath time into another time to get things done, even if they were enjoyable things. I was soaking in a relaxing bath but I was still overloading my nervous system with stimulation.

So, I started a new ritual of doing nothing for the last ten minutes of my bath. Doing nothing allows me to really be in the moment, to feel the warm water, smell the essential oils, and sit in the silence. I often come up with ideas or gain clarity during this time. I always notice myself breathing a bit deeper. Letting go of taking in information, whether from a book or electronic device, has brought me increased relaxation. It also reminded me of the importance of just being in silence with myself on a regular basis.

Spend some time with your journal today. Are you over-functioning during your down time? Can you add a few minutes of doing nothing into one of your self-care rituals?

We All Deserve to Feel Safe and Connected in Our Bodies

It's said that we teach what we need to learn. One of the things I teach most often is listening to and honoring the wisdom of our bodies.

I spent nearly two decades cut off from the wisdom of my body. At first it was subconscious, an automatic response to coping with trauma. My body was a frightening place where abuses were carried out. Understandably, I spent most of my time in my head—learning, thinking, and analyzing. In my teens and early twenties, I began to more purposefully disconnect from my body—drinking alcohol, smoking pot, binge eating or not eating, and over-focusing on school and work. The longer I spent disconnected from my body, the scarier it felt to connect with it.

I began my journey back into my body when I was 24 years old and took my first yoga class. Right around the same time I left an abusive relationship for the last time and restarted therapy. I was blessed to have a therapist who understood the importance of working with the body as well as the mind. Through yoga and therapy, I learned to feel safe inside my body again. I began to pay more attention to my body's signals. I learned to take care of myself—to eat when I was hungry, to pee when I had to pee, and to rest when I was tired. I learned what a "yes" and "no" felt like in my body and began using my body's wisdom to guide my decisions. I learned that tuning into my body helped me to connect more deeply with my intuition. Healing my relationship with my body changed my life.

I think on some level most women struggle with listening to and honoring their bodies. Because we live in a patriarchal society where our bodies are seen as objects or commodities, we are trained to focus on how we look rather than how we feel. We internalize this belief and subsequently begin to think of our own bodies as something to present rather than something to love and protect. Couple this with the fact that so many women do experience some form of violence in their lifetime, complicating their relationship with the body, and it is easy to understand why most of us check out from the neck down to one degree or another. I want us to reclaim our relationship with our bodies. I want us to heal so that we can access the wisdom of our bodies. We all deserve to feel safe and connected in our bodies.

Spend some time with your journal today. Do you feel connected with your body? Are you in tune with your body's signals and sensations? If you are a trauma survivor, it may feel scary to connect with your body. Please know that this is natural and that help is available. Somatic-based therapy (such as Somatic Experiencing or EMDR) and trauma-informed yoga can both be beautiful pathways back to your body.

The First Thing

How we spend our days is, of course, how we spend our lives.
~ Annie Dillard

My typical routine is to get up and write in my journal first thing before I get ready for my day. At times, I get off course and end up sleeping in. When this happens I still write in my journal every day, but it might be after I've taken my daughter to school or on my lunch break at work. I've noticed that writing first thing in the morning has a different impact for me than writing later in the day. When I write as soon as I wake up, it sets the tone for my day and I am able to approach my tasks with mindfulness and intention. That one choice first thing in the day leads me toward other choices that support my mood and decrease my stress level. When I write later in the day on a consistent basis, I start to notice other things suffering in my life, such as my task management, food choices, and physical activity. Shifting just one thing and writing as soon as I wake up has a positive snowball effect on the rest of my day.

Spend some time with your journal today. Does the idea that what you do first thing in the morning impacts the rest of your day resonate with you? What's one thing that will set a positive tone for your day? Some ideas include making your bed, meditating, exercising, spending time in nature, drawing or coloring, or pulling tarot or oracle cards.

november 25

Part of Healthy Boundaries is Compartmentalizing Our Roles

I am a writer, a teacher, and a therapist.
I am a student and a client.
I am a wife and a mom.
I am a sister, a daughter, and a friend.
I am many things to many people.
Above all, I am a woman in her own right.

When I am in my office with a client sitting across from me, I am a professional therapist. Every other role in my life fades away. My own shit fades away. I am fully present and attuned to my client. Conversely, when I am on the couch in my own therapist's office, I am a woman doing the hard work of looking at her personal struggles and patterns. I am knee deep in my own shit. When I am teaching yoga, I am focused externally. I am thinking of my students' experience—which postures do they need, how can I keep them safe, what is the energy in the room today? Conversely, when I am a student in yoga class, I am focused internally. I am having my own experience of breath, body, and mind.

I used to believe that shifting my behavior in different contexts meant that I wasn't being authentic, but now I understand that part of healthy boundaries is compartmentalizing our roles. I am one way at work, another way at home. I am one way with my family, another way with my friends. I am one way in my writing, another way in person. These shifts in behavior aren't about denying parts of myself to conform to people or places. Instead, I am honoring myself by stepping into the many roles in my life and expressing the various parts of myself as appropriate.

Hello Self, You Are Welcome Here Too

I take pleasure in my transformations. I look quiet and consistent, but few know how many women there are in me. ~ Anaïs Nin

Hello self who is resisting what is happening,
You are welcome here too.

Hello self who feels resentful and wants to run away from it all,
You are welcome here too.

Hello self who feels guilty and keeps replaying mistakes of the past,
You are welcome here too.

Hello self who feels sad and doesn't know why,
You are welcome here too.

Hello self who just knows things without any rational explanation,
You are welcome here too.

Hello self who is angry, so angry sometimes that she can't see straight,
You are welcome here too.

Hello self who is tired and just wants to take a nap,
You are welcome here too.

Hello self who is unsure and feels afraid,
You are welcome here too.

Hello self who is embarrassed for sounding so ungrateful,
You are welcome here too.

Hello self who wants more,
You are welcome here too.

Hello self who feels strong and confident,
You are welcome here too.

Hello self who is filled with doubt and worry,
You are welcome here too.

Hello self who is lazy and self-indulgent,
You are welcome here too.

Hello self who has no name and can only be felt,
You are welcome here too.

Hello you holding this book in your hands,
You are welcome here too.

All of you.
Just as you are.
In this moment.

november 27

Prioritize Your Relationship with Yourself

You cannot be lonely if you like the person you're alone with.
~ Wayne Dyer

I believe in prioritizing our relationship with ourselves. The relationship I have with myself is the most important one in my life because it positively impacts all of my other relationships, but that's not why I choose to prioritize it. I prioritize my relationship with myself because I believe I am worthy of being loved. Prioritizing your relationship with yourself looks similar to prioritizing other relationships in your life. What do you do when someone is important to you? Personally, I consistently spend quality time with the person, I listen to them with my whole heart, I support them when they are struggling, and I say kind things to them. These are the same things I do for myself.

Spend some time with your journal today. How can you prioritize your relationship with yourself? List some concrete actions, such as taking yourself on a monthly date; saying kind things to yourself when you look in the mirror; or signing up for that book club you've been wanting to join.

november 28

When You Lose Faith in Yourself

Faith means believing in advance what will only make sense in reverse.
~ Philip Yancey

We all lose faith in ourselves sometimes. Personally, when I lose faith in myself, I fall into anxiety and fear. I am naturally inclined toward those states, so it's easy for me to hang out inside that space. As uncomfortable as it is, I find a familiarity there that creates a false sense of comfort. When I become afraid I turn inward and I stay there. It's just me and my anxious thoughts and fears on repeat. I forget that I have choices. I allow myself to feel helpless. Sometimes for five minutes, sometimes for five days.

What pulls me out of these moments of fear and anxiety is connecting with the wise part within me, the divine center of love that lives within us all. When I pause and connect to the wise part within me, I can see that whatever particular confluence of events I find myself inside of is occurring for a reason. I can trust that something bigger than me has my back. I can see that what is happening is an opportunity for me to learn and evolve and break old patterns. I gain clarity that I am being invited to revisit some old stuff so that I can heal at a deeper level. I find my way back to center, back to believing in myself.

Somewhere along the path you will lose faith in yourself. It might happen when you face an obstacle or a setback. Or it could be that nothing in particular is wrong, you just feel stuck or discouraged. You may wonder why you even bother to be on the path. You may find yourself inside of anxiety and fear. You will likely fall back into old patterns. Know that all of this is normal, an expected part of being on the path. Allow yourself to feel your feelings without getting stuck inside them. Invite yourself to connect with the wise part within, the divine center of love that is always there. Remind yourself that your circumstances are temporary, and when all else fails, breathe deeply, practice trust in the process, and just hang in there as best you can. You will find your way back to having faith in yourself.

november 29

Be Gentle with Yourself

You are not meant to be productive at the expense of your human needs.
~ Mara Glatzel

We can be so hard on ourselves. We push ourselves; we expect more of ourselves than we would ever ask of others. We say harsh things to ourselves in our minds. We deny our needs for rest and relaxation. We keep going when we are sick or tired. We judge ourselves for our mistakes. I believe we do these things in service of being productive. The truth is, being hard on ourselves is unkind, unfair, and unsustainable.

How can you be gentle with yourself today?

We Can Be Both Content and Wanting More

My motto is: Contented with little, yet wishing for more. ~ Charles Lamb

I used to believe that if I were truly content with my life I wouldn't want for more. The truth is I am happy with my life as it is, *and* I dream about an even better version of it. I think this is a very human experience, and I have stopped judging myself for feeling this way. I have learned to open up and hold the paradoxical truth that I am grateful and I want more. I am living the dreams of my past self and my present self yearns for the next iteration. I am content and wishing for more.

Spend some time with your journal today. In what ways are you content with your life? In what ways are you wanting more? Practice allowing yourself to be both content and wishing for more.

Little You, Wise You

We all have different parts inside of us. Sometimes this idea gets pathologized, but really it is simply the truth of being a human. We are complicated beings.

Two parts I think about a lot are Little Mindy and Wise Melinda. Little Mindy is a scared child. She feels everything intensely and worries a lot. Wise Melinda is a grown woman. She is my spiritual center, calm and rational. The holiday season tends to bring Little Mindy to the forefront. It feels like a high-stakes time of year and I struggle with anxiety about forgetting something or messing things up. I worry about disappointing people and being judged by others. Sometimes Little Mindy takes over and I can't sleep or I end up in the fetal position crying my eyes out. When that happens I let myself cry until I feel complete and then I go to my journal and invite Little Mindy to dialogue with Wise Melinda. This is one of my practices for taking care of myself. I allow the wise part of me to reassure the little girl within and guide her toward self-care.

Spend some time with your journal today. Can you relate to the idea of a little girl and a wise woman both existing within you? How can the different parts of yourself support you? What does your little girl need today? What does your wise woman want you to know?

december 2

Gather Words of Encouragement and Kindness

Many women have a hard time accepting compliments. We tend to shrug off or qualify the kind things people say to us. Someone says, *"I love your dress!"* and you reply, *"Oh, I got it on sale."* A friend gives you a wholehearted compliment, *"Your words really spoke to me."* and you say, *"I never know if what I say makes sense."* A relative tells you, *"You are an amazing mom!"* and you respond with, *"Not really. I yell too much and the house is never clean."*

I am a word person; it is my top love language. I have learned to collect compliments, even when I have trouble believing them. I keep a folder of cards and emails that people have sent me. I also keep a handwritten list of nice things people have said to me. When I am having a hard day I re-read the words. The encouraging and kind words from others carry me when I am struggling to believe in myself.

Start a folder of encouraging and kind things people have said to you. Add to it often and allow it to serve as a reminder of your positive qualities and accomplishments.

december 3

Our Breath is a Powerful Resource

Your breathing should flow gracefully, like a river, like a watersnake crossing the water, and not like a chain of rugged mountains or the gallop of a horse. To master our breath is to be in control of our bodies and minds. Each time we find ourselves dispersed and find it difficult to gain control of ourselves by different means, the method of watching the breath should always be used.
~ Thich Nhat Hanh

Our breath is a powerful resource. How we breathe impacts our mood, energy, and nervous system. Breathing is a unique bodily process because it happens automatically *and* we can also voluntarily alter it. There are a variety of breathing techniques and entire books and courses dedicated to breath work. For today, simply consider your relationship with your breath. Do you notice it throughout your day? If you pause right now and bring awareness to your breath, where do you feel it in your body? Are you breathing quickly or slowly? What happens in your mind and body when you rest your attention on your breath? Spending even a few minutes consciously working with the breath has a powerful impact on our physical and emotional experience. In particular, learning to take deep, diaphragmatic breaths is a life-changing practice.

Find a few minutes today to practice diaphragmatic breathing. To begin, lie down and place your hand on your belly. Breathe deeply so that your hand rises as you inhale and falls as you exhale. You can also practice in a sitting position as you become more comfortable with diaphragmatic breathing. Practicing for a few minutes every day has more of an impact than one longer session once in a while.

Deep belly breaths are a tool that can be used at any time to help calm your nervous system. With practice, you will be able to breathe deeply and activate your relaxation response when talking, walking, or doing any of your other daily activities.

december 4

Savor the Good Stuff, Breathe Through the Hard Stuff

Turbulence teaches grounding. The edge teaches breath. Falling teaches rising. Breaking teaches building. Pain teaches healing. Resentment teaches boundaries. Failing teaches rebirth. Harmony continuously seeks itself. Remember, it is simply a circle continuing on, and you are supported.
~ Victoria Erickson

Life is full of opposites,
The ups and the downs,
The good and the bad.

When darkness comes,
Remember the light always returns.

Enjoy the ups,
Accept the downs.

Savor the good stuff,
Breathe through the hard stuff.

december 5

What's On Your Mind?

Some days I have so much on my mind that I feel like my brain might explode. My thoughts race and my mind feels like a computer browser with 50 open tabs. On these days, I can't even think straight enough to write or make a list. The idea of pages upon pages of my thoughts feels overwhelming. These are the days when I find relief from creating a mind map of things on my mind. I take a blank piece of paper and draw a circle in the middle labeled "Things on my Mind." I branch off other circles representing the main categories of what is on my mind (usually things like home stuff, work stuff, my kids, my husband, and myself) and then more small circles from there, listing the specific things I am thinking about in each category (e.g., projects at home, tasks for work, the health and happiness of myself and my family). When I am done, I've visually represented all of the things on my mind on one piece of paper.

Seeing everything in one place immediately helps to calm my mind. Often as I look at what I have created, it strikes me that so much of what is on my mind is actually not mine to be thinking about. I then go back to my mind map and cross off everything I feel is not mine to worry about. Then I go back through again with my priorities in mind and deliberately chose things to release. I actively decide not to give any mental energy to things that aren't a current priority. If I can't immediately do anything about something that's on my mind, I make a plan to do it. Completing this exercise brings me great relief. Our minds aren't meant to hold a bunch of to-do lists, yet women tend to do this a lot. I am a big fan of writing things down because it creates an immediate shift. The mind map is especially useful because of its visual nature.

Grab a piece of paper and create a mind map. What's on your mind today? Is it really yours to be thinking about? If not, cross it off. Next, consider your priorities. Cross off anything that doesn't align with what is currently most important to you. What is left on your mind map? Can you make a plan to address those things that require action? Notice how you feel after completing this exercise.

december 6

Some Things I Want You to Know

There are some things I want you to know.

You are brave.
You are beautiful.
You are brilliant.
Truly.

You don't need to be fixed because you are not broken. You may have forgotten the truth of your innate perfection, but trust me, it is there under the layers of expectations, roles, anxieties, and to-do lists.

You deserve the same kindness you give so freely to others. Practice self-forgiveness, self-love, and self-compassion.

Go ahead and put yourself at the top of your priority list. Taking care of yourself is part of taking care of everyone and everything else in your life. You have to refill the well or there will be nothing left to give.

I invite you to stop saying "I'm sorry" all the time, as if you have to apologize for your very existence. Try "excuse me" or "pardon me" instead. Save "I'm sorry" for the times when you truly feel sorrow.

Please get off the scale and stop obsessing about your body. Eat in a way that makes you feel vibrant. Move your body in ways that make you feel alive. Allow whatever body shape and size results from eating and moving in this way to be just right.

If something feels good and right for you, do it. I don't mean the kind of good and right that is fleeting. I mean the kind of good and right that feels true deep in your bones—the things and people and work that resonate with your soul.

Do not concern yourself with the opinions and judgments of others. Know that they say so much more about those opining and judging than you.

The band Roxette had it right—listen to your heart. And remember your heart shows up through your gut more often than not. You can trust your body's messages; deep wisdom lies within your cells.

No one knows what is best for you more than you do. Talk with people that you love and respect. Listen to their perspectives and advice. *Then decide for yourself.* No one knows what is best for you more than you do.

You have everything you need within you. The answers are not out here. If something brings you closer to that truth or helps you access your inner teacher, do more of that.

Breathe.
Choose love.
Begin again.
You've got this.

december 7

Letting Go of the Safety of People-Pleasing

[I]f you want to live an authentic, meaningful life, you need to master the art of disappointing and upsetting others, hurting feelings, and living with the reality that some people just won't like you. It may not be easy, but it's essential if you want your life to reflect your deepest desires, values, and needs.
~ Cheryl Richardson

I found safety in people-pleasing for much of my life. I was an overachiever who worked hard to earn approval from others. Making other people happy was my primary goal, no matter the impact on me, because I thought it would keep me safe. I believed I would be okay as long as everyone liked me. It took years for me to learn to feel safe to be who I really am, to say what I really mean, and to act in a way that feels aligned with my inner truth even if it might disappoint or upset some people. There have been many layers to the work of owning and feeling safe inside my truth. Big layers like saying out loud that I wanted to be a yoga teacher and quitting my job, and smaller layers like getting tattoos and sharing my stories through my writing.

The truth is I am still on the journey of letting go of the safety of people-pleasing. I think it is particularly hard for women to deal with people not liking us. Perhaps this is because long ago, if we got kicked out of the group, we literally might die on our own in the wilderness. Now we can survive on our own, but we have those same brains from long ago. Maybe this accounts for the fact that I am still so motivated to please others and sometimes feel like I will die when someone is angry with me. Whatever the case, I am continuing to work on staying true to myself even when it disappoints or upsets others because people-pleasing is exhausting and unfulfilling. I want to live inside of my truth.

Spend some time with your journal today. Do you struggle with people-pleasing behavior? What would it take for you to feel safe inside of your truth, even if it might disappoint or upset some people?

december 8

Some Thoughts on How to Navigate Sickness

For many years, when I wasn't feeling well I would simply refuse to believe it. I would not slow down or pause to rest. Despite being sick, I would not cancel appointments, skip my workouts, or go to bed early. Once I hung out in this denial for ten days leading up to a party celebrating my yoga studio's anniversary. I ended up losing my voice for the party. I still kept saying, *"I feel fine. Really. I know I sound terrible but I feel fine."* When I finally decided to rest on day 12 of feeling sick, I had a great big pity party for myself. After I got that out of my system, I spent some time reflecting. I was able to acknowledge some old patterns that I had fallen into— neglecting my needs for fear of disappointing others, minimizing my physical needs, and pushing through discomfort. Then I moved into another old pattern and started berating myself, *"You teach about self-care and you went to work with no voice?"* My mind was starting to feel like a deep, dark hole.

When I notice a pattern that I repeat often, one of my coping techniques it to write myself notes that I can refer to when the situation arises again in the future.

Here's the note I wrote to myself on how to navigate sickness:

Hey Love,

I understand you aren't feeling well. That's okay. It doesn't mean you're a bad person or you messed up. (Sometimes I blame myself when I get sick because I haven't adhered perfectly to every healthy idea I've ever read anywhere.) Everyone gets sick sometimes, probably even Oprah! I want you to know it's okay to rest. As awesome as you are, the world can go on without you for a day or two. (Sometimes I get caught up in my ego and think it will be the end of the world if I cancel my yoga class or client appointments.) I know you are going to want to fight it and insist that you are okay, and I also know that the sooner you surrender to the reality of not feeling well, the sooner you will feel better. I am giving you permission to ask for help too. You are not expected to do everything you would normally do when you are feeling well. Also, about the self-pity party you are planning in your head... Go ahead for a bit and then I encourage you to get some perspective and ground back into gratitude. Now put on your favorite comfy clothes, make yourself a cup of tea, and climb back into bed. It's okay to rest.

XO,

Me

Spend some time with your journal today. How do you navigate sickness? If you struggle with letting yourself rest, write yourself a note (or borrow mine) and let it serve as a reminder.

december 9

Stay with the Good

*There's a traditional saying that the mind takes it shape from
what it rests upon. ~ Rick Hanson*

Human beings have a built-in negativity bias. Our brains are programmed
to notice what is wrong, bad, and dangerous over what is right, good, and
beautiful. Our children play quietly in the corner and we say nothing. The
moment they start wrestling each other for their favorite stuffed animal
we are right there to intervene. Many of us are blessed to wake up each
day with bodies that don't hurt, yet we don't see many social media posts
celebrating the good fortune of feeling well. The moment something
hurts—a pulled muscle, a migraine, a toothache—it has our full attention.
A thousand things go our way each day with no notice on our part, but
one bounced check or stubbed toe and we are definitely paying attention.
We are biologically programmed to ignore the good stuff. Thankfully, we
are not beholden to our biology. We can consciously choose to notice the
good stuff, and by doing so, we change our brains for the better.

Staying with the good is a practice. It can bring up our feelings of
unworthiness, our discomfort with receiving, our obsession with chasing
the next thing, or our fears around having too much. That's okay. Just
allow yourself to notice, without judgment, what comes up for you when
you practice paying attention to the good stuff in your life. A wonderful
and effective practice for staying with the good is to simply rest your
awareness on positive experiences for 30 seconds. When something
positive happens in your day, stay with it and focus on really feeling the

sensations in your body associated with the positive experience. Aim to practice staying with the good at least five times today. You may not notice an immediate shift, but research shows that consistently practicing staying with the good leads to a more positive outlook on life as well as improvements in mood and confidence.

december 10

When Shit Goes Awry

The women whom I love and admire for their strength and grace did not get that way because shit worked out. They got that way because shit went wrong, and they handled it. They handled it in a thousand different ways on a thousand different days, but they handled it. Those women are my superheroes.
~ Elizabeth Gilbert

Life is made up of the good, the bad, and everything in between. Accepting this truth and releasing the expectation that things be any other way than they are creates peace. Shit will go awry. It doesn't mean that you've failed, it just means that you're human like the rest of us. Try to be loving toward yourself inside of the shitstorms. Begin by letting go of any judgment that is arising. Pause for a few deep breaths. This will help you come into a more grounded space so that you can mindfully choose your next steps. You'll know how to handle the shitstorm, you always do. Drink a glass of water and give yourself a few quiet minutes. Reach out to someone who can hold space for you in a healthy way. Don't isolate yourself. You deserve to be seen and loved inside of the hard stuff too. Hang in there, love. It's going to be okay.

december 11

Accept Your Contradictions

Do I contradict myself?
Very well then I contradict myself,
(I am large, I contain multitudes.)
~ Walt Whitman

I love to be alone, and I am often the loudest one in a crowd.
I feel nervous when I meet new people, and I can totally overtake a group
conversation. It drains me to go to a party, and it fills me up to teach yoga
to a packed room.

I used to feel confused by my feelings and behaviors. I resisted my
seemingly dichotomous nature. I really wanted to fit myself into a neat
box of being this or that. The truth is I am both the woman laughing
loudly with the group and the quiet one hiding in the corner. How I feel
and act changes based on internal and external factors such as my mood
and energy or the situation and context. I found freedom and joy when I
learned to accept my contradictions. I let go of the idea that I need to
show up in the world in a consistent way and gave myself permission to
just be who I am, whatever that may look like on any given day.

december 12

Just Breathe

What if we could trust life like we trust the breath? What if we could take in all the nourishment of the moment and then let it go fully, trusting that more nourishment will come? ~ Deborah Adele

For today, just breathe.
Take air in, let air out.
Trust that everything will be okay.
Let your breath be an anchor back to the present moment.
Allow this to be your practice whenever stress or worry arise.
For today, just breathe.

december 13

You Are Not Behind

There is no arriving, ever. It is all a continual becoming. ~ Joan Anderson

So often we cling to timelines. The truth is, when it comes to your personal and spiritual growth, the timeline is your entire life. You are an ever-evolving creature, and the inner work you are doing cannot be put into a neat checklist with boxes to be ticked off. You can trust the timing of your becoming. You are not behind. Relax into the knowing that you are exactly where you are meant to be in this moment.

Your Quirks Are a Gift

*Since you are like no other being ever created since
the beginning of time, you are incomparable.*
~ Brenda Ueland

We all have our quirks, those peculiar pieces of who we are. One of mine is that I make a lot of lists. Over the years I have been teased about my list-making so much that I came to think of my many lists as embarrassing and something to be changed or fixed. But when I get quiet and tune into myself, I can see that my lists are not just about getting things done. The truth is, lists not only keep me organized, they also help me to feel calm. Getting things out of my head and down onto the page brings me peace. Lists are my way of growing, exploring, and becoming. Now I've reframed my list-making quirk as a gift to be embraced rather than a flaw to be fixed. It has been freeing to let go of the idea that I need to be anything other than who I am.

Spend some time with your journal today. What are your quirks? How do you feel about them? What would it be like to reframe them as a gift?

Flip Your View

[Yoga] does not just change the way we see things;
it transforms the person who sees.
~ B.K.S. Iyengar

Today's invitation is to go upside down, literally. The gentlest way to do this is a yoga posture called Legs Up the Wall. To get into the pose, sit with one hip against the wall and swing your legs up the wall as you gently lay back on the floor. Once you are in the pose, make any adjustments that will help you feel more comfortable. You could use a pillow under your head or put a blanket over you for warmth. The closer your hips are to the wall, the more stretch you will feel in the back of your legs. If you'd like less sensation, simply scooch away from the wall. You can also practice this pose in bed. Once you are comfortably situated, close your eyes if it feels supportive. Breathe deeply and allow yourself to sink into the support beneath you. Stay here for five to ten minutes. Take your time when coming out of the pose. Slide your legs down the wall and roll off to one side for a few moments. Allow yourself to transition slowly and mindfully. Observe how you feel after a few minutes spent upside down.

december 16

Enjoy the Full Bloom

A flower blossoms for its own joy.
~ Oscar Wilde

I used to be a person who ran from one goal to the next. I think this is partly because I love so many things and have so many ideas. As soon as something I was working on came to fruition, I would dart off to the next thing. The bud would appear and I was already on to planting a new seed, missing the beauty of the flower in full bloom. In some ways I think it is counter-cultural to pause and bask in the beauty of our achievements. Capitalism encourages us to always be reaching for more. The truth is, slowing down and soaking up the goodness that surrounds us is a powerful practice. Over time, I have learned to stick around for the full bloom and it has brought me joy and contentment.

Spend some time with your journal today. What is in full bloom in your life right now? Can you allow yourself to enjoy the fruits of your labor? Pause today and take in the goodness of the life you have created. Let go of needing to get anywhere else or achieve anything more, even if just for a few moments.

december 17

What Are You Taking for Granted?

If the only prayer you ever say in your entire life is
"Thank you," it will be enough.
~ Meister Eckhart

Many of us have so much that we take for granted. Personally, I forget to pause and be thankful for things like my health, having a safe place to sleep at night, and my car starting each morning. I also do this with things that used to be wild dreams and are now my reality, such as the wellness center and yoga studio. As things become our everyday experience, it is easy to take them for granted. We become desensitized to the goodness that surrounds us; it becomes so commonplace that we have the luxury of not thinking about it. Pausing to acknowledge the goodness inside of our lives helps to shift our perspective and move us into a state of gratitude.

Spend some time with your journal today. What are taking for granted? How does it feel to pause and recognize the good things in your life?

december 18

Appreciate Your Body

*Hating your body is like finding a person you despise and
then choosing to spend the rest of your life with them
while loathing every moment of the partnership.*
~ Sonya Renee Taylor

Women tend to spend a lot of time focused on how their bodies look. We have been socialized to be hyper-aware of our physical appearances and trained that there is one version of a "good" body, namely, light-skinned, thin, and able. This is dangerous messaging for a slew of reasons. Let's take the focus off what our bodies look like and appreciate them instead for all they allow us to be, do, and feel.

Today, I invite you to let go of what your body looks like and instead focus on appreciating all it allows you to experience. Our bodies are the homes of our souls and deserve to be treated as sacred. Say the following out loud or in your mind as you imagine wrapping your body in a beautiful, healing light: "Dear Body, I am so grateful for you. Whatever your limitations, aches, or pains, you allow me to make my way through the world. I appreciate all that I can be, do, and feel because of you. You are loved and appreciated, today and always." If you are able, place your hand on your heart and say thank you, thank you, thank you to your body.

december 19

You Are Enough

The most important day is the day you decide you're good enough for you.
It's the day you set yourself free.
~ Brittany Josephina

If I had to drill down to the core wound that I see plaguing most women I know, including myself, it would be this: We feel like we are not good enough. This feeling manifests in many different ways, some specific (such as thinking "I am not smart enough") and some more general (such as pervasive feelings of insecurity). It leads us into feelings of guilt, sadness, and fear. It's at the root of our body image problems and anxiety disorders. It's the force behind our constant striving toward some elusive ideal. It's the boulder that stands between us and feelings of peace and contentment. The truth is you are enough, simply because you exist. There is nothing for you to earn or prove. You came into this world as enough, and you are enough exactly as you are today.

Spend some time with your journal today. What beliefs do you have that are preventing you from knowing your worth, knowing that you are good enough? What would it feel like to believe that you are enough, exactly as you are in this moment?

december 20

Gift to Self

When you recover or discover something that nourishes your soul and brings joy, care enough about yourself to make room for it in your life.
~ Jean Shinoda Bolen

You deserve beautiful care. Today, I invite you to give yourself a gift. This could be a physical gift such as a new book or pair of earrings. It could also be a gift of time, such as giving yourself space for a walk or nap.

Do something nice for yourself today. What gift will you give yourself?

december 21

We Need Community Care

I believe self-care is essential. I have been working on caring for myself for years and it has been life changing. More recently, I have realized that discussions about self-care often leave out the importance of community care. The truth is we need each other. The notion that we should do everything on our own is dangerous and unhealthy. We can ask for help and allow ourselves to be cared for by our community. Leaning on others is an edge for me. I have a fiercely independent streak and a deeply rooted belief that I should be able to handle whatever comes my way on my own. It's a ridiculous notion. The truth is we need community care. It's okay to lean on each other. We deserve support and connection despite the lies that capitalism and patriarchy tell us.

Spend some time with your journal today. What does community care mean to you? How can you seek support from others? What support do you have to offer?

december 22

Send a Thank You Note

Let us be grateful to people who make us happy, they are the charming gardeners who make our souls blossom.
~ Marcel Proust

It is a rare gift to know the impact we have had on a person. Today, think of someone who has had a positive influence on your life. This could be a recent interaction or something from the past. It might be a small thing, like a customer service person whose attention and kindness meant a lot to you, or a big thing, like a teacher who shaped the course of your career. Take the time to write a heartfelt thank-you note and send it to this individual. Let yourself feel the joy that comes from knowing you are about to brighten someone else's day. More than that, know that your words of gratitude may provide some much-needed soul balm for the recipient. I have often received kind words at just the moment when I was feeling down or discouraged, and it has helped me to persevere.

december 23

Go with Your Flow

Modern life demands that we show up every day to do our work, whether that work is inside the home, outside the home, or both. It can feel like there is very little room for honoring the changing nature of our physical, emotional, and energetic experiences. We are expected to perform the same way each day despite shifts in how we feel and what we need. The more we blindly live by the clock and the calendar, the less we honor our intuition and the changing needs of our bodies. I believe we can find ways to meet the demands of our lives while also honoring our cyclical nature.

As an example, my body asks me to rest as much as possible during the week before my period. She implores me to slow down the pace of my life and reminds me that this is not the time for thinking, planning, or creating. I often resist this pull to take a break from the intense flow that is my usual life. My mind says, *"But there are things I could be doing!"* The truth is there are always more things I could be doing. I have learned that it is okay to let some things go for a period of time. I have learned that emails can go unreturned and tasks undone, and still the world turns. I have learned that I can show up as the B-version of myself for a week and everything will be okay. I have learned that life always feels overwhelming when I have PMS and that this same life feels totally manageable as soon as I begin to bleed. I have learned that when I honor my cycles and go with the flow of my energy, my life unfolds in a beautiful way.

It can feel foreign to release timelines, task lists, and regular expectations in favor of what essentially amounts to going with the flow and trusting that everything will get done when it needs to get done. Yet I have found that the more I work with my natural rhythms and energies, the better things go.

How can you go with your flow today?

december 24

Give Without Expectation

I have found that among its other benefits, giving liberates the soul of the giver.
~ Maya Angelou

So much of our world is transactional that it can be challenging to let go of this programming, even when we want to. I struggle with this myself—getting frustrated when my kids aren't appreciative of me and the things I do for them, feeling hurt when I give my time and energy to a friend who doesn't reciprocate. I think most of us naturally expect certain things in return for our kindness. The truth is that giving with the expectation of getting something back (whether that is a thank-you or a reciprocation) sets us up for frustration and resentment. Moreover, it mucks up the energy of what we are giving. Learning to give with an open heart that expects nothing in return brings joy and freedom to both the giver and the receiver.

What would it be like to give without expectation of receiving anything in return? To give simply because it is what your heart wants to do? Play with this idea today. Simply notice your emotions around giving. Does it feel different when you are giving a physical gift versus the gift of your time or emotional energy? Do your feelings vary based on who you are giving to?

december 25

What Would It Take to Give from a Place of Overflow?

Women tend to give and give without ever pausing to refill our internal well. In fact, somehow we seem to be able to continue giving long after the well has dried up. A powerful question to ask yourself is what would it take to give from a place of overflow? To be so filled up that you have extra to share with others? It can be difficult to fathom what this might look like, but today's journal exercise will help you imagine what it would take in order for you to give from a place of overflow.

Grab your journal. Start by making a list of what fills you up. We are all unique individuals with different needs, but I will share some things from my own list to give you some ideas. Things that fill me up: time alone, nature, salty baths, reading, writing, meditating, walking, yoga, going to the beach, acupuncture, visioning, orgasms, empty space on my calendar, and spending time with my soul friends. Next, imagine what you would need to do (and not do!) in a day in order to create an overflow of energy inside yourself. Write this out, in detail. Extend this vision to a week, a month, a year. We are just playing at this point; don't censor yourself. After you've spent some time imagining what life would need to look like in order for you to give from a place of overflow, come back into the here and now. You may not be able to create exactly what you imagined in your vision, and that's okay. What is one step you can take toward it? Commit to doing what you can to refill your own well.

december 26

Some Thoughts on Grief

There is nothing to fix or save in another; there is only the gift of listening.
~ Deborah Adele

Grief is not only about the experience we have when someone dies. We grieve all kinds of things—change, things that never came to be, things that have ended. We grieve when we lose a job, a friend, a lover. Grief is a complicated, many layered experience. In my experience, grief feels like a swirl of so many feelings happening all at once. I think our society leaves much to be desired when it comes to grief. We seem to greet it with fear, denial, or annoying platitudes. I understand why we do this, and I'm sure I have done it myself. It's because of the discomfort. It's because we care and we want to help people feel better; we want to take away the pain. The truth is we can't, and that can be hard to accept. When it comes to grief, the most healing thing we can offer is our compassionate presence. It can feel challenging to just sit and be with someone without trying to fix or change their pain. But it is profoundly healing to simply be witnessed inside of one's emotional experience.

december 27

What if This is Enough?

Midlife is not a crisis. Midlife is an unraveling.... Midlife is when the universe gently places her hands upon your shoulders, pulls you close, and whispers in your ear: I'm not screwing around. All of this pretending and performing – these coping mechanisms that you've developed to protect yourself from feeling inadequate and getting hurt – has to go. Your armor is preventing you from growing into your gifts.
~ Brené Brown

I found myself on the cusp of 40 feeling like I was having the opposite of a midlife crisis, thinking, *"What if this is enough for me?"*

What if I am already living my dream?
What if I don't want to make more money?
What if I don't care about expanding my business?
What if instead of more, I want less?
What if instead of something different, I am content with exactly what I have?

My cravings at midlife are for things like simplicity, ease, joy, and freedom.

I feel like there is a lot of pressure in our culture to constantly be achieving, accumulating, and wanting more, but I feel great acceptance and awe for this life of mine, as it is. I want to go to yoga class, take my daily walk by the river with my dog, and sit in my backyard and watch the birds. I want to take my daughter to the playground and chat with my mom friends and bake cookies and watch Netflix snuggled up on my husband's chest. I want to do my work in this world and water my plants and clean out my closet and finally hang art on my walls. I want to let go of the hustle for more and just be with what I have and who I am. To just let that be enough. Because, for me, it is.

december 28

Give Yourself the Gift of These Six Words

There is one particular sentence that I lean on when I am struggling—*I love you no matter what.*

For me, *I love you no matter what* is reassurance; it is kindness, love, and compassion. It is medicine for my soul. Sometimes it doesn't feel true. There are days when my anxiety and self-judgment are through the roof and I am replaying things I have said over and over again in my head. There are days when I yell at my kids or make a mistake at work and I find it hard to forgive myself. I lean on this sentence even more on the days when it feels hardest to love myself—because that is when I most need it.

We all deserve unconditional love. Yet, it can feel really challenging to give yourself this gift. That's okay. Remember that self-love is a *practice*. It's not something you do once and check off a list. It is an ongoing practice, and some days are harder than others. Showing up and trying are the most important elements of any practice. We're aiming for progress, not perfection.

Today, practice telling yourself, "I love you no matter what." You could set a reminder for a few times throughout the day to pause and repeat the words to yourself, or you could say the sentence every time you look in a mirror. Don't worry if it feels unnatural or uncomfortable; that will shift with time.

december 29

Both/And

You can be both soft and intense.
Both traditional and rebellious.
Both vulnerable and strong.
Both romantic and realistic.
Both feminine and oceanic,
yet filled with slow. burning. fire.
There is possibility inside of paradox.
There's a universe of different perceptions.
~ Victoria Erickson

It is human nature to want to sort things into categories. We feel the urge to define ourselves and our experiences as either this or that. The truth is, life is full of nuances and complexities. Most things are not either/or, but rather both/and. We can learn to hold two seemingly opposing ideas at once and embrace the full spectrum of our lives.

Both accepting ourselves as we are and wanting to change.
Both the sadness of losing someone and the joy of having known them.
Both showing up for our soul work and letting go of trying to get anywhere.

Both our fear of losing what we have and our gratitude for the goodness in our lives.

Both the effort of working toward our goals and the surrendering of all the pieces that we can't control.

You are a holy container capable of holding the whole truth of your existence. Open up and allow yourself to hold the seemingly paradoxical nature of yourself, of life.

december 30

Are You Performing?

There is the act of *living* our lives, and there is the act of *performing* our lives. We are living our lives when we are tuned into our internal experience and showing up in a way that aligns with our values and priorities. We are performing our lives when we are outwardly focused and showing up in a way that we think will earn us approval. The truth is we are not here to put on a show. Some signs that you are performing include being overly concerned with what other people think of you, saying yes when you want to say no, and making life choices in order to try to please other people. I have done all of these things and more. It's easy to fall into performing our lives, especially inside of a world so heavily focused on social media. The good news is that we can learn to recognize when we are performing our lives, understand why we do it, and mindfully choose a different way to show up.

Spend some time with your journal today. Where in your life are you performing? Does it seem to happen more in certain situations or around particular people?

How can you show up in a way that is more closely aligned with your values and priorities?

december 31

A Sacred Pause on the Eve of a New Year

It is good to have an end to journey towards;
but it is the journey that matters in the end.
~ Ursula K. LeGuin

Today, let's honor where we've come from, who we are now, and where we are headed. As the year comes to a close, take some time to ponder how reading this book and integrating the concepts and suggested practices has impacted you.

Spend some time with your journal today. Who were you at the beginning of the year? How are you different now? What have you learned about yourself? What has shifted in your life? How has the way you show up in the world changed? What old stories have you released? How is your relationship with yourself different? What practices will you continue in order to honor this new version of yourself? Who do you want to become? What's next for you? How will you support yourself through your ongoing growth and evolution?

about the author

Melinda Scime, Ph.D. is a licensed psychologist, certified trauma-informed yoga teacher, and creator of Badass Self-Care®. Melinda earned her doctorate in Counseling and School Psychology from the University at Buffalo where she studied the mind-body connection and its impact on the healing process. In 2008, Melinda founded Tree of Life Yoga Studio and began teaching yoga classes and self-care workshops for women. One year later she realized a long-held dream and opened Living Wellness of Niagara, a holistic health center in her home town of Niagara Falls, NY. Melinda works with sensitive, empathic women who are ready to move beyond exhaustion and overwhelm and into the space of self-care and prioritizing their own needs. Her work is informed by her experience as a therapist and yoga teacher with specialized training in trauma, as well as her lived experience of navigating self-care in this world as a woman, mother, and healer. Her community of badass women is devoted to doing inner work and creating outer change. Learn more about Melinda and her work at www.melindascime.com.

CPSIA information can be obtained
at www.ICGtesting.com
Printed in the USA
LVHW090921100920
665516LV00009B/151